THE BASICS OF
BIOETHICS

ROBERT M. VEATCH

Kennedy Institute of Ethics
Georgetown University

Prentice Hall, Upper Saddle River, New Jersey 07458

Library of Congress Cataloging-in-Publication Data

Veatch, Robert M.
   The basics of bioethics / Robert M. Veatch.
     p. cm.
   Includes bibliographical references and index.
   ISBN 0–13–083976–0
   1. Medical ethics. I. Title.
   R724.V39   1999
   174′.2—dc21   99–045810

Editorial Director: Charlyce Jones Owen
Acquisitions Editor: Karita France
Assistant Editor: Emsal Hasan
Director of Production and Manufacturing: Barbara Kittle
Production Editor: Louise Rothman
Manufacturing Manager: Nick Sklitsis
Prepress and Manufacturing Buyer: Tricia Kenny
Marketing Director: Gina Sluss
Marketing Manager: Ilse Wolfe
Editorial Assistant: Jennifer Ackerman
Cover Designer: Joseph Sengotta
Cover Art: Kamalova/SIS, Inc.

This book was set in 11/13 Minion by Pub-Set
and printed and bound by RR Donnelley & Sons Company
The cover was printed by Phoenix Color Corp.

© 2000 by Prentice-Hall, Inc.
A Pearson Education Company
Upper Saddle River, New Jersey 07458

Printed in the United States of America
10 9 8 7 6 5 4 3 2 1

ISBN 0-13-083976-0

Prentice-Hall International (UK) Limited, *London*
Prentice-Hall of Australia Pty. Limited, *Sydney*
Prentice-Hall Canada Inc., *Toronto*
Prentice-Hall Hispanoamericana, S.A., *Mexico*
Prentice-Hall of India Private Limited, *New Delhi*
Prentice-Hall of Japan, Inc., *Tokyo*
Pearson Education Asia Pte. Ltd., *Singapore*
Editora Prentice-Hall do Brasil, Ltda., *Rio de Janeiro*

Contents

List of Cases

List of Figures

Preface

Bioethics has emerged over the past twenty-five years as a new field of study and controversy. Textbooks, anthologies, casebooks, and single-authored works are available to provide perspectives on the issues of bioethics. But no current, brief survey exists that is a suitable introduction to the field. This volume is designed to fulfill that need. It is intended for health professionals and laypeople who want an introduction to the issues in a relatively small edition. It can be used in short courses in schools of medicine, nursing, and other health professions; continuing professional education; undergraduate courses in philosophy, religion, and the social sciences; and adult education.

Law has in a sense taken over in the practice of medicine. In a way that is too bad. Law is obviously important, but it is not all there is to medicine. Medicine is a profession, and, traditionally, one of the chief characteristics of a profession is that it has its own ethic. At least until recently, self-regulation was one of the definitive signs that medicine was a profession—self-regulation didn't engender much controversy. In this volume, we look at the controversies over self-regulation in medicine and some of the ethical problems that have emerged.

I have taught medical ethics in four medical schools and in several undergraduate and graduate schools. Starting in 1970 I developed the first medical ethics program at the College of Physicians and Surgeons of Columbia University while on the staff of the Hastings Center. Since almost that time I have been doing a one-week version of the same material at a seven-year medical student program at Union College and Albany Medical College, and since 1980 I have been teaching at Georgetown University. Finally, for about ten years I have taught a one-week introduction to medical ethics for the St. George's University School of Medicine in Grenada. I have also taught undergraduates and graduate students at Vasser, Brown, Dartmouth, and Georgetown. It is in those contacts with thousands of students over the years that these chapters have taken shape. Often what was needed was a serious, balanced examination of the issues of biomedical ethics in a format that could be covered in a week or two rather than a semester or a year. This volume is designed to serve that purpose.

The approach is systematic. Rather than discussing issue by issue every topic in the current bioethics literature, we begin with a brief history. We ask why the old Hippocratic Oath is in trouble, and what the alternatives are. In chapter 2 we discuss what may first seem like a disparate collection of topics: abortion, the definition of death, and the welfare of nonhuman animals. We shall see that they all raise the question of who has moral standing and why. Next, in chapter 3, we discuss the ethics of benefiting patients. That may sound like a platitude—of course the health professional's goal must be to benefit his or her patient. However, benefiting patients is increasingly controversial morally. There are in fact many situations in which physicians decide not to provide benefit, at least if they follow more contemporary ethical thinking rather than the traditional Hippocratic Oath.

Next, in chapter 4, we deal with the major challenge to the Hippocratic perspective, what is often referred to as the ethics of respect for persons or the ethics of liberal political philosophy. This approach includes an alternative set of ethical principles that is now being used in place of the Hippocratic Oath. We talk about rights of patients and rights of physicians, particularly in terms of fidelity, autonomy, and veracity, and why these principles are causing big problems for health professionals.

Chapters 5 and 6 deal with one of the hottest issues in medical ethics, the care of the terminally ill. Traditional medical ethics of the past hundred years was committed to preserving life, sometimes preserving it at all costs. In Western cultures, life, at least human life, was deemed sacred or ultimately valuable. We shall see that this notion is enormously complex. Euthanasia has variously been taken as referring to active killing for mercy, the forgoing of medical treatment even though the result is likely to be death, and sometimes simply any good death. In chapter 5 we begin to examine these issues by dealing with competent patients. Then in chapter 6 we grapple with what the real complications are today: dealing with incompetent patients who are terminally ill and considering whether these patients would be better off if they were not treated so aggressively.

We then turn, in chapter 7, to *the* issue of medical ethics for the twenty-first century, the social ethics of health care, including the morality of allocating scarce medical resources. We also discuss other conflicts, such as medical research that pits the interests of the individual against those of society. We examine the role physicians have to play as society's agent, or cost-containment agent, allocating a pie that is too small to give everyone all the health care he or she needs.

Finally, in chapter 8, we step back a bit from the principles of normative medical ethics to ask about an underlying basic value commitment that shapes positions taken on just about every issue in medical ethics: whether humans are going too far in attempting to remake their own basic nature. We ask the question as a dispute between two fundamental value orientations: one group that feels we are in a morally unacceptable way beginning to "play God" by remanufacturing the basics of life and another that relies on another equally religious metaphor, the idea that humans are acting most responsibly when they attempt to use their rationality to redesign their basic biology by "having dominion over the earth and subduing it." Here we focus on genetics and birth technologies—genetic screening and engineering as well as in vitro fertilization and surrogate motherhood—as the areas of medicine that pose this question of fundamental value orientation most dramatically.

These eight brief chapters will give the reader a general framework by which the full range of ethical issues in health care can be addressed. It is not that every topic in contemporary medical ethics will have been examined explicitly; an exhaustive evaluation would be impossible in a volume of this size. Rather the goal is to understand the historical framework of the Hippocratic Oath, which many persons mistakenly believe is still the dominant view in medical ethics, and the alternative religious and secular medical ethical theories that have made the Hippocratic Oath so outdated and so wrong morally. The reader will end with a set of principles that are alternatives to the Hippocratic tradition and that address the major themes of health care ethics of today: confidentiality, informed consent, honesty in communication between patient and provider, the care of the terminally ill, and the allocation of scarce resources. This book provides some sense of who has moral standing and why that question is crucial, not only for the abortion debate and deciding when an individual is dead but also for how animals are treated in research, education, and other spheres of life. It also explores whether the human's role is that of co-creator of a new genetic and reproductive future or would be better seen in a more humble light, if only for fear that we may be playing with Promethean fire.

A large number of people have played a role in the production of this book. I have tried out many of the ideas and chapters on the Scholars of the Kennedy Institute of Ethics and other colleagues in the field of biomedical ethics. David Smith and Cynthia Cohen each provided careful and helpful readings of parts of the manuscript. Kathy McMahon, a former Institute staff member, played a major role in typing and editing early versions of these chapters, and Julie Eddinger has provided administrative assistance more recently. Kier Olsen and David Singh have provided very helpful research assistance. Ashley Fernandes, simultaneously a graduate student in philosophy and a medical student, has carefully reviewed almost the entire manuscript and provided many helpful suggestions as well as completing some of the research for the volume. Most of all I am grateful to the thousands of students who have pursued these issues with me by demanding clarity and enjoying the debate. Many have told me that these are the real issues that will make the health care professions rewarding for them even if they will also make life very difficult. Just as important, others have conveyed that, while they are not planning careers in the health professions, exploring these issues will make them better patients, surrogate decision makers, and participants in the public policy discussion. If so, that is good. I have long held that laypeople are always necessarily the primary medical decision makers in our society and that they must be not only partners in the health care enterprise, but primary in that partnership.

RMV, Washington, D.C.

CHAPTER ONE

The Hippocratic Oath
and Its Challengers

A Brief History

Case 1.1:   *The Boy Who Ate the Pickle*

A nine-year-old youngster named Yusef Camp who lived in inner-city Washington, D.C., ate a pickle that he had bought from a street vendor. Soon after eating it he went into convulsions and collapsed on the sidewalk. A rescue squad took him to the nearest emergency room, where his stomach was pumped. Tests revealed that the pickle contained traces of marijuana and PCP. The boy suffered severe respiratory depression and was left unconscious and unable to breathe.

The emergency room personnel restored respiration by putting him on a ventilator, but that is all they were able to accomplish. They could not restore him to consciousness or get him breathing adequately on his own.

The physicians concluded that his brain function was irreversibly destroyed and that there was no possibility of recovery. They might have simply pronounced him dead and then stopped the ventilator, but the situation soon became more complicated. Two of the attending neurologists were convinced that the patient's brain was totally dead. But one believed that he still had minor brain function, so they could not pronounce the patient dead on the basis of loss of brain function. Now they had to decide what to do. Their patient was still living but was permanently unconscious, breathing only because he was on a ventilator.

The physicians pointed out that there was nothing more they could do except to keep the ventilator running, perhaps indefinitely, and maintain the boy in a persistent, or permanent, vegetative state. (The longest case on record of maintaining a patient in what is called a permanent vegetative state is over thirty-seven years.) The parents were Muslims, members of the Nation of Islam, who firmly believed in the power of Allah. They believed that Allah would

1

determine the fate of the boy and that it was the physicians' job to give Allah that opportunity by keeping the boy on the ventilator. How should the physicians have responded?

Where might a physician, a parent, or a social observer of this scene turn for moral advice about how to handle a case like this? One possibility is to look at a code of ethics. These codes have been prepared by many different cultural, religious, and professional groups. They are meant to summarize the basic principles of ethics from the perspective of the group doing the writing.

The Hippocratic Tradition

The Hippocratic Oath

For many years, some physicians have used the Hippocratic Oath as a summary of moral medical wisdom. It is not, however, a timeless document that has been used throughout history in all parts of the world. It is part of a collection of writings known as the Hippocratic corpus. We really don't know who wrote the oath. Hippocrates, in the fifth century B.C., was one of the original leaders of medicine on the island of Cos in ancient Greece. He was almost certainly not the author of the Hippocratic Oath (Edelstein 1967). The oath is generally believed to have been written about a hundred years later. It is one of several ethical writings along with other, more scientific ones in the Hippocratic corpus.

Most people have not thought extensively about where the oath came from and, more important, about the belief system on which it was based. A provocative observation on the island of Cos should arouse curiosity. On the island is a ruin of a Greek healing temple. According to local folklore the school of Hippocrates was associated with this temple.[1] When local residents are asked what happened to the building, they say the destruction happened during the Christianization of Greece. Apparently, at some point in history, the Hippocratic and Christian schools of thought were sufficiently at odds that they battled to the point that the temple was destroyed. At some point in history Greek ethics and medicine were very different from Christian ethics and medicine (Veatch and Mason 1987), raising questions that should concern moderns who see themselves as standing in the Christian tradition, but affirming the Oath.

---

[1] In fact, there is reason to believe that Hippocrates was not a part of this temple, but rather a challenger to the earlier religious healing system.

The most famous twentieth-century scholar of this period, Ludwig Edelstein (1967), thinks that the Hippocratic tradition arose from the Pythagorean cult (named for the same Pythagoras who gave us the Pythagorean theorem), a cult that was interested in science and philosophy and religion, and, if Edelstein is correct, produced a school of medicine in ancient Greece known as the Hippocratic school.

Even if all this is true, why should a group of twentieth-century secular Western physicians caring for a Muslim patient in Washington, D.C., turn to a 2500-year-old Pythagorean cultic ritual oath for moral guidance? Let us take just a brief look at the content of the Oath (see the Appendix). One will begin to see that however helpful it was for an ancient medical group, for those practicing medicine today it is controversial. The oath is divided into two parts, an oath of initiation followed by a code of conduct.

The Oath of Initiation Section   The oath of initiation contains several elements. For instance, there is a pledge of loyalty to the teacher. If the teacher should ever become short of funds, it is the student's moral duty to come to the rescue. There is also a rather strange oath of secrecy. One pledges, when one takes the Hippocratic Oath, that he or she will not reveal the knowledge of medicine to laypeople. It was believed that the knowledge transmitted to the physician was very powerful and that that power in the hands of someone who does not understand it can do great harm. This was a belief of Pythagoreanism, which also purported that knowledge should not be revealed to anyone outside the cult. We still see this attitude in modern medicine, particularly among some older physicians who are uncomfortable about sharing medical information with patients.[2] This traditional practice is at odds with the current stress on the physician's duty to educate and inform the patient about his or her medical situation and to obtain informed consent.

Still in the oath section, there is a pledge to the Greek gods and goddesses Apollo, Aesclepius, Hygieia, and Panaceia. Modern physicians have felt it necessary to modify that sentence so that they are not actually pledging to the Greek gods and goddesses. They might substitute authorities within their own religious tradition or even secular authorities.

By contrast, various other religious and secular approaches to medical ethics, such as those in Judaism and Christianity, hold that there is a covenant

---

[2]Likewise, until recently, pharmacists were taught that a pharmacist was not to put the name of the prescription medication on the label and should not to tell the patient the name of the drug, because somehow that was information that could harm patients. They might hear that that drug was used for other diseases and become distressed with the thought that they might have such a condition. Or they might read about side effects and become unnecessarily alarmed about them.

relationship between God and his people and no vow of secrecy. The Judeo-Christian belief generally, especially in Protestantism, is that all people are capable of using knowledge responsibly.

In secular liberal political philosophy, education is also important. Liberal political philosophy has its origins in the philosophy of Locke, Hobbes, and Rousseau and reaches its best-known political expression in the documents of the founding fathers of the U.S. political system. It stresses the importance of the individual and commands respect for the liberty of the individual even if other people believe they know what is best. It also incorporates a belief in the equality of moral worth of all persons, providing a basis for various concerns about social justice. Its proponents believe that people have a right to know; the development of an informed consent doctrine illustrates the pervasiveness of this conviction. No discussion of patients' rights appears in any of the Hippocratic writings. We begin to see that the Judeo-Christian attitude and that of secular liberalism as well as other traditions have medical ethical doctrines that differ from the old Pythagorean Hippocratic tradition.

The Code of Conduct Section   The second half of the Oath contains the code of ethics itself. It deals with dietetics, pharmacology, and surgery.[3] The third sentence contains an odd prohibition that requires physicians to swear solemnly that they will never practice surgery. Translations differ a bit, but the best translation prohibits using the knife "even on sufferers from stone," which presumably refers to bladder stone surgery. Because that was relatively simple surgery even in ancient times, the statement seems to emphasize that the prohibition was categorical and did not merely reflect an awareness that complex surgery was too dangerous.

Why would a medical ethical oath forbid its physicians to practice surgery? One explanation is that the original meaning was that the Hippocratic physician should not practice surgery because surgery involves contamination (i.e., touching blood and waste products), which is religiously defiling. Pythagoreans worried about such ritual contaminations. However, the Oath does not say that surgery is inherently dangerous for a patient, but rather that Hippocratic physicians should leave surgery to persons who practiced that particular branch of medicine. In short, there was a moral division of labor like that seen in some traditional cultures, in which those in priestly roles were kept "pure." This interpretation is supported by the fact that the Oath holds out "purity and holiness" as the two key Hippocratic virtues.

---

[3]One of the reasons we are convinced that the Oath is Pythagorean in origin is that it reflects exactly the way the Pythagoreans divided the world of medicine, and most other Greek schools of thought did it differently.

The oath also contains other prohibitions. The Hippocratic physician will not give deadly drugs. Euthanasia is proscribed, as are abortifacients.[4] Most important, the Oath contains what can be called its core principle, namely, that the physician should *benefit the patient according to his ability and judgment*.[5] Decisions as to what will benefit the patient are made on the basis of the *physician's* ability and judgment, not the patient's. Hence, the Hippocratic ethic is often considered *paternalistic;* that is, it approves of actions intended to benefit another person even if that person does not want the benefit. While some interpret the Oath to deal with total patient well-being, often in medicine this paternalism arises because the health professional is focusing exclusively on the medical benefits of treatments while the patient may be willing to sacrifice those medical benefits in order to obtain nonmedical benefits considered more important or desirable. (Smoking, consuming unhealthy foods, and failing to exercise are all possible examples.)

By contrast, other ethics are of a different style. Some interpretations of Judeo-Christianity, for example, are less paternalistic and are different from the Hippocratic Oath in other significant ways. The other major religious and secular traditions of the world—Hinduism, Buddhism, various Chinese traditions, Marxist thought, and, for our purposes probably the most significant, the liberal political philosophy of the modern West—all have something that can be called an ethic for medicine. All of these will be seen as contrasting to the Hippocratic tradition that has been so prominent in medical ethics at various times over the past 2500 years. Hence, physicians or parents or anyone else seeking moral guidance for a case such as that of Yusef Camp will need to determine on which of the many ethical systems that are available they wish to rely.

Modern Codes in the Hippocratic Tradition

Percival's Code of 1803   Several modern professional ethical codes stand in the Hippocratic tradition, at least in the sense that they stress the duty of the physician to benefit the patient. By far the most important for the English-speaking world is the code of Thomas Percival, published in 1803 (Percival 1927). The need for a written ethics code for medicine arose from a typhoid

---

[4]Some people say that the Hippocratic prohibition on abortion dovetails with Christian objections to abortion (Edelstein 1967, pp. 62–63; Carrick 1985, p. 159; Temkin 1991, p. 182) and that is why the two traditions came together. But if one looks at the ancient tradition of Christianity, one will see that in all the documents that exist from the first eight centuries of Christianity only eleven references are made to the Hippocratic writings (Veatch and Mason 1987). Nine of those eleven had nothing to do with the Oath. They praise the quality of the writing, holding it as a model of classical Greek writing style. Only two references mention the Hippocratic Oath in eight centuries of the Christian era. Both were rather hostile to Hippocratic concepts, reflecting a difference between the Christian and Hippocratic traditions.

[5]In Hippocratic medicine, physicians were always male.

and typhus epidemic in Manchester, England, that occurred in the 1790s. As a result the Manchester infirmary staff were overworked. Medicine in the eighteenth century in Britain was divided very much the way it was in the Hippocratic tradition. There were physicians, who specialized in dietetics; surgeons; and apothecaries, who did the pharmacology work. The pressure of this epidemic was more than they could handle. They began to fight among themselves about who should be doing what.

As it happens, a physician named Thomas Percival had quit practicing medicine around the time of this epidemic because of a physical disability. He was well educated, and everybody thought well of him. The physicians embroiled in the dispute asked him to mediate. The result was a volume of ethical guidance. Thus the purpose of the code was originally to mediate fights among physicians, not to deal with relationships with patients. Percival's code was published in revised form in 1803. It was in the Hippocratic tradition in that it stressed the duty of the physician to benefit the patient and placed no emphasis on the rights of patients in matters such as informed consent or open disclosure.[6]

This duty to benefit the patient combined with the absence of any recognition of the rights of patients is the hallmark of the Hippocratic tradition. It is one of the major differences between a medical ethics that is Hippocratic and many of the other religious and secular ethics we shall be considering. The focus on benefit to the patient became the foundation not only of British, but also of American, professionally sponsored medical ethics.

The AMA Code of 1847 In the United States at the beginning of the nineteenth century, several schools of medical thought existed side by side, just as there had been in ancient Greece. Members of these schools began to fight among themselves, each wanting to establish theirs as the dominant school. In 1847, one group, representing what we now call allopathic (or orthodox and scientific) medicine, founded the American Medical Association to accomplish this end and to combat what they thought of as quackery.

They recognized that if theirs was going to be a profession, as opposed to a mere business, they had to have a code of ethics. (Sociologists of the professions note that writing a code of ethics is often a distinguishing mark of a

---

[6]Classifying Percival's work as in the Hippocratic tradition is the now-standard reading of his ethics. That is the position taken by Chauncey Leake (Percival 1927; Berlant 1975; Waddington 1975, 1984). More recent scholarship is now questioning this reading of Percival. Whereas the Hippocratic Oath focuses on the individual isolated patient-physician relation, Percival differs by including extensive discussion of social relations, including the duty of the physician to society. It is also now becoming clear that Percival was much more conversant with the contemporary philosophical literature of the time and not just repeating Hippocratic formulas (Baker 1995).

profession.) In writing one, they turned to Percival's code, taking whole sections of it and incorporating them into their original 1847 Code of Ethics of the AMA (AMA 1848). So both Britain (with Percival) and the United States (with the AMA) had codes of ethics that are essentially Hippocratic in their content, focusing on benefit to the patient. However, they both also discussed the duties of physicians to benefit society, something the Hippocratic ethic never mentioned.

The World Medical Association Declaration of Geneva, 1948   Just after World War II, the World Medical Association, a conglomeration of national medical societies, needed a code to respond to the medical experiments in the Nazi concentration camps. In 1948 this group developed the Declaration of Geneva (World Medical Association). Its contents are remarkably similar to the Hippocratic Oath. Deleting from the old oath the references to Hygieia and Panaceia and all the old gods and goddesses and the prohibition on surgery and abortifacients, it still includes the key sentence that is a slightly modified version of the Hippocratic principle. It now reads "the health of my patient will be my first consideration." Essentially, then, a Hippocratic Oath in modern language governs this organization of world medical associations. The World Medical Association is no more cognizant than the Hippocratic Oath of the problem that arises when the patient does not want her health maximized; that is, when she has something else on her agenda other than health, or when she disagrees with the physician about what would count as improving her health.

Other Contemporary Oaths or Codes in the Hippocratic Tradition   Just under half of the medical schools in the United States and Canada (47 percent) still administer some version of the Hippocratic Oath to their graduates, but only one school (State University of New York at Syracuse) was reported in a 1997 article still to use the original version (Orr et al. 1997). Similar patterns appear in other countries, with some schools using the Hippocratic form, usually modified, and others using an oath of entirely different origin.

In post-Soviet Russia, physicians have recently constructed an oath for the Russian physician ("Solemn Oath of a Physician of Russia" 1993). Wanting to replace the Soviet oath, which had significant Marxist overtones, Russian physicians took the old Hippocratic Oath and translated it into Russian, cleaning it up in a manner similar to that of the World Medical Association. Another example is the Academic Oath of St. George's University School of Medicine in Grenada. It also uses a rewrite of the Hippocratic Oath. Their version, however, requires the graduating medical student to work for the benefit of the patient rather than merely for the patient's health. The key sentence reads, "The regimen I prescribe will be for the good of my patients, according to my ability and judgment." We shall see in chapter 3 that there can be a difference between working for the patient's total welfare and focusing more narrowly only on the patient's health.

There are other rewritings, such as the Florence Nightingale Pledge for nurses. It was not written by Florence Nightingale any more than the Hippocratic Oath was written by Hippocrates; it is a thinly modified rewriting of the Hippocratic Oath.

Until the later decades of the twentieth century, then, physicians often used some version the Hippocratic Oath as their ethical code (and some continue to do so to this day). The definitive feature is a commitment of the physician to benefiting the patient without any acknowledgment of patients' rights, such as the right to be told the truth or to give consent before being treated. The more purely Hippocratic codes also pay no attention to the welfare of society or other individuals (although we have seen that both Percival and the AMA depart slightly from the standard Hippocratic formula by secondarily mentioning some concern for social benefits).

But beginning about 1970, the Hippocratic tradition started to collapse. Observing this collapse is in a way quite exciting; it must be like being with Galileo during the revolution in astronomy, or Albert Einstein when atomic physics was emerging. A new medical ethics emerged on the horizon, particularly for Western culture. The new ethics has its roots in ancient Judeo-Christianity, but more explicitly in secular liberal political philosophy.

The Collapse of the Hippocratic Tradition

The Hippocratic Oath is being challenged in three ways. One preliminary challenge deals with the way in which benefits are assessed. The oath makes an enormous presumption when it says that a physician should judge what is best for his or her patient according to the physician's ability and judgment. In some cases, the physician's colleagues, who are competent in their field, may not concur. Even if they do, the patient may prefer some other course. In this sense, the Oath's assessment of benefit is subjective. In chapter 3 we shall discuss further the problems with the subjective notion that it is the physician's standard of benefit that is decisive.

A second challenge involves problems that arise when benefits conflict with other kinds of moral duties, particularly those related to rights and obligations to the patient. Many ethical theories hold that there is more to ethics than merely producing good consequences. They affirm moral obligations and rights that are relevant to deciding what is ethically right conduct regardless of the consequences. In chapter 4 we shall talk about conflicts between benefiting the patient and respecting certain rights of the patient, including the right to the truth, the right to have one's autonomy respected, and the right to have promises kept. Then in chapters 5 and 6 we shall talk about the rights of the dying.

The third challenge to the Hippocratic tradition arises when there is a conflict between the interests of the patient and those of other individuals or of society. The Oath, at least in its original form, focuses exclusively on the individual patient. In chapter 7 we will look at the way in which this focus on the individual conflicts with the health professional's duty to others in society in the areas of research medicine, public health, or cost containment.

Codes and Oaths That Break with the Hippocratic Tradition

The Nuremberg Code, 1946   Several kinds of medical codes or oaths break with the Hippocratic tradition. The first and most dramatic challenge in modern times came shortly after World War II with the Nuremberg trials. People began to question Nazi physicians about the painful, sometimes lethal, studies they had been doing on unwilling concentration camp prisoners. It became obvious that research on humans could be ethically controversial. The agenda pursued in these studies had been set by the Nazi state. The experiments were not for the benefit of prisoners in concentration camps. It is the very nature of medical research (as opposed to innovative therapy) that the goal is to produce knowledge, not to benefit the subject. On the other hand, the Hippocratic ethic requires action only for the individual patient's benefit.

The Nazi physicians had abandoned the traditional ethical commitment of the physician to the individual patient's welfare. The Nuremberg trials uncovered a serious problem; Nazi physicians had not been working for the benefit of their patients. One option would be to go back to the Hippocratic formula, requiring that physicians focus only on individual patient welfare, but that would mean that no physician could ever do any research, even for the good of society. The Hippocratic ethic would have prohibited the Nazi experiments, but it would also have foreclosed even the most benign and defensible research.

Instead of returning to a Hippocratic model, spokespersons for Western society acknowledged that research was necessary for the benefit of humankind but that some protection was needed for the individual patient. This protection came in the form of requiring informed consent from subjects so they could look out for their own interests. The resulting Nuremberg Code ("Nuremberg Code 1946") was the first medical ethical document in the 2500 years after Hippocrates that mentioned the concept of informed consent: that is, the notion that the patient or subject has the right to be informed of the relevant facts of what is being proposed and to approve or disapprove before the physician proceeds.

There is a second important difference between the Nuremberg Code and the codes in the Hippocratic form. It is a public document of international law, not one written by the medical profession and bestowed on the public. We are beginning to see the clash of two different perspectives that represent two radically different ethical traditions. The collision that resulted beginning in about 1970 was dramatic. One element, represented by the Nuremberg Code, is grounded in liberal political philosophy and another element from the Hippocratic tradition shows no manifestation of liberalism. This latter tradition is older, more paternalistic, and, as we are beginning to discover, is incompatible with the liberalism on which the Nuremberg Code is based, at least in certain areas such as research medicine.

The American Hospital Association Patient Bill of Rights, 1973   Another document that breaks with the Hippocratic view came in 1973 from the American Hospital Association (1978) right at the beginning of the collision between the Hippocratic and liberal traditions. The American Hospital Association's Patient Bill of Rights goes a long way toward focusing on the rights of patients. It includes informed consent and a right to information. Nothing like that ever appeared in the Hippocratic tradition. Notice, though, that this affirmation of patient rights came not from the Medical Association but from the Hospital Association.

The American Medical Association Principles of 1980   It was not until 1980 that the AMA changed its code in a dramatic, significant way. The new version (see the Appendix), adopted that year and published in 1981, finally began speaking of the rights of patients. The use of the word *rights* is a signal that something new was going on. A right is a moral or legal entitlement that cannot be defeated merely by appeals to good consequences that would result from failing to honor the claim. The Hippocratic Oath never mentions anyone's rights. The language of rights is grounded in the liberal political philosophy of Locke, Hobbes, Rousseau, and the framers of the U.S. Constitution.

Sources from Outside Professional Medicine

We also begin to see the emergence of medical ethical documents from other sources to which physicians, parents, or others confronting difficult decisions, such as that involving Yusef Camp, might turn.

Judaism, Catholicism, and Protestantism   It has already been mentioned that the Nuremberg Code is a document of international law—that is, from outside organized professional medicine. Religious traditions also have medical ethical doctrine, such as Talmudic Judaism (Rosner and Bleich 1979) and Catholic moral theology (National Conference of Catholic Bishops 1995). Protestant ethics has positions on many medical ethical issues including abortion, euthanasia, and the right of access to medical care that come from moral sources fundamentally different from that of organized medicine.

Hinduism   Outside of the West, many ancient religious traditions have developed medical ethical positions. The Hindu Vedic scriptures, for instance, contain a medical ethic. The Vedic texts are classical religious writings. One branch of those writings, the Ayur Veda, contains medical material, including a code of ethics called the Caraka Samhita ("Oath of Initiation [Caraka Samhita 1978]"). This code required that the physician not injure or abandon the patient and not cause his death. One of the provisions in that document that makes very little sense to Westerners but is understood within the Vedic tradition is a pledge of the physician that it is his duty not to treat haters of the king. There is nothing like this provision in Western medical ethics, but it is perhaps more understandable against the backdrop of the religious traditions of ancient India.

Buddhism   The classical Buddhist ethic involves an eightfold path in which there are five precepts. These precepts include prohibitions on killing, lying, and drinking intoxicants. So, within the Buddhist tradition an ethic exists with definite implications for the practice of medicine.

Ancient Chinese Thought   Ancient China developed a complex, rich culture that included the thought of Confucianism as well as strands of Buddhist and Taoist thinking. By the seventh century A.D., Chinese writing began to focus explicitly on medicine. Sun Simiao wrote a famous treatise, "On the Absolute Sincerity of Great Physicians," in his work *The Important Prescriptions Worth a Thousand Pieces of Gold*. It affirms special moral duties for professional physicians. It is widely believed to reflect Buddhist and Taoist influences.

Islam   There are a number of Muslim oaths for physicians. The Islamic Code of Medical Ethics was prepared in Kuwait in an international meeting of Islamic scholars in 1981 (International Organization of Islamic Medicine 1981). Islamic medicine has a strong prohibition on killing, including mercy killing and abortion. There is an affirmation of Allah's will, the concept that we saw in the case of Yusef Camp.

Japan   Japanese ethics also has rich traditions relevant to medical ethics. Consider the following case.

Case 1.2: Physician Assistance in a Merciful Homicide

A young woman had just given birth, in Tokyo. She was unmarried, had no close relatives who could help her raise this child, and had a malignancy of the breast. In fact, it had now metastasized. The oncologist told her she probably only had a few more months to live. The woman said to the oncologist, "I want you to help me to do the most loving thing that I can do for my child. I would like you to tell me how I can mercifully kill my child so that when I die, the child will not be condemned to the life of an orphan."

The physician pointed out that there were other possibilities. For instance, someone could adopt the child. The mother understood all this. She said, "My child is a girl. My child has a deformed hip. That close bond between mother and child is destroyed forever with my death. So my child will never be able to do well."

There is a concept in Japanese culture called *amae,* which is roughly translated as dependency, a close bond between a mother and child that would be irretrievably destroyed with the mother's death (Doi 1981). There is also in Japanese culture a concept called *joshi. Joshi* is what we would probably translate as "love killing," or mercy killing. It is sometimes used by the head of a household who is disgraced in business. He might, as a merciful act, not only kill himself in suicide but also have the kindness to take his wife and children with him so they will not be disgraced. Though illegal today, this practice, which comes out of the more traditional *edo* period in Japan, still occurs. This woman's request obviously reflected those old beliefs. Japanese people today understand the concept, and it doesn't surprise them that a mother could ask for help from her physician to kill not only herself but also her infant child. The striking thing about this story was that the physician understood. Most physicians, even in Japan, would not have cooperated, but this physician did. It is impossible to understand that story without knowing a great deal about traditional Shinto doctrine and beliefs in Japan. It is the exception rather than the rule, but it does happen.

The Oath of the Soviet Physician   All of these traditions in medical ethics leave us with the realization that those facing a choice in Yusef Camp's case and in similar situations cannot assume that the Hippocratic ethic and the professional consensus about what is ethical are automatically correct. There are many different theories of what is ethical in medical decision making, many views of what is ethical in the practice of medicine. These are not limited to the religious traditions. In secular philosophy a number of philosophical systems contain implications for medical ethics that contrast with the Hippocratic tradition. One example is the Soviet Oath from 1971 ("Oath of Soviet Physicians" 1971). It contains, among other things, a pledge of loyalty to the communist society.

Liberal Political Philosophy   Another example is seen in the most important intellectual movement for modern Western culture, the tradition of liberal political philosophy, which is the dominant commitment of secular society in the United States and most other nations of the West. Liberalism emerged as a major challenger of the more paternalistic Hippocratic tradition in the last quarter of the twentieth century.

Summary

Figure 1.1 on page 14 lists the traditions discussed in this chapter that either do or do not follow the Hippocratic tradition.

In the next chapter, we will explore the question of who it is who has full moral standing, and in chapter 3 we will begin with the Hippocratic approach to ethics and medicine. We will ask what complications arise if we assume that our goal is to produce benefits—benefits for the patient—and to protect the patient from harm.

Key Concepts

Hippocratic Oath: The code of physician ethics attributed to the Greek physician Hippocrates but more likely written by his followers in the fourth century B.C. Often believed to be related to a Pythagorean cultic belief system.

Hippocratic principle: The core principle of the Hippocratic Oath holding that the physician pledges to benefit his patient according to his ability and judgment and to protect the patient from harm. Compare Social consequentialist ethics (Key Concepts, chapter 3) and Deontological ethics (Key Concepts, chapter 3).

Liberal political philosophy: The dominant commitment of secular society in the United States and most other nations of the West that has its origins in the philosophy of Locke, Hobbes, and Rousseau and reaches its best-known political expression in the documents of the founding fathers of the U.S. political system. It stresses the place of the individual and commands respect for the liberty of the individual. It also incorporates a belief in the equality of moral worth of all persons, providing a basis for various concerns about social justice.

Rights: Moral or legal claims often associated with deontological ethics (see Key Concepts, chapter 3), including the view that these claims cannot be defeated by appeals to good consequences that would accrue from failing to act on the claims.

Figure 1.1: *Types of Codifications of Medical Ethics*

Hippocratic Codes or Oaths

Closely within the Hippocratic Tradition

The Hippocratic Oath
The Hippocratic Oath insofar as a Christian May Swear It
The Florence Nightingale Pledge
The Declaration of Geneva
The St. George's University Academic Oath
The Oath of the Russian Physician

Qualified Hippocratic Content

Percival's Code of 1803
The AMA Principles of 1847

Non-Hippocratic Codes and Oaths

Professionally Generated Codes Significantly Departing from the Hippocratic Tradition

The AMA Principles of 1980
American Nurses' Association. *Code for Nurses, with Interpretive Statements,* 1985

Medical Ethical Systems Based on Nonprofessional Ethical Traditions

Ten Maxims for Physicians and Ten Maxims for Patients, China
The Ethical and Religious Directives for Catholic Health Facilities
The Caraka Samhita of the Hindu Ayur Veda
The Seventeen Rules of Enjuin, Japan, Seventeenth Century
The Islamic Code of Medical Ethics
The Oath of Maimonides (Jewish)
The Oath of the Soviet Physician (1971)
The AHA Patient's Bill of Rights
The Consumers' Bill of Rights of the President's Advisory Commission on Consumer Protection and Quality in the Health Care Industry (1997)

Bibliography

American Hospital Association. 1978. "A Patient's Bill of Rights." *Encyclopedia of Bioethics*, vol. 4, edited by Warren T. Reich. New York: The Free Press. pp. 1782–1783.

American Medical Association. 1848. *Code of Medical Ethics: Adopted by the American Medical Association at Philadelphia, May, 1847, and by the New York Academy of Medicine in October, 1847.* New York: H. Ludwig and Company.

American Medical Association. 1981. *Current Opinions of the Judicial Council of the American Medical Association.* Chicago: American Medical Association.

Baker, Robert. 1995. Introduction to *The Codification of Medical Morality: Historical and Philosophical Studies of the Formalization of Western Medical Morality in the Eighteenth and Nineteenth Centuries. Vol. Two: Anglo-American Medical Ethics and Medical Jurisprudence in the Nineteenth Century,* edited by Robert Baker. Dordrecht, The Netherlands: Kluwer Academic Publishers. pp. 1–22.

Baker, Robert, Dorothy Parker, and Roy Porter, eds. 1993. *The Codification of Medical Morality: Historical and Philosophical Studies of the Formalization of Western Medical Morality in the Eighteenth and Nineteenth Centuries. Vol. One: Medical Ethics and Etiquette in the Eighteenth Century.* Dordrecht, The Netherlands: Kluwer Academic Publishers.

Berlant, Jeffrey L. 1975. *Profession and Monopoly: A Study of Medicine in the United States and Great Britain.* Berkeley, University of California Press.

Carrick, Paul. 1985. *Medical Ethics in Antiquity: Philosophical Perspectives on Abortion and Euthanasia.* Dordrecht, Holland: D. Reidel Publishing Company.

Doi, Takeo. 1981. *The Anatomy of Dependence.* Tokyo: Kodansha International.

Edelstein, Ludwig. 1967. "The Hippocratic Oath: Text, Translation and Interpretation." Pages 3–64 in *Ancient Medicine: Selected Papers of Ludwig Edelstein,* edited by Owsei Temkin and C. Lilian Temkin. Baltimore: The Johns Hopkins University Press.

International Organization of Islamic Medicine. 1981. *Islamic Code of Medical Ethics.* [Kuwait]: International Organization of Islamic Medicine.

National Conference of Catholic Bishops. 1995. *Ethical and Religious Directives for Catholic Health Care Services.* Washington, D.C.: United States Catholic Conference.

"Nuremberg Code, 1946." 1978. *Encyclopedia of Bioethics,* vol. 4. Edited by Warren T. Reich. New York: The Free Press. pp. 1764–1765.

"Oath of Initiation (Caraka Samhita)." 1978. *Encyclopedia of Bioethics,* vol. 4. Edited by Warren T. Reich. New York: The Free Press. pp. 1732–1733.

"Oath of Soviet Physicians (1971)." 1978. *Encyclopedia of Bioethics,* vol. 4. Edited by Warren T. Reich. New York: The Free Press. pp. 1754–1755.

Orr, Robert D., Norman Pang, Edmund D. Pellegrino, and Mark Siegler. "Use of the Hippocratic Oath: A Review of Twentieth Century Practice and a Content Analysis of Oath Administered in Medical Schools in the U.S. and Canada in 1993." *Journal of Clinical Ethics* 8 (1997):377–88.

Percival, Thomas. 1927. *Percival's Medical Ethics, 1803.* Edited by Chauncey D. Leake. Reprint, Baltimore: Williams and Wilkins.

Rosner, Fred, and J. David Bleich. 1979. *Jewish Bioethics.* New York: Sanhedrin Press.

"Solemn Oath of a Physician of Russia." 1993. *Kennedy Institute of Ethics Journal* 3, no. 4:419.

Temkin, Owsei. 1991. *Hippocrates in a World of Pagans and Christians.* Baltimore: Johns Hopkins University Press.

Veatch, Robert M., and Carol G. Mason. 1987. "Hippocratic vs. Judeo-Christian Medical Ethics: Principles in Conflict." *The Journal of Religious Ethics* 15 (Spring):86–105.

Waddington, Ivan. 1975. "The Development of Medical Ethics—a Sociological Analysis." *Medical History* 19(1): 36–51.

Waddington, Ivan. 1984. *The Medical Profession in the Industrial Revolution.* Atlantic Highlands, N.J.: Humanities Press.

World Medical Association. 1956. "Declaration of Geneva." *World Medical Journal* 3 (Supplement): 10–12.

CHAPTER TWO

Defining Death, Abortion, and Animal Welfare

The Basis of Moral Standing

In the previous chapter we saw that different cultures and social groups have different medical ethical codes or oaths. One way or another they provide compilations of ethical principles, virtues, or rules that specify the norms of morally right conduct and character. In addition to the question of which set of norms should be used, another major issue must be addressed. To whom do these norms apply? That might seem to be a question with an obvious answer: They apply to human beings. The question is, however, far more complex. At least four problems arise.

First, some codes are written as if they apply only to members of certain professional groups. They delineate norms of conduct for physicians, nurses, or other health professionals. But even they raise troublesome questions. Are the writers claiming that they apply to all members of the relevant profession or only to those who are members of the organization that adopted the code? For example, the American Medical Association's code prohibits active mercy killing. Does that prohibition apply to all physicians, even those who are not members of the AMA? Certainly, it does not make sense for it to apply to physicians who are not American. Also, some codes written by professional groups specify behavior that is morally required for patients and other laypeople. Can these professional organizations claim authority to specify what is morally right conduct for those who are not even in the profession and cannot be members of these organizations?

A second problem arises with the fact that professional groups are not the only ones who write codes purporting to state norms of professional conduct. Religious groups and governmental agencies do as well. One can imagine a religious group claiming authority to articulate norms for its members and even claiming to know what the norms of conduct are for those outside the group. Secular philosophies might make similar claims. Ethical norms are usually thought to be universal; that is, a single system of ethics applies to all. But there are many different groups claiming to know what those norms are. For example, religious groups claim to be able to articulate the norms of conduct for physicians and other health professionals just as professional groups do. This means that a physician may be subject to the norms articulated not only by the professional group but also by his or her religion, and the two may not approve of or permit the same conduct.

Third, ethical duties in the biomedical world may extend beyond living human beings. In the era of organ transplantation, even bodies of newly dead humans have become extremely valuable. In the era of genetic manipulation and test tube babies, the same can be said for human gametes and embryos. There seem to be moral limits on how these are treated, even if they are not considered living human beings. Whether an embryo—or for that matter a fetus—has the same moral standing as (other) living human beings is a matter of enormous controversy. Whether the moral principles—such as the principle of beneficence or avoidance of killing—should apply (or could apply) to these entities with a human genetic endowment will require much more philosophical work. Also, some nonhuman animals appear to most people to have some kinds of moral claims on us. Those claims may not be as weighty, but they exist nonetheless. We need to understand to whom the principles apply—to which humans (if not to all) and to which beings that are not human (if any).

Finally, the very language of morality and moral standing is complex. We speak in casual conversation of humans, persons, individuals, and beings sometimes interchangeably and sometimes with important moral differences presumed or implied. We need to understand how these terms should be used in more careful ethical discourse. In this chapter we first look at these linguistic questions. Then we examine three major areas of biomedical ethics that play key roles in deciding to whom the moral principles apply and to what extent. We examine the debate on the definition of death to see when we believe we should quit treating a human as having the full moral standing that is attributed to normal humans. Next, we look at the other end of life, to the even more controversial area of abortion to see when we should begin treating humans as having full moral standing. The link between the two will quickly become clear. Finally, we look at the controversy over animals to see whether any nonhuman animals have moral standing and, if so, how much.

Persons, Humans, and Individuals:
The Language of Moral Standing

The Concept of Moral Standing

We need to identify those to whom the moral norms apply: that is, those to whom duties of beneficence, nonmaleficence, and the other moral principles apply. One way of speaking is to refer to any being or object to whom we owe some kind of duty as having a moral claim on us or as having *moral standing*. We usually believe that humans (at least normal humans) have moral standing. But other beings do as well. Extremely abnormal humans—the permanently unconscious and severely retarded, for example—pose some difficult problems. Nevertheless, most people believe they have moral claims as well. It is also widely believed that nonhuman animals are owed at least something. Almost everyone believes we should not cause them pain, at least not without good reason. Whether we have a duty not to kill them is more controversial. Some even believe that we have duties toward plants and inanimate objects.

If we do have such duties toward nonhuman animals, plants, and inanimate objects, the reason we have them is the cause of further controversy. It may be because they are the possessions of another, in which case the moral standing may be indirect. Both religious and secular people often speak as if we have duties toward trees, ecological systems, or natural landscapes. For religious people, it may be because they believe that these are God's creation or God's possessions. For secular ecologists, the reasons why we have such duties are harder to articulate. It may be because other human beings have claims to enjoy the rest of nature, but often ecologists speak as if the duties toward the environment were more direct, that there is something intrinsically wrong with destroying a gene sequence even if humans have no interest in it and get no benefit from it. Perhaps we believe that, even if these genes are not useful now, we may find that genetic material useful to humans in the future. Or, perhaps we believe that it is intrinsically valuable and simply deserves protection.

When we claim that we have a duty to animals, plants, and inanimate objects we can say that they too have moral standing. Clearly, not all the moral principles can apply in each case, however. It is hard to imagine what it would mean, for example, to speak of a duty to respect the autonomy of trees or to tell the truth to them, although we can imagine what it might mean to have a duty to avoid killing them.

It is common to speak as if humans have a special moral standing. Some say that each person has maximum moral standing. Moreover, if each human has maximum standing, the standing of all is equal. The duties we owe to each person, we owe to all equally. Those who hold such a view would say that these humans have *full and equal moral standing.*

It is not that those outside this group have no standing at all. For example, it seems as if we owe lower animals, such as rabbits, something. It appears that we can divide the world into those who have full standing and those to whom we owe some lesser duties. Thus, all but the most extreme animal rights advocates would be quite willing to sacrifice a rabbit for the welfare of a human child but unwilling to sacrifice a child for the welfare of rabbits, even if the amount of good we could do the rabbits of the world were enormous. Likewise, if a human child and a bobcat were both starving and we had enough food only for one, certainly most people would favor giving the food to the child. (In fact, many would support killing the bobcat to feed to the child, but no one would favor killing the child to feed to the bobcat.) We can say of that special moral status that we give the child that he or she has full moral standing. One of the critical questions in biomedical ethics is to whom do we owe this full moral standing. It is that problem that is addressed in this chapter.

Moral and Nonmoral Uses of the Term Person

The English language has done us a disservice by giving us so many ways of referring to humans while at the same time often lacking precision in how those terms are used. We speak of human beings, persons, and individuals, as well as using more technical terms such as "moral agents." In the field of ethics, sometimes these terms do important moral work, signifying our commitment that the being referred to either has or does not have some kind of moral standing. The language may signal that we have duties toward it as called for by the various ethical principles or that it has a particular type of moral standing. In other cases, however, these words can be used in a way conveying no moral implication at all. To make matters particularly confusing, sometimes the same word can be used both morally and nonmorally, even by the same speaker and in the same paragraph or sentence. Figure 2.1 shows the distinction between a nonmoral and a moral definition of *person.*

Persons Defined as "Those Who Possess Some Nonmoral Characteristic"
The word *person* is particularly confusing when used in the nonmoral sense. Sometimes the word is used in ways that do not necessarily convey any moral status. Thus a *person* can be defined as any self-aware or rational living being. (Other physical or mental characteristics that do not necessarily imply a moral status are also sometimes used, such as possessing an opposing thumb, a unique genetic code, or self-awareness.) It should be clear that, if *person* is *defined*

Person (nonmoral definition)

Humans (and other beings) who possess some critical physical or mental capacity such as self-consciousness, self-awareness, or rationality

Person (moral definition)

Humans (and other beings) who possess full or maximal moral standing

---

Figure 2.1: *Two Definitions of* **Person**

by the possession of one or more of these characteristics, no moral status is necessarily implied. Thus it could be a correct use of the language to say, "Even though a baby is not a person in the sense of possessing self-awareness, nevertheless, babies have full moral standing." Such a statement would simply convey that the speaker based moral standing on something other than that on which he or she bases personhood. When the language is used in this way, there could be human living nonpersons with full moral standing. Likewise, although it would be an unusual moral view, it would not be a linguistic contradiction to say that some individuals are persons in the sense that they possess self-awareness and yet they lack full moral standing. (Certain racists might hold such a view, for example.) Those who use the word *person* in this way are also using it in a nonmoral sense.

Persons Defined as "Those with Full Moral Standing" The word *person* is also used in a way that attributes moral standing to its referents by definition. According to this view, we must first determine who has full moral standing (and who does not) and then call all in the first group *persons*. Hence, one might say, "I believe that embryos have full moral standing and therefore are persons even though they obviously lack self-awareness." Or someone might say, "Even though small children possess self-awareness, they are nevertheless not persons because they do not have full moral standing." This would be an unusual view about the moral status of children, but if being a person means nothing more than having moral standing, it is a linguistically comprehensible statement. On the other hand, such a statement would be self-contradictory if the speaker defined *person* as meaning "one who possesses self-awareness."

The bottom line is that some people use the term *person* to identify those with certain physical or mental characteristics and others use the term to identify those who, by definition, have moral standing regardless of whether they possess any particular mental or physical characteristics.

Confusion Resulting from Shifting from a Nonmoral to a Moral Use of the Term Person   The problem arises when someone tries to say something like the following:

> Late-term fetuses are not persons because they lack self-awareness (or self-consciousness or the ability to reason). And, since lacking personhood means that one lacks full moral standing, fetuses can be aborted.

Although it may be morally correct to hold that fetuses can be aborted to serve the interests of others, one cannot validly get to that conclusion using the reasoning just presented. The speaker, using the nonmoral definition, first claims that fetuses are not persons. The speaker wants us to accept as obvious that fetuses do not possess some key nonmoral characteristic such as self-awareness. He then shifts to the moral meaning of the term *person,* claiming that only persons have moral standing. Notice that, as long as one defines *person* without any reference to moral standing, one has not established that only persons have moral standing. This linguistic sleight of hand seems to suggest a proof that fetuses lack full moral standing, but it is merely a linguistic shift from a nonmoral to a moral definition of persons. What is never established is that only those with self-awareness possess full moral standing and that, after all, is what the whole abortion debate is all about.

This confusion between the position that persons have moral standing by definition and the position that personhood can be defined on the basis of certain nonmoral characteristics leads to enormous confusion in medical ethics debates. The easiest way to eliminate this confusion is simply to exclude the use of personhood language, requiring those arguing for one or another position about moral standing to make their claim in a straightforward way. Hence, if one wants to hold that fetuses lack moral standing, it won't do to claim that they are not persons and that only persons have standing. Or, if one wants to hold that they possess moral standing, it won't do to claim that they are persons and therefore they must have moral standing. Either persons have moral standing by definition, in which case little is established, or persons possess some nonmoral physical or mental characteristic, in which case claiming someone is a person tells us nothing about that person's moral status.

Proving that some nonmoral characteristic such as self-awareness or a unique genetic code is what it takes to establish full moral standing is extremely difficult to do. Many would hold that if such a link could be proved, someone would have done so by now and the abortion, definition of death, and animal rights debates would be over. Apparently, there are no definitive secular proofs of what characteristics establish full moral standing. Instead, we rely on firmly held beliefs—either secular or religious—that can not be proved to others who do not share those beliefs. Nevertheless, virtually everybody accepts the idea that some beings have full moral standing while others do not. We continue to have controversy over the definition of death (when full moral standing ceases), abortion (when full moral standing begins), and the moral standing of non-human animals precisely because we are unable to prove what characteristic establishes full moral standing.

Moral and Nonmoral Uses of the Word Human

A similar problem arises with the use of the word *human*. Sometimes those who adopt liberal views on abortion will say that human life does not begin until quickening or the third trimester of gestation or even birth. Similarly, those who are skeptical about the moral standing of anencephalic infants or the persistently vegetative may claim that such beings are not "human." Clearly, they are not challenging the genetic makeup of such beings; they are merely making claims about their lack of full moral standing.

On the other hand, conservatives may respond by pointing out that these beings clearly are "human" since they possess the genetic code of the human species. (They are not cats or dogs.) In making these claims they are relying on our consensus that the anencephalics or fetuses or persistently vegetative adults in question possess some nonmoral characteristic that makes them a part of the human species. They trade on the consensus on the characteristics of humans defined nonmorally to attempt to establish that all those with these characteristics are also humans defined as having full moral standing. Once again, it seems that one can only add confusion by sliding from a nonmoral definition to one that establishes moral status by definition. To be a human in a nonmoral sense clearly establishes nothing one way or another about whether that being also has full moral standing. Doing so requires a belief that all who are humans in the nonmoral sense also possess full moral standing. Or, to point out the liberal's problem, establishing that one lacks some nonmoral characteristic of humanness, such as self-consciousness, does not prove that one lacks moral standing.

The issue in this chapter is how people have attributed moral standing to individuals and, further, how they have attributed what we call *full moral standing*.

Defining Death

It is probably best to start by examining what it means to lose full moral standing. A good case could be made that when there is a quantum change so that full moral standing is lost we say that the individual has died. At least for humans, the fight over the definition of death is really a fight over when we should no longer treat someone the way we normally treat living humans. Once an individual is said to have died, our moral (and legal) duties toward that individual are not the same as they were when the individual was alive. One cannot kill a corpse. Other rights claims are also terminated. To say that someone has died therefore means, among other things, that we no longer attribute full moral standing to the individual. To be sure, even a corpse is thought to retain some attenuated moral standing. There are things we could do even to a corpse that would be considered immoral.

In chapter 5 we will encounter the principle of avoidance of killing. A critical problem with the principle of avoidance of killing—the idea that it is wrong to kill people—is that we need to figure out what it means to be dead. Until recently, we all knew who was dead and who was alive; it was straightforward. But in the last twenty or thirty years it has become increasingly difficult to decide whether someone is really dead or alive. Since one can not be guilty of killing a corpse, if we are going to discuss the ethics of killing, we need to first figure out what it means to be dead.

Remember Yusef Camp, the boy we encountered in chapter 1 who ate the pickle and was left possibly brain-dead in a hospital bed. If we cannot agree on whether he is dead or alive, we are going to have a real problem figuring out how to handle such a case. We need to determine whether the clinicians who favor cessation of treatment can stop it on the grounds that their patient is deceased, on the basis of brain criteria, or whether they believe that it is acceptable to stop treatment even though he is still alive.

There are three major positions regarding what it means to be dead (Law Reform Commission of Canada 1979, President's Commission for the Study of Ethical Problems in Medicine and Biomedical and Behavioral Research 1981, Lamb 1985, Gervais 1986). They are defined in Figure 2.2.

A Cardiac Definition of Death

The first, the traditional definition, can be called the *cardiac definition of death*. According to this view, an individual dies when there is irreversible cessation of circulatory and respiratory function. This is more accurately referred to as a *cardiac-oriented* definition, keeping in mind that we are referring not just to the functioning of the heart but also to the functioning of the circulatory and respiratory systems. It is possible for someone to be alive even with a dead heart. As the following case shows, those who favor the cardiac definition of death can recognize that an individual can be alive even if his heart has been removed and discarded.

Cardiac-oriented

Irreversible loss of cardiac and respiratory function

Whole-brain-oriented

Irreversible loss of all functions of the entire brain

Higher-brain-oriented

Irreversible loss of higher brain functions (those responsible for consciousness or feelings)

Figure 2.2: *Three Definitions of Death*

Case 2.1: The Man Living without a Heart

Some years ago, a dentist named Barney Clark was a heart patient at the University of Utah, where clinicians were experimenting with artificial hearts. He was at death's door and was awaiting a heart transplant. The physicians had removed his heart and connected his aorta and veins back up to an artificial heart pump running right next to him, pumping as a heart would pump blood. Barney Clark lived for four months on that artificial heart. At times he was doing quite well with this machine. At times he would sit up in bed, even get out of bed and go for a stroll, pulling this machine along with him on a cart. Sometimes he carried on a conversation, smiling and discussing things with those at his side. Would anyone, even believers in a cardiac definition of death, have considered him dead?

This was an unusual case, but it seems clear that Barney Clark was not dead during this period. What we mean by a cardiac-oriented death is that an individual has irreversibly lost the cardiac and respiratory functions that normally are controlled by the heart. The fact that these functions are being maintained by some artificial device does not make one dead.

The Problem of Irreversibility Notice that for a individual to be dead by the cardiac definition, the stoppage of the circulatory and respiratory functions must be *irreversible*. It is very common but very wrong for clinicians and others to refer to someone who has suffered a cardiac arrest and been successfully resuscitated as having been "clinically dead." According to the cardiac definition, being dead means *irreversible* loss of cardiac function. If one suffers a cardiac arrest and then is brought back, that individual was never dead. His or her tissues continued to live. We potentially can save that individual. Such individuals have suffered a cardiac arrest, and would have died had we not intervened with CPR, but it is incorrect to say that they were ever dead during that episode.

If we understand being dead as signaling a critical change in moral status, it is easy to see why it is important that such persons do not die temporarily only to be brought back to life. If they are dead, many behaviors become appropriate that are totally inappropriate for living people, even unconscious people who are not breathing and temporarily have no heartbeat. We can do things such as read the person's will, transfer assets, and, with appropriate permission, remove organs for transplant. The individual's spouse becomes a widow. None of that happens with a temporary cardiac arrest. For those who do not believe in reincarnation, we get only one death per individual, at least in this world.

If death is pronounced in such a case and then the patient's cardiac and respiratory functions return, we must say that we made a mistake. Death was erroneously pronounced—at least in the eyes of those who hold a cardiac-oriented definition of death.

Problems with a Cardiac-Oriented Definition of Death   There are some serious problems with a cardiac-oriented definition of death. For one, there are bad consequences in continuing to use the cardiac definition. Thousands and thousands of people around the world are awaiting organs for transplant. In the United States alone, there were 64,000 people on the waiting list for organs as of July 1999. If we waited until cardiac function ceased, the organs of most potential donors would no longer be usable in transplants.

It would be nice to be able to get these organs to be used for life-saving transplants, but it is clear we cannot change the definition of death just in order to get wanted organs. In fact, if we wanted to get more organs and could do so by changing the definition of death, we might as well, for example, define all medical students as dead. Then we would get young, healthy organs for the most part, rather than waiting for people to have automobile accidents or strokes or to die of age-related problems. It is obvious that we can not just pick a definition out of thin air simply because it would be useful in saving lives. On the other hand, if there are reasons why the cardiac-oriented definition is wrong, then we should begin the task of determining when we believe people lose their full moral status and die.

Many people believe that the cardiac-oriented definition of death is no longer appropriate. To claim that people die when their fluids stop flowing is to elevate blood flow to too lofty a place. Instead there is another, more complicated, explanation of what it means to die.

A Whole-Brain-Oriented Definition of Death

In about 1970, we began talking about what is today sometimes called the *whole-brain-oriented* definition of death. An individual dies, according to this view, when there is irreversible cessation of all functions of the entire brain, including the brain stem (Harvard Medical School 1968; Task Force on Death and Dying, Institute of Society, Ethics and the Life Sciences 1972; see also President's Commission for the Study of Ethical Problems in Medicine and Biomedical and Behavioral Research 1981). This is a belief based on the claim that the essence of humans is their ability to integrate bodily functions, and, insofar as we believe that the brain is responsible for those integrations of bodily function, one is dead when and only when the brain irreversibly stops functioning. Of course, according to this view one can lose individual functions and still be alive. It is the integrating capacity that counts.

Whole-brain death is the current law in most jurisdictions of the world. The exceptions include some Asian countries. Japan adopted a brain-oriented definition of death only in 1997, limiting it to cases in which organs will be procured for transplant. The resistance to the brain-oriented definition of death in Asia can be traced mainly to the fact that it does not square well with traditional Buddhist and Shinto beliefs. Some members of these groups believe the soul is dispersed throughout the body. Also, the very first organs procured for transplant in Japan, at the end of the 1960s, may well have been taken from a patient who was not dead. By either a cardiac or a brain definition, he may still have been alive. So there is a lot of nervousness in the country about procuring organs from the deceased. The Japanese do not object to procuring organs from a living patient, for instance taking one kidney from a parent to transplant to a child. It is the problem of pronouncing death on the basis of whole-brain death that is the difficulty.[1]

There is one jurisdiction in the United States that still accepts some death pronouncements based on cardiac criteria. That is New Jersey. Policy makers in that state recognize that picking exactly what it means to be dead is not totally a scientific question—that some people could choose one view, some could choose another. In New Jersey, death is based on whole-brain criteria

---

[1]Denmark has an ongoing debate. It has been the primary site of controversy on this issue in Europe. In Denmark, it is legal to pronounce death by brain criteria, but some scholars and policy makers there are not willing to accept that conclusion.

unless the individual had executed a document expressing a religious objection to the use of the whole-brain death concept. This exception was incorporated primarily to deal with Orthodox Jews, who hold to a cardiac definition of death in many cases, but other groups, including many Native Americans and Japanese, also prefer the more traditional definition.

If his entire brain had been destroyed, as two of the neurologists believed it had, Yusef Camp would have been dead by whole-brain criteria even though the ventilator was maintaining his heart and respiratory function. Once death has been pronounced the normal practice is to stop treatment if it has not already been stopped. Most people hold that treatment can be stopped on one who is dead even against the wishes of the family. Family members have no right, according to this view, to insist that clinicians continue to ventilate a corpse. However, in Yusef Camp's case, the neurologists could not reach an agreement that the entire brain was destroyed, so they could not use whole-brain death as a way of pronouncing death.

A brain-dead patient on a ventilator does, of course, make for an unusual corpse. On the ventilator, he is respiring and his heart is beating. But if his whole brain is dead, and it is not a New Jersey case, the law in most jurisdictions says that the patient is deceased.

A Higher-Brain Definition of Death

Yusef Camp could not be pronounced dead according to the whole-brain–oriented definition of death, because some brain function might have remained. This situation brings us to the third and final definition, sometimes called the *higher-brain* definition. Suppose Yusef Camp were permanently unconscious, with most brain functions gone but limited reflexes remaining in the brain stem. He would not be dead by whole-brain criteria. According to the whole-brain formulation, every last function must be gone. People have begun to say that perhaps there are some brain functions that are not absolutely essential to being considered alive. In that case, we might pronounce somebody dead, according to a newer definition of death, if his "higher functions" are permanently lost. For instance, if the cerebrum is gone, but the brain stem remains so that brain stem reflexes are present, one might, under a higher-brain definition of death, claim the patient is dead. An individual dies, according to this view, when there is an irreversible loss of higher brain functions.

Defining exactly which functions are "higher" is controversial. Some have claimed that the critical function is the function of the cerebrum. But it is theoretically possible for some motor functions to remain in the cerebrum even though all sensory function has been lost. Most defenders of the higher-brain formulations consider some sensory function to be crucial for being alive. Some of them simply equate death to an irreversible loss of consciousness.

Anybody who is permanently unconscious, according to this latter view, would be considered dead. Since considering someone dead is, in reality, claiming that the person has undergone a major change in moral status, many behaviors appropriate with regard to dead people would become acceptable at this point.

The higher-brain definition of death is not yet legal any place in the world. But it is an idea that is debated increasingly. A number of philosophers and neurologists are beginning to endorse this idea. Somebody will eventually propose that it be the legal definition of death. Had it been the legal definition of death, Yusef Camp would have been dead from the moment he became irreversibly unconscious. Nancy Cruzan, Karen Quinlan (two young women left in a vegetative state from accidents, whose families led battles for the right to forgo life support), and Baby Theresa (a permanently unconscious anencephalic infant whose parents wanted to donate her organs) would have been dead by this higher-brain definition even though they were legally alive according to the present whole-brain definition.

Definitions and Moral Standing

Almost everyone holds some version of one of these three major definitions of death. They believe that once one has irreversibly lost the critical function—cardiac, whole-brain, or higher-brain—a major moral shift has taken place as well as a biological one. They believe that the individual no longer has the full moral standing that he or she once possessed. Thus, they hold that many behaviors become acceptable that are not appropriate for individuals considered living. They may have some moral standing, but full standing no longer exists.

Abortion

Symmetry between Definition of Death and of Abortion

If calling someone dead is, in fact, a social symbol that we are declaring a major change in moral status, then the debate over the definition of death is really a great moral debate. Moreover, it may have direct relevance to the even more controversial debate over abortion. Whatever factor signals the end of full moral standing would appear to be relevant as a marker of when full moral standing begins. It is possible we can do things before full moral standing is attributed that we will not be able to do later in a human's life. We might, for example, be able to trade off interests, do laboratory manipulations, perhaps even end biological life.

The moral problems with manipulation of sperm and egg cells are often believed to be less troublesome than are those arising from manipulating a late-term fetus or a postnatal infant. It is important to know why. It must be that, no matter how we attribute value and moral status to sperm and egg cells, we view them has having a moral standing that is different from that of the late-term fetus or the postnatal infant. If we can identify what it is that is responsible for this perceived shift in moral status, perhaps we can understand better the ethics of the moral treatment of the fetus and when full moral standing accrues.

Can we use the criterion for the end of life as a signal of when full moral standing begins? Some people think we can. Let us see what the implications of each of the three definitions of death might be for the issue of the moral standing of fetuses. (For a range of well-developed positions on abortion see Callahan 1970, Noonan 1970, Feinberg 1973, and Dworkin 1994.)

First, the higher-brain death formulation implies that full moral standing accrues only when the requisite higher functions appear. For many holders of this position that means the capacity for mental function, or consciousness. These appear late in fetal development, perhaps, at about twenty-four weeks of gestation. Holders of this view would accept a lesser moral status for fetuses before that time but would not attribute the same moral status that is assigned to postnatal humans. This concept is probably what underlies the most liberal view on abortion.

Second, the whole-brain death definition implies that full moral standing accrues when the capacity for neurological bodily integration develops. This is earlier, perhaps, in about the eighth to twelfth week. Those who believe that full moral standing accrues at the point at which neurological integrating capacity appears would probably accept abortion up to the eighth or even the twelfth week, perhaps later, depending on exactly what they understand integration to mean.

The cardiac definition of death implies that full moral standing accrues when the capacity for cardiac function appears. That, in turn, depends on exactly which cardiac function is critical. Cardiac muscle contraction occurs quite early in fetal development; full pumping of blood occurs much later, perhaps at a time similar to the occurrence of the neurological integrating capacity.

Each definition of death has a corresponding notion of when full moral standing begins and implications for the moral status of fetuses before that time. None of this implies that a fetus has no moral status before the emergence of the critical function; just as a corpse commands respect even after the critical function has ceased, so even liberals on abortion may recognize that early fetuses are not merely meaningless pieces of tissue. There are moral limits on what can be done to a corpse. But those limits are not as constraining as for a being with full moral status. In the case of a dead body, we may transplant organs, do research solely for the benefit of others, perform a respectful autopsy, and so on. So, likewise, those who identify a point later in fetal development at which full moral standing begins may still believe that fetuses at an earlier stage of development have some intermediate moral status.

Notice that there is no scientific way to choose among these functions to determine which function is an absolute criterion for full moral standing. That choice requires a religious or philosophical judgment. Most people in Western society have chosen the whole-brain function as critical in the definition of death. Should they also use that as the critical point in deciding when in fetal development full moral standing accrues? Should those who accept a higher-brain definition of death likewise accept the beginning of these functions as the beginning of full moral standing?

Possible Basis for a Breakdown in the Symmetry

It is striking to note that none of these positions has anything directly to do with the fixing of the genetic code. None seems to imply full moral standing at moment of conception. How do conservatives on abortion, those who would oppose all abortion from the beginning, defend their position? What is the position of those who believe that if one kills an embryo it counts as morally equal to killing a postnatal child?

Thus far we have assumed that it is the actual capacity to perform some function that is morally critical. That function might be cardiac function, neurological integrating capacity, or consciousness, but it is the *ability to perform* the function that is decisive morally. There are people, however, who hold that it is the *potential* for these functions that is morally critical. They say that once the genetic code has been determined, the eventual development of the critical function has been determined. Barring some injury or other untoward event, the capacity will eventually emerge. In death, one loses potential when one loses capacity irreversibly. At the beginning of full moral standing, the potential is present long before the actual capacity is. Potential is present at conception or soon thereafter. If it is potential for an individual with either cardiac, whole-brain, or higher-brain function that is morally critical, then full moral standing will arise once that potential has been established.

Liberal critics may claim at this point that potential is present even before conception. The genes are present in sperm and egg, and the potential for combining exists before conception. This claim would appear to give egg and sperm cells full standing, a position almost no one finds plausible. But defenders of the potentiality position claim that what is critical is the potential for these functions' occurring *in a unique and individual way*. This potential occurs only when the genetic code is determined, at least insofar as these functions are determined genetically. If one believes that unique potential is what is morally critical to establishing full moral standing, then the moment when the genetic code is fixed becomes critical. A more moderate defender of the potentiality position may recognize that there is at least the possibility for changes in the genetic makeup of an individual for several days after conception (Hellegers 1970, McCormick 1991), perhaps, up to the point at which twinning can take place. Regardless of when they believe the genetic code is fixed, their ethic is shaped by the belief that full moral standing is contingent on the establishment of the genetically unique individual. This position would lead to attributing full moral standing at or near conception no matter which function is critical.

There is one possible exception. If the embryo or fetus has a major defect so that we could determine that it could never develop the critical function, then it lacks the potential and would never attain the full moral standing we are discussing. If a fetus is diagnosed as an anencephalic, then holders of a higher-brain view would conclude that the fetus never has the potential for the development of consciousness. Termination of such a pregnancy would theoretically be acceptable even to one who has unalterably opposed abortion of all "living" fetuses. This decision would, of course, require reliance on the higher-brain view and the unique potential view simultaneously. On the other hand, holders of the whole-brain view would still view the anencephalic fetus as having full moral standing. It could not licitly be killed. They would, however, seem logically committed to the view that a fetus so genetically abnormal that it had no potential for the development of *any* brain function (cerebral or lower) would lack full moral standing. Likewise, the holder of the cardiac view would be committed to the view that a fetus with no potential for any heart function would lack full moral standing.

The Moral Status of Nonhuman Animals

This discussion leads directly into another controversial issue in medicine: the moral status of nonhuman animals (Singer 1975, Regan and Singer 1989, Orlans 1993, DeGrazia 1996). Clinicians and scientists who do research or educational projects using nonhuman animals must confront the question of the moral limits of using them. Radical protesters destroy labs and assault medical personnel in their fight over the moral status of nonhuman animals. In the United States, federal regulations control animal use carefully (U.S. National Institutes of Health 1985, 1986). The Animal Care and Use Committee of the research sponsor's institution must approve animal research just as institutional review boards must approve research on humans.

Do any animals have the "full moral standing" we give to humans, and what would it mean if they did? Western culture has viewed nonhuman animals as subordinate to humans. They are used for food, medicine, religious ritual, and even sport. This status is reflected in the Judeo-Christian creation story, in which man is to have dominion over the earth and subdue it. Thus, non-human animals are morally subordinate to humans. They are believed to deserve protection from needless suffering, but the interests of humans take precedence. Xenografts (transplantation of organs from one species to another) are accepted; in some forms of Judaism they are even imperative. The radical separation between the status of humans and that of animals is seen in the zealous controversy over creation versus evolution. Creationists insist that God has a special relation with humans, who did not merely evolve from other animals.

By contrast, Eastern thought often gives a higher moral status to animals than most Westerners do, and animal suffering causes greater concern. For example, the Hindu doctrine of *ahimsa* (avoidance of suffering) applies to all species. Jains believe that no animal should be killed. Their priests actually sweep the ground ahead of them before they walk, to brush insects out of the way.

Western secular thinking has traditionally followed its religious thought in subordinating the moral status of nonhuman animals, but recently some people have taken a different position. Western secular thought is sometimes utilitarian. The focus is exclusively on the amount of good and harm done by an action. Many utilitarians treat pain as an evil and pleasure as a good, regardless of the species. An identical kind and quantity of pain always counts the same morally regardless of whether it is suffered by a human or a nonhuman. Utilitarians claim that anyone who treats individuals differently solely on the basis of species is guilty of "speciesism" (Singer 1975). They see it as comparable to racism or sexism or ageism.

Two other current views about the moral status of nonhumans support concern about animals. One view, the animal rights perspective of philosophers such as Tom Regan (1989), holds that sentient animals have a sacredness or right to life just as humans do. The argument is not driven by concern for consequences. Animals simply have rights, including a right to live. The second position, held by philosophers such as Ray Frey (1989), could be called the "degrees-of-pleasure-and-pain" view. It reflects a utilitarian perspective. According to Frey, two animals of different species who experience the same kind and quantity of pain do have equal moral claim to be relieved of that pain. But he emphasizes humans and rats may experience pain differently. Even though a human and a nonhuman who experienced identical kind and quantity of pain would deserve to be treated equally, if they experience it differently their moral claim would differ.

Frey's view suggests a puzzle: If a chimpanzee has developed mentally to the point that his experiences are richer than those of a severely retarded human, what would justify using him, rather than the human, for research or xenograft or food? How could one defend a priority for the human in such a case? Is species itself a morally defensible dividing line? That is, is speciesism acceptable after all? Or are we prepared to grant to nonhuman animals who have the functional capacities of severely impaired humans all the moral status we grant humans?

Key Concepts

Cardiac-oriented definition of death: The view that an individual dies when there is irreversible cessation of all cardiac and respiratory functions.

Higher-brain-oriented definition of death: The view that an individual dies when there is irreversible cessation of all "higher" functions of the brain, often believed to be functions related to consciousness and feelings.

Moral standing: The status of humans (and other beings) who have moral claims on others or to whom others have duties.

Person (moral definition): Humans (and other beings) who possess full or maximal moral standing.

Person (nonmoral definition): Humans (and other beings) who possess some critical physical or mental capacity such as self-consciousness, self-awareness, or rationality.

Rights-based defense of the moral status of animals: The view that sentient animals have a sacredness or right to life just as humans do. The argument is not driven by concern for consequences.

Speciesism: The view that species itself is a morally relevant factor in deciding moral standing; that humans, just by being humans, have greater moral standing than nonhuman animals, even those capable of having a similar kind and quantity of experience.

Utilitarian defense of the moral status of animals ("the degrees-of-pleasure-and-pain" view): The view that animals of different species who experience the same kind and quantity of pleasure or pain have equal moral claim to have the pleasure promoted or to be relieved of the pain.

Whole-brain-oriented definition of death: The view that an individual dies when there is irreversible cessation of all functions of the entire brain, including the brain stem.

Bibliography

The Definition of Death

Gervais, Karen Grandstand. 1986. *Redefining Death*. New Haven, Conn.: Yale University Press.

Harvard Medical School. 1968. "A Definition of Irreversible Coma. Report of the Ad Hoc Committee of the Harvard Medical School to Examine the Definition of Brain Death." *Journal of the American Medical Association* 205:337–340.

Lamb, David. 1985. *Death, Brain Death and Ethics*. Albany, N.Y.: State University of New York Press.

Law Reform Commission of Canada. 1979. *Criteria for the Determination of Death*. Ottawa: Ministry of Supply and Services.

President's Commission for the Study of Ethical Problems in Medicine and Biomedical and Behavioral Research. 1981. *Defining Death: Medical, Legal and Ethical Issues in the Definition of Death*. Washington, D.C.: U.S. Government Printing Office.

Task Force on Death and Dying, Institute of Society, Ethics and the Life Sciences. 1972. "Refinements in Criteria for the Determination of Death: An Appraisal." *Journal of the American Medical Association* 221:48–53.

Veatch, Robert M. 1975. "The Whole-Brain-Oriented Concept of Death: An Outmoded Philosophical Formulation." *Journal of Thanatology* 3:13–30.

Abortion

Callahan, Daniel. 1970. *Abortion: Law, Choice and Morality*. New York: Macmillan.

Dworkin, Ronald. 1994. *Life's Dominion: An Argument about Abortion, Euthanasia, and Individual Freedom*. New York: Vintage Books.

Feinberg, Joel, ed. 1973. *The Problem of Abortion*. Belmont, Calif.: Wadsworth Publishing.

Hellegers, A. 1970. "Fetal Development." *Theological Studies* 31 (March):3–9.

McCormick, Richard A. 1991. "Who or What is the Preembryo?" *Kennedy Institute of Ethics Journal* 1:1–15, esp. 4, 9, 11–12.

Noonan, John T. 1970. *The Morality of Abortion: Legal and Historical Perspectives*. Cambridge, Mass.: Harvard University Press.

Moral Standing of Non-human Animals

DeGrazia, David. 1996. *Taking Animals Seriously: Mental Life and Moral Status*. Cambridge, England: Cambridge University Press.

Frey, R. G. 1989. "The Case against Animal Rights." Pages 115–118 in Tom Regan and Peter Singer, *Animal Rights and Human Obligations*. second edition. Englewood Cliffs, NJ: Prentice Hall, 1989.

Orlans, F. Barbara. 1993. *In the Name of Science: Issues in Responsible Animal Experimentation*. New York: Oxford University Press.

Regan, Tom, and Peter Singer, eds. 1989. *Animal Rights and Human Obligations,* 2d ed. Englewood Cliffs, N.J.: Prentice Hall.

Regan, Tom. 1989. "The Case for Animal Rights." Pages 105–114 in Regan and Singer, *Animal Rights and Human Obligations.*

Singer, Peter. 1975. *Animal Liberation: A New Ethics For Our Treatment of Animals.* New York: Avon Books.

U.S. National Institutes of Health, Office for Protection from Research Risks. 1986. *Public Health Service Policy on Humane Care and Use of Laboratory Animals.* Bethesda, Md.: Office for Protection from Research Risks.

U.S. National Institutes of Health. 1985. "Laboratory Animal Welfare: Public Health Service Policy on Humane Care and Use of Laboratory Animals by Awardee Institutions; Notice." *Federal Register* 50, no. 90 (May 9):19584–19585.

CHAPTER THREE

Problems in Benefiting
and Avoiding Harm
to the Patient

What Counts as a Benefit?

Even if a health professional decided to remain committed to the Hippocratic principle of benefiting the patient and protecting the patient from harm, he or she would still face some serious problems. Some of these problems are increasingly difficult to solve. They concern the subjective nature of the Hippocratic commitment (that the physician should benefit and avoid harm *according to his ability and judgment* rather than some more objective standard); the trade-offs that must be made between medical and other elements of personal welfare; the different kinds of medical benefit that a physician might pursue; and, most critically, the controversial nature of medical paternalism.

Subjective vs. Objective Estimates of Benefit and Harm

First, if a health professional is to be Hippocratic and work only for the welfare of the patient, he or she must face the problem of whether to rely on subjective or objective assessments of benefit. A judgment of benefit is *subjective* if it is based on the perspective of the one making the assessment. On the other hand, a judgment can be considered *objective* if it would be true regardless of who was making it. There is considerable dispute over whether evaluative judgments (such as judgments about whether a given outcome is a good or a harm) can be thought to be objective at all. Some people believe that, by their very nature, value judgments are always subjective. They might define the "good" as "desired by the speaker" or as "preferred by the speaker." Others believe that at least some values are objective: that certain states are good or bad independent of who is making the assessment. If we believe that some value judgments, including some medical value judgments, can be objective, we might seek to discern what is truly a good outcome. We might do this by trying to eliminate or at least neutralize biases and special perspectives when we decide what a good outcome would be. We might for example, involve many different people in the assessment and use the consensus of a large group of people rather than relying solely on the judgment of an individual physician about what counts as a good outcome. For our purposes, the important point is that there are different ways of assessing how good or bad an outcome is. If we are striving objectively to determine what is good, we will probably use a different method of assessment than if we are striving subjectively to determine the good. In the case of subjective assessments, in medicine we have traditionally relied on the physician's judgment, but, as we shall see later, we might also consider the judgment of the patient or some other party.

Case 3.1:   The Physician Who Favors Hysterectomies

Dr. Morton Westerman is a gynecologist who has been in practice for thirty years. He sees an ambiguous Pap smear with some abnormal cell development, something that he has seen for thirty years. In such cases his rule is: When in doubt, do a hysterectomy. But recently his professional peers have done studies that reveal that there is no documentation that a hysterectomy does any good. But Dr. Westerman has been in practice for a long time, and his gut feeling is that this woman should have a hysterectomy—better to be safe than sorry. The Hippocratic Oath tells us that the physician is to benefit the patient according to his ability and judgment. Thus, the Oath is telling Dr. Westerman that, even if his colleagues disagree with his clinical judgment and have an abundance of empirical studies and data to support their position, it is his moral duty to do what he thinks is beneficial. Should he follow his own judgment or that of his peers?

The view that the physician should decide on the basis of subjective criteria grounded in his or her own judgment is increasingly hard to defend today. In fact, Dr. Westerman could be prosecuted for doing a hysterectomy that none of his colleagues thinks is worth doing. The mere fact that he believes something subjectively is not enough to settle the matter.

One can refer to the approach in which the physician bases a decision about patient benefit on his or her own judgment as *subjective Hippocratic utility*. *Utility* refers to assessments of benefit and harm. The principle of utility holds that an action is morally right insofar as it increases net utility: that is, the net amount of good that results when the harm that may be done is taken into account as well. Sometimes the benefits and the harms are considered separately, and we then refer to the principles of *beneficence* and *nonmaleficence* (that actions are morally right insofar as they, respectively, increase the good and avoid harm). *Beneficence* is the philosopher's word that simply means doing the good. *Nonmaleficence* means avoiding doing harm. Taken together we can speak of utility. Subjective Hippocratic utility, then, is based on the clinician's individual judgment. Figure 3.1 shows that the principles of medical ethics can be formulated with two dichotomous variables. The two columns of the chart represent the fact that some ethics are *consequentialist* (meaning they focus on producing benefits and avoiding harms, doing good and avoiding evil), whereas others are *duty-based* (that is, they hold that some actions are morally required as one's duty regardless of the consequences). This latter group of ethics is sometimes called *deontological ethics,* which is a term derived from the Greek word for duty. The Hippocratic ethic is consequentialist in that it focuses on benefiting the patient. Both consequentialist and duty-based ethics can apply either to the individual or to the society or community. Hippocratic utility is individual and consequentialist.

The individual, consequentialist quadrant is labeled Hippocratic utility. The original form of Hippocratic utility is subjective. The clinician's judgment is what counts. Increasingly, this emphasis on personal physician judgment is being replaced with a more objective form of Hippocratic utility in which judgment of benefit is based on peer review, utilization review, quality assurance, outcomes research, and treatment protocols—all examples of more collegial consensus about what the objective consequences of a particular treatment

Figure 3.1: *Where Hippocratic Utility Fits in a Grid of Types of Ethical Principles*

	Consequentialist Principles	**Duty-Based Principles**
Individual	Subjective 1. Beneficence 2. Nonmaleficence ....Hippocratic Utility......... Objective 1. Beneficence 2. Nonmaleficence	
Social		

decision will be. If the consensus of his colleagues is that there is no evidence that a hysterectomy would have an effect on the patient, the more modern form of Hippocratic utility requires that the clinician not do the hysterectomy. He must be guided and influenced by the more objective data about outcomes. This is no major moral change. It is still consequentialist, and it still focuses on the individual patient. But now the clinician is no longer the sole standard of benefit. There is no reason to assume, according to this new view, that the individual physician's judgment of benefit is right when his or her colleagues disagree.

There is a remaining question: What happens when the entire medical profession reaches a consensus about what is beneficial that conflicts with the convictions of other groups or individuals in the society? Maybe physicians believe the hysterectomy will help, but others in the society believe it will not. Imagine that it is 1970, and there is an issue involving a patient with metastatic cancer who develops pneumonia. The physician's colleagues all say that penicillin will be beneficial in fighting the pneumonia. In 1970, the members of the medical profession as a whole believed penicillin was beneficial because they believed that even if one suffered from metastatic cancer life was worthwhile, intrinsically good. But more and more laypeople, such as Karen Quinlan's family, were beginning to recognize that there comes a point when it no longer serves a good purpose to keep the patient alive.

Here an important distinction must be made. The claim that penicillin is beneficial in fighting pneumonia really involves two different kinds of propositions. First, it involves an empirical claim about medical science: that penicillin is likely to change the course of the pneumonia, decreasing the effects of the disease. That is a pharmacological claim about which we generally recognize an expertise. Physicians and pharmacologists are usually presumed to be more expert than laypeople in judging such factual claims. For these kinds of scientific claims, objective evidence, peer review, and outcomes research are considered legitimate.

But the claim that penicillin is beneficial in fighting pneumonia also involves a second proposition: that the change that penicillin is likely to produce is a beneficial one. Normally, that judgment may be obvious, but not always. For example, if the patient with pneumonia also has metastatic cancer and is ready to die, pneumonia can be considered "the old man's friend." Whether the consequences of penicillin are good or bad in such a case is not something medical science can determine. It is a value judgment, pure and simple. It is not an issue about which physicians or other experts and medical science can be expected to be authorities. For now, the central issue is the shift to an objective standard for deciding what the effects of an intervention will be on the patient. Recent years have seen a shift from a subjective basis rooted in the individual physician's judgment to a more objective basis as articulated by a physician's peers, in the scientific literature, and in the peer review process.

Medical vs. Other Personal Benefits

There is a second problem. Is the goal really to promote the total well-being of the patient? Or is the goal to promote only the *medical* well-being of the patient? Either way, there is a major problem for a physician. If the goal is total well-being, no physician can be expected to be able to be skilled in all aspects of living well. But if the goal of the physician is medical well-being, one has to recognize that no rational patient wants to maximize his or her medical well-being at least if it comes at the expense of other goods in life. People have goals for well-being that have nothing to do with their health. Health is an important goal for most people, but it is not the only goal. What should the physician do when a patient says she understands that a certain behavior—smoking or eating fatty foods or mountain climbing—is not good for her medical well-being but that she nevertheless gets such pleasure from it that the medical risks are justified? If the physician's duty, following the Hippocratic Oath, is to promote the total well-being of the patient, he or she should recognize that determining what will maximize it requires skill well beyond that of the ordinary health care professional. The patient may not need the physician's medical skills to increase her well-being; she may need a chef, an art critic, a book salesman, or a television repair person. In some cases she may even be willing to take some risks with her medical well-being in order to promote her total well-being.

Suppose that the circle in Figure 3.2 represents total personal well-being. This pie can be divided into several slices, or spheres, of well-being. Let's call one organic and another psychological. There are also legal, economic, religious, familial, and aesthetic spheres of well-being, among others. According to most interpretations of the Hippocratic formula, the physician's duty is to promote the total well-being of the patient. But that is an unrealistic demand in light of the skills that physicians possess. On the other hand, if a physician focuses only on the organic, he or she is obviously attending to only one sphere of the patient's concerns.[1] It becomes increasingly clear that it would be irrational for the patient always to maximize one sector of this pie at the expense of others.

---

[1] It is debatable whether the medical sphere includes both organic and psychological dimensions of well-being. A case can be made that the psychological and organic are different and that medicine in its traditional form is restricted to the organic. Under that view, psychiatry would be an interdisciplinary speciality that deals with the problems at the borderline between the psychological and the organic. Of course, the physician, as a specialist in the organic under this view, would be responsible for recognizing patient problems in other spheres of life, including the psychological, but, just as the clergyman should be aware of the possibility of an organic cause of what might at first appear to be a religious problem (but not attempt to treat the organic), so the physician should be aware of the possible links between the organic and the psychological but not claim expertise in the treatment of the psychological. The psychiatrist or psychologist should deal with these. However, regardless of whether the medical sphere ought to include the psychological, the problem remains the same: Some elements of well-being will clearly be beyond the physician's expertise, and, even within the medical sphere, there will always be potential goals that can conflict with one another.

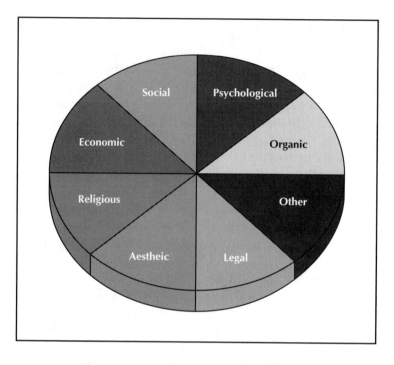

Figure 3.2: *Spheres of Well-being*

At first, one might be inclined to reject this conclusion. We sometimes think we need to follow the physician's recommendation about what will maximize our health in order to be able to enjoy any other spheres of well-being. But that really is not true. Consider a person who is diagnosed as suffering from diabetes. Imagine what a physician would recommend if she were committed to doing literally what was medically best for the patient. The absolutely best course might include an impossibly strict diet, a terribly disrupting exercise program, frequent monitoring of blood sugar, and perhaps multiple daily injections of insulin to maintain tight control. Now, a rational person would take these recommendations seriously and would try to comply with most of them most of the time. But no rational person would at all times follow what is literally the perfect diet; no one would monitor blood sugar quite as often as the best possible regimen. If the physician recommends what is absolutely the best possible course, the reasonable patient will perhaps come close to following those recommendations but will back off a little from time to time in order to accomplish other valued experiences in life.

The reasonable person will also be receiving advice from advisers in other spheres of life: from a lawyer, dentist, accountant, clergyperson, insurance agent, auto mechanic, and others. If each recommended literally what was best in his or her sphere, the poor person would face impossibly complex demands. Moreover, no obviously correct formula exists for exactly how much one should back away from the recommended course for making one's life "best" in each sphere. One thing is clear, however; no person will lead an ideally perfect life in any sphere if the goal is to maximize overall well-being rather than merely well-being in one sphere.

It is the patient's job to balance these spheres against one another so that the total size of the pie, or total well-being, is as large as possible.

In contrast to the Hippocratic Oath, members of the World Medical Association pledge to work only for the *health* of their patients. The problem here is that if they focus on only one piece of well-being, they have to recognize that rational patients will trade off that piece against all the others. The total resources the person needs to maximize well-being in all spheres is going to exceed the total available. The rational patient will have to conclude that the advice given by a physician targeted on maximizing health is advice that ought not to be followed completely. Whether the goal is medical well-being or total well-being, all professional advisers have to realize that rational patients should not follow professional advice completely.

Conflicting Goals within the Medical Sphere

A third problem that Hippocratic physicians will face is deciding what counts as a benefit within the medical, or organic, sphere. Assume, for the moment, that we accept the position that the physician's duty is to focus on medical benefits for the patient. Is there a consensus in medicine about what counts as a medical benefit? The notion of medical benefit turns out to be incredibly vague. As seen in Figure 3.3, there are no fewer than four different goals that a physician or a patient may want to pursue. Before about 1950 or 1960, the gold standard was that the purpose of medicine was to preserve life. It had not always been that way, but for most of the twentieth century that was the goal. On this basis, keeping oxygen flowing into permanently unconscious Yusef Camp's lungs would count as a benefit, because the goal was to keep that youngster alive. This notion had become controversial by the late 1960s.

In addition to preventing death, medicine strives to cure disease, relieve suffering, and promote the well-being of the patient. The problem is that sometimes one cannot accomplish all four of these goals in a given patient at the same time. The only way to relieve suffering in the metastatic cancer patient with pneumonia may be to withhold the penicillin and let the patient die. The goal of preserving life has not been achieved, but the goal of relieving suffering has.

No definitive way exists to combine all four of these goals of medicine into a single all-purpose goal that will indicate definitively what the health professional ought to do for each patient. Some may see it one way; some another.

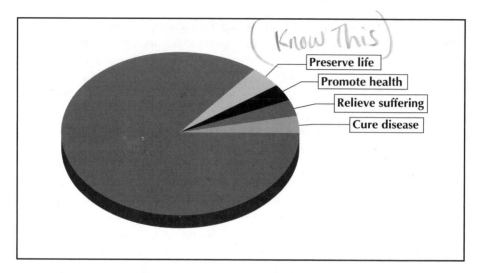

Figure 3.3: *Elements of Medical (Organic) Well-being*

Different physicians will balance these goals differently just as patients will. Even if there are objective facts upon which a physician must base judgments about possible outcomes of treatments, there may be no such thing as an objective, factual way to determine which types of benefits to pursue or no definitive way to correctly balance these four competing medical goals.

Ways to Balance Benefits and Harms

Even if the decision maker determines which types of benefits and harms count and just how beneficial or harmful each is, there is still a serious problem. Any reasonable estimate of benefits and harms will end with several different types of benefits—some medical and some not—and, likewise, several different types of harms. For each possible intervention alternative, the benefits and harms have to be combined in some way (at least by rough intuition) into a single estimate so that the clinician can attempt to do that which produces the best outcome. But there is no single definitive way for these benefit and harm estimates to be combined. At least three major possibilities exist: arithmetic summing, the ratio of benefits to harm, and giving priority to avoiding harm.

Bentham and Arithmetic Summing

Jeremy Bentham was a late-eighteenth-century philosopher who is often considered the father of classical utilitarianism, the moral philosophy that is committed to the view that the correct action or rule is the one that produces the best consequences. Classical utilitarianism is like Hippocratic ethics except that, whereas Hippocratic utility focuses only on the individual patient, classical utilitarians would consider the effects on all parties. Classical utilitarianism is thus social consequentialism. Its proponents often put forward a specific method of calculating (sometimes called a utilitarian, or Benthamite, "calculus").

Bentham proposed that a decision maker should consider the amount of benefit to each person affected and then the amount of harm. He or she should then subtract the benefit from the harm to reach a net figure for that individual. Then, after repeating this calculation for each person affected, the individual numbers should be summed to get an overall estimate of the effect of that option. Then the whole process should be completed for every alternative course being considered—for example, every treatment option in medicine. The decision maker morally ought to choose the option with the greatest net aggregate good consequences.

In Hippocratic medicine, the same process of combining estimated benefits and harms is undertaken except that the estimate is made only of the net benefit to the individual patient. Properly speaking, this process should be undertaken after deciding whether it is medical good or total good to be estimated and after deciding what counts as medical good. The method used in each case is adding and subtracting.

Comparing the Ratio of Benefits to Harms

Consider the following problem faced by a physician who is contemplating placing her patient into a randomized clinical trial of a new chemotherapeutic combination for her patient's cancer.

Case 3.2: Risks and Benefits in a Randomized Clinical Trial

Dr. Sally Satherwaite had cared for Mr. Jerome Jenkins for some years. He had been diagnosed with cancer of the prostate two years ago. Dr. Satherwaite was in contact with the Oncology Center of a nearby teaching hospital, which had offered to place Mr. Jenkins in a randomized clinical trial.

If he entered the trial he would be placed in either the standard treatment (control) group or the group given an experimental combination of potent new agents. The standard treatment posed only minor risks, but, unfortunately, only modest benefits. Two-year survival rates were as low as 3 percent. On the basis of this information, Dr. Satherwaite figured that the benefits of the standard treatment were nonetheless greater than the risks—perhaps two times as great. If she had only the standard treatment available she would recommend it to Mr. Jenkins.

The experimental agent was more promising. Preliminary data showed better two-year survival rates, perhaps ten times as great. Unfortunately, the side effects were also greater, about ten times as bad. Mr. Jenkins asked her for her recommendation about whether to enter the trial.

On the basis of Dr. Satherwaite's estimates, the standard treatment has twice as much benefit as potential harm (considering both severity and probability). But so does the experimental treatment. The clinician could view this as a choice between two options, which, if we used some imaginary unit of benefit and harm, could be said to offer the choice presented in Figure 3.4.

One choice has a benefit of 2 and harm of −1, and a second choice has a benefit of 20 and a harm of −10. Of course these are only rough intuitive estimates, but often that is all the bedside clinician has to go on.

If Dr. Satherwaite follows Bentham's method of calculating, subtracting harms from benefits in each case, she reaches the surprising conclusion that the standard treatment has a net good of 1 while the experimental treatment has a net good of 10. In general, in comparisons of high-risk/high-gain options with low-risk/low-gain options, the difference between plausible alternatives will be greater in the high-risk/high-gain option. Bentham's arithmetic combining has the surprising effect of tending to favor more aggressive interventions. Dr. Satherwaite would probably urge Mr. Jenkins to enter the trial with the hope of getting the experimental treatment. She might even try to get it for him off protocol so he does not have the risk of being placed in the group getting the standard treatment.

However, Dr. Satherwaite might try to integrate her estimate in a different way. She could calculate the ratio of benefits to harms in each case. Strikingly,

Figure 3.4: ***High-Risk/High-Gain vs. Low-Risk/ Low-Gain Therapy Choices***

	Standard	Experimental
Benefits Harms	2 units 1 unit	20 units 10 units

she would find that the ratios for the two options are the same. She would presumably be at the "indifference point" (the point at which she had no basis for favoring one treatment or the other) and might endorse entry into the trial on a randomized basis. It is when benefit/harm ratios of treatment options seem the same that many consider the randomized trial to be morally acceptable. Likewise, many health planners attempt to arrange limited health resources so as to maximize the ratio of benefits to harms. (This method of allocating scarce resources will be discussed further in chapter 7.)

First of All, Do No Harm

There is still a third possibility for combining benefits and harms that is even more conservative than using ratios. The folk ethics of physicians often includes a slogan that is meant to address problems of comparing benefits and harms of alternative treatments. *Primum non nocere,* or "first of all, do no harm" is a slogan popular among physicians. Often it is presumed to come from the Hippocratic Oath, but, as we have already seen, all the Oath says is to benefit *and* do no harm; a coordinating conjunction indicates no priority for avoiding harm. Those who have looked for the origins of this slogan cannot find any use of it before the nineteenth century, at which time medicine began to realize that sometimes physicians' interventions caused harm rather than good (Sandulescu 1965, Jonsen 1978, Veatch, 1991).

Some take *primum non nocere* to mean that avoiding harm gets first priority. If a physician realizes that he or she may do good but may also do harm, then the priority for not harming should lead the physician not to intervene. This, clearly, is the most conservative of all the methods of combining benefits and harms. If loyal to this particular method, Dr. Satherwaite would have a clear preference for the standard treatment. She would direct her attention to the second line of the table in Figure 3.4, striving to minimize harm. In fact, taken to the extreme, she would not even recommend the standard treatment, since it would pose the risk of at least some harm. Locking oneself in the office and never doing anything would guarantee that no harm would be done. Of course, much good would be forgone as well.

Perhaps what some who invoke the *primum non nocere* slogan mean is that the physician should *intend* no harm. That would at least be more plausible than an instruction to *do* no harm. This is part of the idea behind what is sometimes called the *doctrine of double effect,* a notion we shall discuss in chapter 5. If that is what is meant, it is quite different from the injunction to do no harm; much harm can be done even if it is not intended. The doctrine of double effect holds that harms may even be foreseen and still be morally tolerable provided they were not intended.

We are left with the question of whether a physician can ever do harm in the process of doing good for patients and, if so, how one ought to combine the benefits and the harms: whether one should look at the arithmetic result, calculate ratios, or give an absolute priority to avoiding harm. None of these methods of combining benefits and harms is obviously the correct one. Different physicians and patients with different risk aversiveness will use different methods. It seems that, even if the data with which physicians can predict outcomes could be made more or less objective through peer review, there is, in principle, no way that quantifying benefits and harms and combining those into an integrated estimate of the value of alternatives can be made objective. In such cases a critical question is whether it is the physician's judgment that should count rather than the judgment of the professional group, the larger social community, or the individual patient.

The Problem of Medical Paternalism

In addition to the practical problems of identifying which types of benefits and harms count and how they should be compared, a serious moral issue raised by the Hippocratic ethic has come to light in the current generation of medical ethics. We have seen that there are good reasons why the typical physician, especially one who does not know the patient well, ought not to be able to figure out what will benefit the patient. If different people have different values and priorities, it would be expecting too much to ask even the very talented and dedicated physician to be able to figure out what will really promote the patient's well-being the most. But even if the physician can succeed in that difficult task, there still remains a problem. The Hippocratic ethic, even at its best, is paternalistic.

Paternalism, as we saw in chapter 1, is an action taken to benefit another person and done for the welfare of that person, but against his or her will. It should not be assumed that all paternalistic actions are necessarily immoral. Most people, for example, favor some instances of what is often called "weak" paternalism: that is, paternalism regarding persons who are not (or may not be) mentally competent to make substantially autonomous choices—small children, the severely mentally retarded, and the incapacitated, for example. Moreover, even among those who usually find "strong" paternalism (that is, paternalism toward those who are substantially autonomous) morally troublesome, there may be overriding considerations that could justify it.

The Hippocratic Oath tells the clinician, whether using his own personal judgment or that of peers, to do what appears to benefit the patient—even if the patient is not in agreement or does not want the offered benefit. Other ethical systems have other principles that move beyond consideration of the consequences to the patient.

Medical paternalism is rampant in the old Hippocratic tradition. The health care professional was instructed to do what is beneficial according to his ability and judgment. It did not factor in benefit based on the patients' judgment of what was good. It did not consider the possibility that the patient might have a right to choose even if that choice did not produce the most good for the patient.

The Hippocratic Oath says that the physician should benefit the patient and protect him or her from harm. However, scholars have asked, "What is this harm with which the Hippocratic position is concerned?" Some suggested that it was harm instigated by enemies. In Greek medicine, occasionally an enemy of the patient would bribe a physician to prescribe a medicine for the patient that was actually a poison. But it is not a great moral insight to recognize that one should not take bribes from the patient's enemy in order to poison the patient. In fact, there is no historical evidence that this is what the Hippocratic author meant. Another possibility is somewhat more promising. Sometimes the Hippocratic Oath is interpreted to mean that patients may have family and friends that come around in a time of illness who mean well, but actually do more harm than good. Remember the view of knowledge in the Pythagorean system: Well-meaning uneducated do-gooders may do more harm than good. So when laypeople gather around the patient and start to make recommendations, it is the physician's duty, according to this interpretation, to make sure they do not harm the patient.

That at least makes a little more sense, but there is no evidence that that is what the Hippocratic writer meant, either. Edelstein (1967), the scholar mentioned earlier, believes that what the Hippocratic author meant was that the physician's duty is to protect the patient from harm that the patient may do to himself. Remember, the patient is ignorant; he or she does not have the knowledge that comes with initiation into the cult.

The best interpretation of the Hippocratic Oath was that the physician's duty was to protect the patient from herself. Even if one shifts to a more objective standard of what counts as a benefit by using peer review, one still may end up being paternalistic. The peers may not reach the same conclusion about the penicillin for the pneumonia that the patient reaches. And to the extent that modern philosophical thought is skeptical about paternalism, problems will arise in taking the Hippocratic Oath at face value. To get us oriented toward the alternative to Hippocratic utility, consider the following case that arose in 1970 just as birth control began to be widely used and medical paternalism was starting to be seen as problematic. It is a case that changed the history of medical ethics, at least in the Anglo-American West.

Case 3.3: Is Birth Control Bad for One's Health?

In 1970 Dr. Browne was a kindly, 63-year-old British general practitioner. He had been the family physician of a 16-year-old woman since she was born. This young woman thought she should get some contraceptive counseling. She realized that Dr. Browne might not look too favorably upon this plan, so she went to a place called the Birmingham Brook Advisory Centre. This was a local birth control counseling clinic. She got contraceptive counseling, a physical examination, and a prescription for oral contraceptives. It is standard medical practice to inform a family physician if one writes a prescription for someone who normally sees another physician. The clinic's physician asked if he could notify her physician, Dr. Browne. Perhaps without thinking, she gave her consent.

Dr. Browne received in the mail, unsolicited, a letter informing him that his patient was on the pill. Dr. Browne expressed two concerns. First, he was concerned about her pharmacological well-being. In 1970 the pill had not been on the market very long. Nobody understood what the effects might be, especially in a 16-year-old. But he was also worried about her total well-being: in particular, about what he called her "moral health."

Dr. Browne consulted with some colleagues, got their advice, and finally came up with a plan. One day when the young woman's father was in the doctor's office, Dr. Browne told him the whole story.

The young woman was not pleased with this turn of events. The clinic physician was not pleased either. Dr. Browne was charged before the General Medical Council in Great Britain with the violation of patient confidentiality (General Medical Council 1971). Dr. Browne, in his defense, introduced two documents: the Hippocratic Oath and the British Medical Association (BMA) code. The Oath says that the physician should not disclose "that which should not be spread abroad." That, in turn, has traditionally been interpreted as confirming the core Hippocratic principle: that his moral duty is to do what he thinks will benefit the patient. Likewise, the BMA code explicitly permits disclosures when doing so is believed to be for the benefit of the patient. Dr. Browne claimed that, having struggled with his conscience and consulted with colleagues, he did what he thought was best for his patient. He may have had a somewhat archaic view about what would benefit her, but he really believed that this was the most beneficial course. Should the General Medical Council have exonerated him?

Dr. Browne was acquitted of any violation of the British standard of confidentiality. He followed both the Hippocratic Oath and the British Medical

Association code. If he had been an American physician, he could have consulted the AMA code in effect at the time. This code was consistent with the Hippocratic Oath and the British code: the physician's duty was to keep confidence, with certain exceptions, including when the physician believes that it is in the patient's interest to disclose.

The current generation of medical ethics has seen a dramatic move away from Hippocratic paternalism toward a new set of principles that is based on duty rather than on maximizing good consequences for the patient. These principles involve respect for the autonomy of the individual patient, fidelity to promises, and veracity. Sometimes they are collected together under the heading, "respect for persons." It is widely held that these duty-based principles would give physicians much less leeway to act paternalistically than the Hippocratic Oath does. Together, they offer an alternative to Hippocratic utility when dealing at the level of the individual. In the next chapter, we shall see how these principles affect the patient-physician relation.

Key Concepts

Beneficence: The moral principle that actions or practices are right insofar as they produce good consequences. Compare Nonmaleficence.

Consequentialist ethics: Normative ethical theories that focus on producing good consequences. See Hippocratic ethics, Social consequentialist ethics, and Utilitarianism.

Deontological ethics: Any of a group of normative ethical theories that base assessment of rightness or wrongness of actions on duties, "inherent right-making characteristics" of actions, or rules rather than on consequences. See Duty-based principles. See also Formalism (Key Concepts, chapter 4). Compare Consequentialist ethics.

Duty-based principles: Ethical principles based on formal obligations to act in certain ways toward others regardless of the consequences. These are sometimes referred to as "deontological," a term derived from the Greek term for duty. Among the deontological, or duty-based, principles are fidelity, autonomy, veracity, and avoidance of killing (sometimes collectively referred to as the principles of "respect for persons") as well as the social ethical principle of justice. See Justice (Key Concepts, chapter 7).

Hippocratic ethics: The kind of consequentialist ethics that limit the relevant consequences to those that affect the individual patient.

Nonmaleficence: The moral principle that actions or practices are right insofar as they avoid producing bad consequences. Compare Beneficence.

Objective Hippocratic beneficence: A form of beneficence that determines consequences by some objective standard of benefit.

Paternalism: The view that it is ethical to take action to benefit another person for the welfare of that person but against his or her will. "Strong paternalism" involves taking such action even though the individual benefited is mentally competent; "weak paternalism" involves actions taken for the benefit of an individual who is either known to be incompetent or who is suspected of being so.

Social (or classical) consequentialist ethics: Consequentialist ethics that include all consequences for all parties affected by an action.

Subjective Hippocratic beneficence: A form of beneficence that limits consequences to those judged by the physician (or some other party) to be beneficial to the patient.

Utilitarianism: The normative ethical theory that is committed to the view that the correct action or rule is the one that produces the best consequences considering all parties affected; often limited to those forms of consequentialist ethics that envision calculations of anticipated benefits and harms by subtracting expected amount and probability of harm from expected amount and probability of benefit for each affected party and then summing the net benefits for all those affected.

Bibliography

Bentham, Jeremy. 1967. "An Introduction to the Principles of Morals and Legislation." Pages 367–390 in *Ethical Theories: A Book of Readings,* edited by A. I. Melden. Englewood Cliffs, New Jersey: Prentice-Hall.

Edelstein, Ludwig. 1967. "The Hippocratic Oath: Text, Translation, and Interpretation." Pages 3–64 in *Ancient Medicine: Selected Papers of Ludwig Edelstein,* edited by Owsei Temkin and C. Lilian Temkin. Baltimore: The Johns Hopkins Press.

General Medical Council Disciplinary Committee. 1971. *British Medical Journal Supplement,* no. 3442 (March 20):79–80.

Jonsen, Albert R. 1978. "Do No Harm." *Annals of Internal Medicine* 88:827–832.

Sandulescu, C. 1965. "*Primum non nocere:* Philological Commentaries on a Medical Aphorism." *Acta Antiqua Hungarica* 13:359–368.

Veatch, Robert M. 1991. *The Patient-Physician Relation: The Patient as Partner, Part 2.* Bloomington, Ind.: Indiana University Press.

CHAPTER FOUR

The Ethics of Respect for Persons

Breaking Promises, Cheating and Lying, and Why Physicians Have Considered Them Ethical

In the case at the end of the last chapter, Dr. Browne felt justified (and indeed was exonerated by the British General Medical Council) in breaking a confidence because he followed the Hippocratic dictum that the clinician should always act in a way that he believes will benefit the patient and protect the patient from harm. Reflection on cases such as this one have increasingly led critics of the Hippocratic ethic to doubt that the physician's subjective judgment of patient benefit is the definitive standard for clinician action. The ethic focuses only on the welfare of the patient and excludes any consideration of the welfare of other parties. The problem of the interests as well as the rights of other patients is to be taken up in chapter 7. The Hippocratic principle also poses problems even if we consider the rights of only the individual patient. Increasingly, medical ethics is taking up duties and rights in the patient-physician relation as well as benefits and harms. The general problem is one of whether sometimes an action can be morally wrong even if it maximizes good consequences.

We are starting to talk about the ethic based on duty. When that ethic focuses on duties to individuals it is often called an ethic of *respect for persons.* Respect for persons is an ethic that derives to a great degree from the philosopher Immanuel Kant (1964). Kant stressed that it was important to treat human beings as ends-in-themselves. He affirmed that human life has intrinsic value and therefore that humans deserve respect independent of the consequences of actions. We show respect for them by observing certain duties toward them.

The ethic of respect for persons, being a type of ethic based on duty, differs from ethics that focus on production of good consequences and avoiding evil ones. Whereas consequentialist ethics determine what is morally right by examining the consequences of actions, an ethic of respect for persons considers certain behaviors simply to be one's duty—regardless of the consequences. If an action includes lying, cheating, breaking a promise, or violating another's autonomy, it is morally wrong—even if the consequences are good. Such an ethic focuses on the intrinsic nature of the action, its moral structure or form, and hence is sometimes called *formalism.* According to this view, actions (or sets of actions) are right or wrong not because of the consequences they produce but because of their inherent content or form. Some people also call this kind of ethic *deontological,* derived from the Greek word for duty. Deontological, or formalist, approaches to ethics such as an ethic of respect for persons stand as a major alternative to ethics that decide what is morally right or wrong on the basis of consequences.

In modern Western society those who emphasize more deontological or formalist approaches sometimes use the language of *rights* rather than of duties, but there is a close connection between the two. If one person has a right—for example, a right to refuse medical treatment—then other people have a reciprocal duty, in this case, the duty to leave the individual alone when he or she refuses treatment.

Figure 4.1 modifies Figure 3.1 by adding the ethic of respect for persons, an alternative to the Hippocratic ethic. The figure indicates four principles that are sometimes included under the rubric of respect for persons. The first

Figure 4.1: *Types of Ethical Principles*

	Consequentialist Principles	**Duty-Based Principles**
Individual	Subjective 1. Beneficence 2. Nonmaleficence ....Hippocratic Utility......... Objective 1. Beneficence 2. Nonmaleficence	**The Ethic of Respect for Persons** 1. Fidelity 2. Autonomy 3. Veracity 4. Avoidance of killing
Social		

is the principle of *fidelity*: that is, fidelity to commitments made in relations with others, to promises made and contracts to be kept. Anyone who feels some moral duty to keep a promise even if the consequences are not the best is reflecting this principle. But this is only one aspect of respecting persons. The second is the principle of *autonomy,* which in turn gives rise to the notion of informed consent in a very vigorous way. Third is the principle of *veracity,* or simply the duty to tell the truth. The fourth, which we will take up in detail in chapter 5, is the principle of *avoidance of killing.* In some religious systems, this is referred to as the sacredness of life or the ideal that life is precious and to be respected. Kant derived from that the idea that not only should one not kill other people but even that one should not take one's own life. So for Kant, suicide was prohibited because suicide was failing to show adequate respect for one's own person, for one's own life, or for failing to treat life as an end in itself.

The Principle of Fidelity

We will start comparing the ethics of Hippocratic benefit with the ethics of respect for persons. The problem was encountered in the case of Dr. Browne. The general form of the problem is that one course of action is believed by the physician to benefit that patient the most while another course, often expressed in terms of either rights or duties, appears to be morally required by some principle or rule related to respect for persons. The cases are ones in which the clinician feels required in some moral way to do something other than what he or she believes is the most beneficial course.

Many people, when reflecting on Dr. Browne's choice to disclose the use of contraceptives to the young woman's father, may believe he simply had a duty of confidentiality. Or to put it in other language that amounts to the same thing, the girl had a right to confidentiality. Either duties or rights language is meant to describe a moral concern that more was involved than Dr. Browne's notion that he simply should act so as to benefit his patient.

The general idea of the ethics of fidelity in the patient-physician relation is one of loyalty. A special type of relationship is created between a patient and a physician. Each owes the other some loyalty. Most attention is focused on the loyalty of the physician to the patient, but in some settings we are increasingly talking about the obligations or duties of loyalty of the patient to the physician as well (Benjamin 1985). The troublesome cases are those in which keeping a commitment to the patient is not the way to produce the best consequences for the patient; consequences incline one toward one action, and duty inclines one toward another.

Case 4.1: The Promised Internship

A senior medical student, using the national matching program, is promised what she considers the perfect residency position. She receives and signs a contract for the position. But just before July 1, the day when residency programs begin, the physician/administrator from the hospital calls and says, "I'm very sorry to tell you this, but we have found somebody we think will be better for our hospital and our patients. Even though you have excellent skills, this candidate is just exactly what we need. He has already done a clerkship in the area where we have special need. We're sorry, but we won't be able to accept you after all."

The medical student may feel she has a legal claim against the hospital. That may depend on the exact wording of the legal contract. But she may also feel she has been wronged morally. Given the traditional Hippocratic ethical notion that physicians have a duty to do what is best for their patients, the physician who administers the program claims that, regardless of the legal implications, he is merely doing what his professional ethics requires. Assuming that the physician/administrator really believed that the other person would be better for the patients of his hospital, did this medical student have any moral grounds for protest?

Many would feel that the medical student had been treated improperly. Something was promised, and the hospital's administrators reneged. Anyone who has such a feeling has the idea of ethics of fidelity. Something was promised; a commitment was made. The general idea is that one owes something to the person to whom a promise has been made. Those who hold to the principle of fidelity claim that the mere fact that better consequences will result if one reneges on the promise does not necessarily justify breaking the promise. The striking thing about this case is that many persons would feel that the hospital administrators owed something to this medical student even if the hospital's patients really would be somewhat better off if the promise were broken.

Fidelity gives rise to an independent duty to keep promises or contracts. This is an ethic that is particularly visible in classical Judeo-Christian ethics. The ethic of contract, or covenant keeping, is the central motif of ancient Jewish ethics; Yahweh made a covenant with a people who bear obligations independent of the consequences. This ethic of fidelity has carried into the secular ethics of Immanuel Kant and others in the formalist or deontological tradition in the notion that there is reason to keep a promise simply because it is a promise.

Different Concepts of Duty

A word is needed here about the idea of duty. Duty, according to Kant and deontologists in general, is independent of consequences. For example, the duty of promise keeping does not hold just in the situation where the consequences will be best if the promise is kept. We talk about several different kinds of duties in medical ethics.

Absolute, Exceptionless Duties   Sometimes we talk about *absolute, exceptionless duties.* In a mature, adult world, very few people believe that there are very many exceptionless, absolutely binding, rules. Parents may have said, "It is your duty to keep a promise no matter what." They got the point across that keeping promises was important. They may have at first conveyed the idea that never, under any circumstances, should one ever break a promise. Immanuel Kant is often believed to have held something like that view. He believed that every single time one breaks a promise one has done something that is morally incorrect. Most people don't quite hold to that view, however.

Case 4.2: Conflicting Promises: A Physician in a Bind

Dr. Lewis Hammonds has a patient, Florence Yasmin, who is suffering from a serious malignancy. Ms. Yasmin, after months of pain and increasing incapacity, says to Dr. Hammonds, "Doctor, if this pain gets so unbearable I can't stand it any more, promise me you'll put me out of my misery and kill me."

This is a weak moment for Dr. Hammonds, who responds, "All right, I promise you I will end your life if you are that miserable. I will actively, mercifully kill you."

Normally, he would not have made such a promise, but in this instance for some reason he does. Two months later, the disease progresses to the point that Ms. Yasmin is in constant misery, and she says, "This is that moment, Doctor. I really need your help now. Will you mercifully put me out of my misery?"

It happens that Dr. Hammonds, like many people of the day, also believes that it is morally wrong for a physician to kill, even for mercy. Moreover, he believes that, even if it were not wrong in principle, it would be wrong to violate the law that prohibits physician mercy killings. So now Dr. Hammonds has gotten himself into a bind. He has made a promise, which he believes it is his duty to keep, but he also holds that it is his duty as a physician not to engage in mercy killing even when the patient is mentally competent and voluntarily requests such help. He has made two commitments, not to kill and to keep promises. As long as he believes these duties are exceptionless, he has no way out of his bind.

Prima Facie *Duties*   In a case like this one, ethical theorists contrast absolute or exceptionless duties with what are called *prima facie* duties. *Prima facie* duties are duties that are morally binding, other things being equal. So, in general, if one makes a promise, it is one's *prima facie* duty to keep the promise. But, generally it is also a *prima facie* duty not to kill people. That is to say that if nothing else were at stake, if there were no exceptional circumstances, it would be one's duty not to kill, at least not to kill human beings.

One can analyze the promise made to kill this patient into two moral components. There is the component of the promise made, and there is the component of the act of killing. Much as in physics, a physicist might analyze a force into two or more vectors, so in ethics we can separate a moral action into two or more analytically distinguishable components. Looking at only one of those dimensions, say the act of promising, we would say it is one's *prima facie* duty to keep promises. That is, if we look only at the dimension of promise keeping, the physician has a duty to do what he said he would do. If there were no other moral dimension involved, he should keep his promise. On the other hand, looking at the situation only from the dimension of killing, we might conclude it is his duty not to kill. If there were no other moral dimension involved, he should not kill. We could then say there are two *prima facie* duties and that, in this case, they conflict with each other. Just as in physics two vectors of force may pull in opposite directions, so in ethics two *prima facie* duties may "pull" in opposite directions.

When someone feels in a moral bind the way Dr. Hammonds did, it may be because he feels two *prima facie* moral principles pulling him in different directions. Each of them conveys a *prima facie* duty. In such cases, we need a method of resolving conflict between opposing principles or duties.

Duty Proper   Somehow Dr. Hammonds needs to come to some answer, some course of action. That calls for a theory of resolution of conflict among principles, an area of great controversy and importance in contemporary medical ethics. Each theory of conflict resolution will lead to some answer, some account of which conflicting principle deserves priority. Whichever course of action is determined to have priority is labeled the *duty proper.*

Theories of Conflict Resolution

Different ethical theories of conflict resolution lead to the conclusion that one or another principle wins out. Four general approaches are available.

Single-Principle Theories   One solution is to deny that there are two *prima facie* principles in conflict. The Hippocratic principle that the physician's only duty is to do what he thinks will benefit the patient is a good example. If Dr. Hammonds held such a view, he would feel bound neither to keep promises nor to avoid killing in all cases; he would only be bound to try to benefit the patient. If keeping his promise and euthanizing the patient would be most beneficial for her, then that would be his duty proper. If breaking the promise would be more beneficial to the patient, then that would be the duty proper. If there is only one principle, whatever it may be, then there can be no conflict, at least at this level.

Ranking (Lexically Ordering) Principles   The problem with the single-principle approach is that it seems to many people to be too simplistic. It would mean, in this case, that there is nothing intrinsically wrong with either breaking a promise or with killing. Many people believe that there is more than one right-making characteristic of actions. For example, we may have a duty both to avoid killing people and to keep promises. In such cases we might be able to rank the principles in order of priority. If the choice is between the principle of fidelity with its derivative duty to keep promises on the one hand and the principle of avoiding killing on the other, perhaps we can rank one categorically above the other. Perhaps the notion of never killing takes precedence over the duty of fidelity to promises, for example. If so, then the conflict between the two *prima facie* duties is resolved; avoidance of killing is the duty proper.

This attempt to rank principles is sometimes called *lexical ordering,* referring to ordering as in a dictionary, or lexicon; that is, all instances of one principle before any of the next just as in a dictionary all *a*s come before any *b*s. The term was introduced by the philosopher John Rawls (1971), who has argued that between his two principles of justice (which we will explore in Chapter 7), the first must be satisfied before the second.[1] That approach would solve the problem of finding a duty proper without reducing all ethics to a single principle. The problem, however, is that most people find it about as implausible to rank any one principle in first priority in all possible cases as it is to identify a single, all-purpose principle. In our example, some people may believe that in all circumstances either fidelity or avoidance of killing should always take priority, but others would find that implausible.

Balancing   The approach that has particularly wide appeal at the present time is one that denies that a single principle can be found to resolve all conflict and also denies the possibility of an exceptionless ranking. Instead, it relies on the metaphor of *balancing* competing *prima facie* principles (see, for

---

[1]Rawls's first principle of justice is that "Each person is to have an equal right to the most extensive total system of equal basic liberties compatible with a similar system of liberty for all." That requirement must be satisfied before the second principle comes into play, which is that "Social and economic inequalities are to be arranged so that they are both: (a) to the greatest benefit of the least advantaged, consistent with the just savings principle, and (b) attached to offices and positions open to all under conditions of fair equality of opportunity." (Rawls 1971, p. 302). The second part of the second principle must be satisfied before the first part of it. Hence, some have said that there is really a rank, or lexical, ordering among three conditions.

example, Beauchamp and Childress 1994).[2] Sometimes one *prima facie* principle may be perceived as the most "weighty," sometimes another. Balancing permits either fidelity to promises or avoidance of killing to win out depending on the circumstances.

The problem with the balancing approach is that it seems to rely on the intuition of the decision maker and just about any preexisting intuition can be claimed to be "weightier."[3] Each of the opponents in a moral dispute may discern that his or her principle is the weightier. Balancing may end up providing very little help in resolving moral disputes.

Combining Ranking and Balancing One other possible solution has been proposed to the problem of how to resolve conflict among principles in medical ethics. This attempts to combine ranking and balancing strategies. Perhaps some principles can be grouped into clusters. Within the clusters, individual principles might be considered co-equal in importance so that they can only be balanced against one another. Even if that is the case, it is possible that one cluster might, when taken together, be weightier, more significant, than another (Veatch 1981, 1995).

Such an approach might, for example, treat the consequentialist principles—beneficence and nonmaleficence—as a cluster that cannot be ranked unvaryingly one over the other. According to this position, beneficence and nonmaleficence must be balanced against each other rather than, for example, giving nonmaleficence priority as the slogan *primum non nocere* suggests. Thus the principles on the left half of Figure 4.1 are balanced against each other.

Likewise, the principles that give rise to duties that are not based on consequence maximizing, those on the right half of Figure 4.1, are to be balanced against one another. But, in contrast to more straightforward balancing approaches, in the combination approach, the nonconsequentialist, or duty-based, cluster of principles—including fidelity, autonomy, and veracity as well as avoidance of killing and justice, which will be added in later chapters—is, in aggregate, ranked above the consequentialist cluster. Thus balancing within clusters is combined with lexical ordering between the two clusters.

---

[2]Some ethicists, such as Baruch Brody (1989), object to the numerical quantification of the balancing image, claiming that ethics cannot be reduced to such quantification. Brody prefers, instead, the image of "conflicting appeals," but the result is similar; sometimes one appeal will win out, sometimes another, depending on the power or force of the appeal.

[3]Recently, efforts have been made to add more reason to the balancing by claiming that a process of *specification* of abstract principles can be applied. That is, for particular "domains," or spheres of action, one principle will take precedence without necessarily being ranked as prior for all domains (Richardson 1990, DeGrazia 1992). The problem with specification, however, is that, if one reason can be found for giving priority for one principle over another in one domain, it is hard to see why the same reason wouldn't give it lexical priority over the other in other domains as well. In the end balancing with specification would look essentially like ranking approaches.

The Ethics of Confidentiality

One approach to confidentiality is to view the duty of confidentiality as an example of the ethic of promise keeping. Not everybody views it that way.

The Hippocratic Approach to Confidentiality   The Hippocratic Oath commits the physician not to disclose "that which ought not be spread abroad." This admonition sounds like an oath of confidentiality, but it implies that some things may be spread abroad, perhaps even that some things should be. If one asks how to determine what should be spread abroad, the answer is found in the Hippocratic principle: Benefit the patient and protect the patient from harm. Hippocratic confidentiality is driven by beneficence. Whenever it will serve the patient's good to keep information confidential, then it should not be disclosed. But, on the other hand, in the standard Hippocratic stance, whenever, according to the clinician's judgment, disclosure would be better for the patient, the physician should release the information. Any confidentiality commitment is voided. That was also the ethic of the British Medical Association before the Dr. Browne case. It was the position of the American Medical Association until 1980. It remains the ethic of some codes, such as that of the St. George's University School of Medicine. That oath essentially echoes the Hippocratic Oath, saying, "All things seen or heard in the exercise of my profession, which ought not to be divulged, I will keep secret and will never reveal." So far, that sounds like an oath or a promise for confidentiality. But then a final clause appears: "excepting for most weighty reasons." If one interprets the "most weighty reason" to be the benefit of the patient, then it becomes Hippocratic. And given that many of the elements of the St. George's oath are Hippocratic, it is open to this paternalistic interpretation.

According to the Hippocratic interpretation, confidences should not be broken to benefit other people. For instance, if a patient were to tell her physician that she was abusing her child, that information could not be disclosed (unless the disclosure somehow benefited her). But the Hippocratic physician would be free to disclose even against the wishes of the patient if some benefit to the patient could be discerned.

Non-Hippocratic Prohibitions on Disclosure   A number of codes have more rigorous confidentiality requirements. They prohibit disclosure even if the breaking of confidence is believed to benefit the patient. One might ask why a physician should not break confidence if she believes doing so will benefit the patient in the end. Confidences, according to the respect for persons view derived from fidelity to commitments, go beyond patient benefit. The duty to keep medical information confidential can be seen as grounded in fidelity to the patient. A promise of confidentiality is, at least by implication, made when the relation is created. Views that find a duty of confidentiality that goes beyond patient benefit hold that, at least *prima facie,* confidences are to be kept whenever confidentiality is promised.

The World Medical Association Declaration of Geneva is generally seen as Hippocratic; it is a rewriting and modernizing of the Hippocratic Oath. On this issue, however, it breaks with the Hippocratic Oath. It gives a flat pledge of confidentiality. No exception clauses are implied or specified.

In 1971, just after the Dr. Browne case, the British Medical Association rewrote its code to deal with cases such as Dr. Browne's in which the physician believes it is in the patient's interest to disclose confidential information to a third party. It said that in such cases "it is the doctor's duty to make every effort to persuade the patient to allow the information to be given to the third party, but where the patient refuses, that refusal must be respected."[4]

Some more-recent codes go beyond the Hippocratic Oath in *requiring* disclosure of confidential information—not to benefit the patient but to protect others from serious harm. The BMA, for example, says that, according to its opinion, confidences may be broken when the law requires doing so or when the physician has an overriding duty to society. Depending on the jurisdiction, this might include the legal duty to report gunshot wounds, sexually transmitted or other infectious diseases, or a diagnosis of epilepsy. It is the physician's obligation to make sure the patient understands that exception. There is a public interest in reporting certain medical conditions.

The issue of controversy today is whether the law should require reporting of HIV-positive diagnoses. Some jurisdictions require reporting; others do not. When a physician is facing a patient in whom tests for HIV are contemplated in a jurisdiction that requires reporting, fidelity to the patient requires mentioning the reporting requirement. A physician who is committed to practicing within the constraints of the law and who is practicing in a jurisdiction with a reporting requirement will have to disclose a positive diagnosis. If the patient at that point cannot continue the relation on that basis, she has the right to end the relation.

---

[4]"Central Ethical Committee," *British Medical Journal Supplement* (May 1, 1971), p. 30. The British Medical Association (BMA) appears to have since backtracked on its overturning of the paternalistic exception, perhaps attempting to conform to the General Medical Council, which in Britain has the legal authority to discipline physicians. The BMA by the 1980s (*Handbook of Medical Ethics,* London: British Medical Association, 1981, p. 12) was publishing a list of five exceptions to the duty of confidentiality. One was when the patient consented to disclosure. Three additional exceptions all involve disclosing to serve various interests of society (research, legal requirements to disclose, and "the doctor's overriding duty to society"). The fifth exception can only be seen as paternalistic: "When it is undesirable on medical grounds to seek a patient's consent, but is in the patient's own interest that confidentiality should be broken." This is compatible with the British General Medical Council's position, which reads, "only in exceptional cases should the doctor feel entitled to disregard his [the patient's] refusal" (see General Medical Council, *Professional Conduct and Discipline: Fitness to Practise,* London: The Council, 1990).

If confidentiality is part of the ethics of promise keeping, what is crucial is what the clinician promises the patient. The corollary is that physicians should not promise more than they can deliver. Consider the following case in which a physician may imply too much to his patients (based on Veatch 1977):

Case 4.3: The Case of the Homosexual Husband

A family physician had a general practice at the time when the law still required physical exams as part of a premarital medical examination. He had a 21-year-old male patient whom he had known for a long time. Because he had previously treated him for sexually transmitted diseases, the physician was aware of the patient's sexual history and knew he was gay. Over the course of the years, the patient had discussed his lifestyle with the physician.

When this patient came to the physician requesting a premarital physical examination, the physician was surprised, but he believed it was really none of his business. He knew that, at least sometimes, persons living a gay lifestyle are bisexual, so perhaps the marriage would work out.

Just to make conversation, he asked the patient who his fiancée was and was shocked to discover it is one of his own patients, someone he had known for many years. He began to realize that he was facing a dilemma. If he followed the Hippocratic principle, it was his duty to do what he believed would be beneficial to the patient. In this case, the woman who was about to marry this man was herself a patient. On the other hand, if he had promised confidentiality, it was his duty to the male patient not to disclose without the man's permission.

At this moment the physician found himself in a bind. He believed that the young woman was at some risk. First, he knew that her future husband had a history of sexually transmitted diseases. If he remained actively bisexual, he was going to bring those diseases into the marriage. Second, from what he knew of the man, the physician was rather confident that this woman was going to be in for a very unpleasant marriage. Her marrying someone whom the physician knew was gay seemed to him to doom the marriage to a quick divorce.

This physician concluded it was his duty to his female patient to find out from the man whether his fiancée knew about his lifestyle, and, if she didn't, to inform her. He might be lucky and discover that she already knew the situation or that the man was willing to have the physician help the couple discuss it. If, as seems more likely, the man was not willing to discuss it with his fiancée, then the physician's problem would remain because he also concluded that his duty to his male patient was to keep confidentiality.

He believed he had implicitly promised confidentiality to the male patient and Hippocratic beneficence to the female, but he could not deliver on both promises. He found himself in a spot in which he had two duties and had to determine which one was his duty proper. Once he had made two contradictory commitments, there was no solution to the problem. If he had been more cautious in what he promised to either the woman or the man—for instance, if he had promised the woman that he would work for what was in her interests unless it involved breaching confidentiality with another patient—then the problem would have been solved. Or, alternatively, if he had promised the man to keep information confidential unless it was crucial to the welfare of another patient, the problem would have been solved as well. But this physician had gotten himself into a bind by making commitments on which he could not deliver simultaneously.

The striking thing about this case is that the Hippocratic solution does not satisfy most people. First, it poses a serious problem because the clinician has two patients who may have significantly different interests. In that case, it is impossible to be Hippocratic to both patients simultaneously. Second, even if that problem is avoided, as long as the clinician believes it is in the woman's interest to know about her fiancé's sexual orientation, he has a duty to tell her and that does not square with many people's moral judgment about what is the right thing to do.

Those who hold that the promise of confidentiality must be kept must be willing to yield on their commitment to the Hippocratic notion that the physician's primary duty is to benefit the patient. If there is reason to keep the confidence, it must stem from the obligation owed to the male patient, one best understood as deriving from a promise made. Respect for persons and the principle of fidelity under that notion appear to generate obligations, in this case the obligation of confidentiality, that cannot be overridden by mere considerations of the consequences to another patient.

Non-Hippocratic Requirements to Disclose   There is another dimension to the confidentiality controversy. Even if confidences cannot be broken merely to do what the clinician believes will be beneficial to the patient, it is possible they may be broken in some cases to benefit others. The American Medical Association's Principles of Medical Ethics have been interpreted by its Judicial Council (1984, p. 19) to permit disclosure when "a patient threatens to inflict serious bodily harm to another person and there is a reasonable probability that the patient may carry out the threat." This is clearly not a

Hippocratic paternalistic provision.[5] It could easily justify breaking confidence when it is not in the patient's interest to do so. Contrary to the Hippocratic perspective, it introduces a social dimension: consideration of other persons. Whether it is the rights or the interests of the other party that justify disclosures is a matter that we will take up in chapter 7. Now we need to see how, at the level of an individual patient, there may be other principles derived from the notion of respect for persons that place limits on the health professional's duty to do what he or she thinks will benefit the patient.

The Principle of Autonomy and the Doctrine of Informed Consent

Keeping faith in relations, indicated by the principle of fidelity, is not the only characteristic of respect for persons. But once one understands the relation between duties derived from fidelity and those derived from beneficence and nonmaleficence, the implications of the other principles under the rubric of respect for persons will be easy to grasp. The most visible principle of the medical ethics of the past generation has been the principle of autonomy—another aspect of showing respect for persons. In fact, respecting autonomy is so central to respect for persons that some ethicists (see Beauchamp and Childress 1994) are inclined to treat autonomy as the only principle related to respect for persons. It seems clear, however, that even persons who are not substantially autonomous can still command respect. For instance, promises made to the nonautonomous still must be kept according to the principle of fidelity. Likewise, in the following sections, we shall see that many people hold that respect for persons calls for two further principles: veracity and avoidance of killing. Under these principles, duties to deal honestly and to avoid killing humans, even if they are not substantially autonomous, will be discussed.

The Concept of Autonomy

The principle of autonomy comes, not from the Hippocratic tradition, but from the traditions of Kant and liberal political philosophy. Liberal political philosophy (the term *liberalism* has within it a respect for liberty) has dominated the medical ethics of the United States and much of the rest of the Western

---

[5]In 1994, in a little-noticed modification, the AMA's Council on Ethical and Judicial Affairs (the new name for the Judicial Council) changed the wording to read, "Where a patient threatens to inflict serious bodily harm to another person *or himself or herself*. . ." [italics added], thus reverting to the older notion of Hippocratic paternalism, while still including the non-Hippocratic authorization to break confidence to protect third parties (American Medical Association, 1994, p. 72).

world since the radical rethinking of medical ethics began about 1970. The liberty of the individual is very frequently a key part of the principle of autonomy. We see it dominating liberal political philosophy (though not professionally articulated medical ethics) from the eighteenth century in Western liberal thought. We frequently see this philosophy represented by the use of "rights" language. Recall that rights have a reciprocal relation with duties. If one person has a right, then others normally have duties. Controversy remains over whether rights or duties are conceptually prior (Macklin 1976), but they are clearly closely related. Normally, when an appeal is made to a *right*, this claim is seen as having a special priority or standing such that mere appeals to consequences cannot be used to override the right.

We often talk about the right of a patient to give informed consent before being touched, for example, before surgery. That's just one example of playing out this respect for the autonomy of the patient. We can express this principle in either duty language or rights language, but in either case, the language signals a priority for the claim being made. Sometimes philosophers will say that rights "trump" appeals to consequences, implying that they are of the school that the principles upon which the rights claim is based take priority over appeals to consequences. Thus, when philosophers say rights and duties are correlative they mean that this priority might be expressed in two different ways. I can say that a physician has a duty to get informed consent before touching the patient, or I can say that the patient has a right to give informed consent before being touched. They mean exactly the same.

Sometimes, in Western thought, we talk about a woman's *right* to procure an abortion. As long as we assume for a moment that there is no competing duty (for example a duty to preserve the life of the fetus), such talk makes sense. When a woman expresses this right, she is claiming that under the principle of autonomy she should be free to proceed. Of course, if one believes that the fetus has full moral standing so that duties, such as the duty to avoid killing it, apply, then the woman would be acting in a way that is depriving someone else of rights. We would, once again, have a clash, in this case between the principles of autonomy and avoidance of killing.

Positive and Negative Rights

Rights come in two different forms: *negative rights* and *positive rights*. A negative right is a right to be left alone, to be free from the interference of others to act autonomously. Autonomy is primarily related to negative rights. A positive right implies much more, a right not only to act autonomously but also to have access to the means necessary to carry out one's actions. Some people talk about liberty rights and entitlement rights, implying the same distinction. For our purposes we can assume they mean the same thing.

We can illustrate the difference in the case of an abortion. In the United States, after the 1973 decision of *Roe v. Wade,* the woman has a legal right to an abortion—meaning she has a liberty right, or a negative right. All that means is that she is legally free to pursue an abortion using whatever means she has available within the constraints of the law. If she can find a physician and has enough money to pay for the procedure, she has the autonomy, or liberty, to make an arrangement with that physician to get an abortion. She is free from state interference. That does not imply a positive entitlement right. If she had an entitlement right, she would have the right, not only to make that deal, but also to the resources necessary: access to a physician and the resources to procure the abortion. One may believe that a woman ought to have both a liberty right and an entitlement right, but that is not presently the law in the United States, although certain states and certain insurance plans may have included abortion in their basic health insurance coverage. Legal cases since *Roe v. Wade* have clarified that what *Roe* established was a liberty right; that is, the legal freedom to try to make a deal with a physician to procure an abortion. Of course, the existence of a legal right, either a liberty right or an entitlement right, does not settle the question of whether either form of right exists at the moral level. A liberty right gives one the right to be left alone, free from state interference, to try to make whatever arrangements in private she is able to make. Claiming an entitlement right is a more extensive claim; it implies that the state or somebody has the obligation not only to refrain from interfering but also to provide the resources. Liberty rights are generally grounded in the principle of autonomy: that is, the duty to permit others to live their lives according to their own life plans. By contrast, a claim to an entitlement right will not be grounded in autonomy; it will be based on some principle that imposes an affirmative duty to act, perhaps the principle of beneficence or justice.

Although the primary source of the principle of autonomy is liberal political philosophy, Judeo-Christianity figures in a complicated way in its prehistory. Early Judaism and Christianity had no principle of autonomy any more than any other ancient culture did. No culture in that day held a moral principle that required respecting life-plan choices made by individuals. That required an evolution of a concept of individual choice that did not emerge until much later. Until this day, Jewish Talmudic ethics has no principle of autonomy, at least in the most traditional forms of rabbinical interpretation. Thus, in more traditional Talmudic interpretation, a patient does not even have the right to refuse a recommended treatment (Bleich 1979). Early Christianity had no principle of autonomy in a full-blown sense, but what it did have was a remarkable recognition of the importance of the individual and of personal decisions, even when the religious choice of the individual caused separation from one's family. That seems to be the historical precursor to the development of the principle of autonomy. By the Protestant era in the sixteenth century and the centuries immediately preceding, we begin seeing developments in Christianity pointing in the direction of the affirmation of the individual as a decision maker. In the fourteenth century, John Wycliffe and John Huss as well as the Catholic mystic Johann Tauler recognized this idea of the importance of the individual. The Protestant Reformation went further in affirming the authority of the individual. We were headed in the direction of a concept of autonomy even though it did not surface in a full-blown way until the eighteenth century.

Kant, writing in the eighteenth century, is a manifestation. Kant was a German Pietist, and many people believe this Protestant affirmation of the individual and the authority of the individual is the historical basis for Kant's secular affirmation of autonomy.

By contrast, a number of other philosophical and religious systems in the world do not emphasize autonomy. Marxism does not; neither do Hinduism, Buddhism, Confucianism, and Islam. There are, of course, various levels of sophistication and modernization in any tradition. Moreover, there are certain individuals who may have their origin in a culture that has a traditional religious commitment but who have been exposed to other views of the world and have adopted some amalgam of cultural commitments. Thus, in modern Japan a Western-educated physician or lawyer may use language that is constantly peppered with expressions such as "the right of self-determination" and "individual autonomy." They are not getting that from Buddhism or Shintoism; it comes from their Western exposure.

Informed Consent and Its Relation to the Principle of Autonomy and Therapeutic Privilege

Informed consent is a critical element of any theory that gives weight to autonomy. Hippocratic beneficence might incorporate some minimal informed consent, but only when the clinician believes informed consent will benefit the patient. For example, if a physician is about to write a prescription for diphenylhydantoin, a seizure medication, she might feel obliged to say to that patient, "Be careful about driving until we are sure we have your seizures under control." She might also say that one of the side effects of diphenylhydantoin is that it can make one drowsy. She might warn the patient not to operate dangerous equipment until he is sure he knows how he responds to this drug. That would be informing the patient. The clinician might even go so far as to ask the patient, "Is this something you really want?" This appearance of asking for consent, however, is only because she is terribly worried that if she did not tell the patient this information, he might injure or kill himself or somebody else. There is certain information the clinician has to tell patients, just to protect the patient's welfare.

In liberal political philosophy, the key idea is that meaningful information must be disclosed even if the clinician does not believe that it will be beneficial. Hippocratic ethics includes what is known as *therapeutic privilege*. It is the privilege that a Hippocratic physician will claim when withholding information that the physician believes would be harmful or upsetting to the patient. That privilege makes sense in an ethic based on paternalistic patient benefit, but it is contrary to an ethic giving important place to the principle of autonomy.

In the conflict between liberal political philosophy and Hippocratic ethics a major clash emerges over cases of informed consent. The case of *Natanson v. Kline* suggests the continuing evolution of the principle of autonomy as a replacement for the Hippocratic ethic and the related doctrine of therapeutic privilege.

Case 4.4: Natanson v. Kline: *When May Information Be Withheld?*

In 1960 in the state of Kansas, a woman named Irma Natanson was diagnosed as having breast cancer. She needed to have a radical left mastectomy, followed by radiation. This was standard procedure at the time; it is frequently standard still today. She suffered terrible radiation burns, after which she sued her doctor, Dr. Kline, for the injury. One of the counts was that she had not consented to the risk of the radiation burn.

At this point the question of therapeutic privilege arises. Dr. Kline did not deny that he failed to tell Mrs. Natanson about the risk of the burns. Often physicians in this position claim that such information might disturb the patient; perhaps even lead her irrationally to refuse consent to the needed treatment. Did Dr. Kline have the right to withhold the risk of burns from radiation if he believed it would upset her or make her do something irrational? Or, alternatively, did he have a duty to explain all of those risks?

Justice Schroeder, the judge in this case, gave the definitive response of Anglo-American liberal political philosophy:

> Anglo-American law starts with a premise of a thorough-going self-determination. It follows that each man is considered the master of his own body, and he may, if he be of sound mind, expressly prohibit the performance of life-saving surgery or other medical treatment.

It followed that, if this information was important for her to decide whether she wanted the radiation, she had a right to the information. When she charged

Dr. Kline with failure to get informed consent, the dispute was not over whether she had signed a form. The issue was whether the consent was informed and voluntary and whether the information was understood. We don't really care, from the point of view of ethics, whether a piece of paper has a signature. The piece of paper with a signature may help to demonstrate that the patient has at least seen the paper. It will not prove that the patient read the paper, much less that the signer understood it. The court will, in some cases, throw the consent form out if it is believed that the patient never understood what was on the paper.

Thus, back as far as 1960, Justice Schroeder appeared to be rejecting the therapeutic privilege. In 1960, we were just at the beginning of the era when liberal political philosophy was exerting its influence on medical ethics and challenging the therapeutic privilege. We were in a period of transition in which judges and others sometimes reverted to Hippocratic language and sometimes talked as if autonomy were all that counted. Additional text from Justice Schroeder's opinion reveals the confusion. Despite the bold appeal to autonomy, Justice Schroeder also said:

> The physician's choice of plausible courses should not be called into question if it appears, all circumstances considered, that the physician was motivated only by the patient's best therapeutic interest and he proceeded as a competent medical man would have done under a similar situation.

That sounds very much like the therapeutic privilege doctrine of an earlier era and appears to contradict the just-quoted reference to a "thorough-going self-determination." It sounds as if the judge was about to say that as long as the physician was worried about Mrs. Natanson's welfare, he had acted acceptably. Justice Shroeder said both that the patient had an absolute right to self-determination and that the physician should not be questioned if he had the patient's best therapeutic interest in mind and acted as competent medical men would have in the circumstances. The latter sounds like therapeutic privilege; the former, more like the principle of autonomy.

Just before the sentence quoted immediately above, however, there is an opening clause that conveys that, even as far back as 1960, autonomy was really dominant in Justice Schroeder's mind. He introduced the therapeutic privilege language with the clause, "So long as the disclosure is sufficient to assure an informed consent." On balance he appears to have been insisting on an adequately informed consent, not just a consent without information. But in 1960 therapeutic privilege was so common that the judge was still inserting therapeutic privilege language. He was part of the way down the road toward a conversion to autonomy, and he liked to talk self-determination language, but he still included into the talk therapeutic privilege. In the end, the judge insisted that the consent be informed. The case presents an ambiguous combination of two points of view and, on balance, it seems to be tipping in the direction of requiring information, even if it is upsetting to the patient and even if it is not the common practice among physicians of the day.

It was a series of cases from 1969 to 1972 that really set the pattern of the shift from the more paternalistic Hippocratic basis for consent to one grounded squarely in respect for patient autonomy (*Berkey v. Anderson* 1969, *Canterbury v. Spence* 1972, *Cobbs v. Grant* 1972). *Canterbury v. Spence* (1972) is a good example.

Case 4.5: Canterbury v. Spence

A 19-year-old youth named Canterbury suffered from back pain. He had an operation called a laminectomy to repair a ruptured disc. Afterward he fell from bed and suffered an injury that resulted in lower-body paralysis. For our purposes, the question that was critical was whether Dr. Spence should have explained to Mr. Canterbury the risk of falling out of bed. Dr. Spence made a therapeutic privilege claim, saying he did not think that disclosure was appropriate. Disclosure might have lead the patient irrationally to refuse to consent to the procedure he really needed and might have produced "adverse psychological reactions which could preclude the success of the operation."

The court affirmed the right of self-determination, holding that the patient needed to have the information necessary to make an informed decision. At this level the court did not say that Dr. Spence needed to inform about the risk of falling out of bed. The question of whether that needed to be disclosed was referred back to a lower court. What the higher court said was that Dr. Spence had to tell the patient everything that the patient would deem significant to his decision. Dr. Spence still had available the possibility that he could convince a lower court that falling out of bed is such a rare event that the patient would not need to be told about it to make a rational decision or that the risk was so obvious that it would not have changed this patient's mind had he been told. What this court said was that the physician cannot use therapeutic privilege to justify withholding relevant information.

Standards of Disclosure for Consent
to Be Adequately Informed

Note that no one is insisting that consent be "fully" informed. It is not even clear what that could mean. Certainly, telling the patient everything about a procedure is an impossible task. All that is being called for is adequate information. The key question addressed in this series of court cases is what standard should be used in deciding how much information must be transferred for a consent to be adequately informed. Three different standards are considered: the professional standard, the reasonable person standard, and the subjective standard.

The Professional Standard   The first is the traditional standard, often referred to as the *professional standard*. The professional standard requires that a physician disclose what colleagues similarly situated would have disclosed in similar circumstances. This standard appears to be built on the presumption that deciding how much information to disclose is something that only professionals can know. It is related to the Hippocratic ideology. If one thinks about it, that position does not necessarily serve patient autonomy. It could be that colleagues would not disclose everything about a procedure that a patient would find important. The physician accused of failing to get an informed consent might be able to bring in a number of his or her colleagues who might testify that they also would not have disclosed the disputed information. On the basis of the old professional standard, their testimony would settle the matter in court.

The Reasonable Person Standard   What *Canterbury v. Spence* and other cases of that period established is the adoption of a new standard called the *reasonable person standard*. (It used to be called the reasonable man standard.) The reasonable person standard provides that the physician must disclose what a reasonable patient would want to be told or find significant, even if none of the physician's colleagues would agree.

Ruth Faden and her colleagues (1981) conducted a study in a seizure clinic at Johns Hopkins Hospital in Baltimore. She asked the physicians in the clinic how many side effects to the medicine Dilantin they would disclose. Although the responses were somewhat different for pediatricians, the majority of the physicians for adult patients identified three: ataxia (defective muscle coordination), sedation, and skin rash. These side effects required some immediate patient action—care in operating equipment or checking with the physician—to control them.

Dr. Faden then went to the patients in the clinic waiting room and gave them a long list of possible side effects asking which of them they would like to have been told about. The patients said that they wanted to know about a lot more than those three side effects. For example, one of the risks is hirsutism; Dilantin will make hair grow, a problem that could be of concern, especially to some female patients. They might agree that this was not a crucial problem and if that, if necessary, in order to prevent epilepsy, it was a risk worth taking, but the vast majority of patients said they wanted to know about it anyway. By contrast, the majority of the physicians believed that patients did not need to know about it. Patients also said they wanted to know about very serious effects, even if they were rare, such as drug-related mortality, lupus, and teratogenic effects.

Thus, it is now documented that the patients said in the survey that they wanted to know certain risks that the physicians in the same clinic said were not appropriate to disclose. Studies such as this one suggest that reasonable laypeople may want to know certain information that the professional standard would not require. If a patient were to sue a physician for failure to disclose certain side effects, the reasonable person standard would support the patient. If reasonable patients want the information, then, according to the reasonable person standard, the clinician is obliged to disclose it.

From the point of view of the principle of autonomy, self-determination of the patient would not be promoted by the professional standard. Surely, the fact that a physician and his or her colleagues would not disclose does not establish that patients would not want the information or find it relevant to making choices. Disclosing what the reasonable person would want to know seems to come closer. Of course, some patients may not be "reasonable." They may need more or less information than typical, reasonable people. That fact suggests a third standard of disclosure.

The Subjective Standard   If the goal is to give the patient the information he or she would personally find meaningful in deciding among treatment options, then, to the extent that that information is known or can be known, it seems that the standard should be more subjective in the sense of being based on the life plan and interests of the individual patient. This is what is called the *subjective standard.* It is subjective in that it is based on the actual subjective interests of the patient, not on those of some more hypothetical reasonable patient or reasonable physician. Thus, even if the ordinary reasonable person might not want to know of a one-in-a-hundred-thousand risk of paralysis of the fingers, the patient who is a concert pianist might. Of course, this standard creates a difficult, if not impossible, task for the clinician. In order to know which risks and benefits to present, the clinician would have to learn all the idiosyncratic interests and tastes of the patient. He or she cannot just tell the patient "everything" because there is an enormous, perhaps infinite, amount of information that could be said about any treatment. In addition to information about the side effects of any particular treatment, information about all available treatment options would have to be given. Some treatment options that are conceivable are terribly implausible. Indeed, they may even be immoral in the eyes of most people. Nevertheless, they might be very important to some people with unusual lifestyles and preferences. For every condition, suicide is theoretically an option, although normally clinicians will not suggest that possibility.

There is no way that a clinician can guess at all of the possible areas of concern for each patient. He or she can, however, take into account what is known about the patient. If he or she knows about unusual interests, such as the career of the concert pianist, then the clinician must take that information into account. Moreover, he or she must encourage the patient to make special interests known.

Perhaps the optimal approach would be a combination of the reasonable person standard and the subjective standard as the proper basis for deciding what information must be transmitted in order for a consent to be adequately informed. The clinician must disclose what the reasonable person would want to know or find material in choosing among potential treatment options adjusted by what the clinician knows or should know about the unique interests of the individual patient.

The Principle of Veracity: Lying and the Duty to Tell the Truth

A third way to show respect for persons is by being truthful with them. In addition to the principles of fidelity and autonomy, the principle of veracity is an essential characteristic of human action that shows respect by telling the truth. (It is the third element of respect for persons in Figure 4.1.) Moral conflicts involving the principle of veracity follow the same pattern as the other principles grouped under the heading of respect for persons. Once again, we have a conflict between doing what is going to be best for the patient, in terms of benefit and harm, and fulfilling some general obligation, in this case the obligation to tell the truth.

The Change in Physician Attitudes

In the United States, two studies of physician attitudes about telling the truth to patients reveal an intriguing pattern. In 1961, Donald Oken published a study in which he asked U.S. physicians what their usual policy was about telling the truth to terminally ill cancer patients. Eighty-eight percent of the physicians surveyed said that it was their usual policy not to tell the patient if the patient was diagnosed with a malignancy. The reason is easy to understand if one understands the Hippocratic principle and the depth of the commitment of 1960s physicians to that principle. They were afraid that if they told the patient, the patient would become psychologically upset, and the Hippocratic oath says not to do things that will upset the patient. Almost uniformly, as recently as the 1960s, physicians would not tell patients about cancer.

Something dramatic happened in the late 1960s and early 1970s. That was the period when respect for persons emerged as a dominant principle in medical ethics—the time of the *Roe v. Wade* case involving abortion, the *Natanson* case involving informed consent, and the Karen Quinlan case involving the right to refuse life support. In 1979, Dennis Novack and a group of colleagues published a study (Novack et al. 1979) in which they replicated Oken's questions, asking an essentially similar population of physicians. Less than twenty years later they found that 98 percent followed a usual policy of telling.

Accounting for the Change in Attitudes

Changes in Judgments about Benefit and Harm   The question is, What accounts for this moral shift? Why are physicians now inclined to tell the truth? The original Hippocratic approach stressed doing what will benefit the patient, so that Bernard Meyer (1968), a physician writing in the 1960s, gave the following explanation. (Notice the Hippocratic quality.)

> What is imparted to the patient about his illness should be planned with the same care and executed with the same skill that are demanded by any potentially therapeutic measure. Like the transfusion of blood, the dispensing of certain information must be distinctly indicated, the amount given consonant to the needs of the recipient, and the type chosen with a view towards avoiding untoward reactions (Meyer 1968, p. 172).

According to this Hippocratic ethic, the physician should tell only things that are going to help the patient and should withhold those things that are going to hurt. The logic is identical to the old idea of the therapeutic privilege, radically different from the attitude found by Novack's group. Now, how did the change come about?

One possibility is that physicians had remained consequentialist but had recalculated the consequences. The medical ethicist Joseph Fletcher (1954) illustrated the kind of change that could take place without abandoning the focus on consequences. He was a consequentialist; he believed in benefiting patients and protecting them from harm. But according to him, awful things will happen if the physician does not tell the patient the truth. Particularly as we move to complex medicine in a hospital setting, maintaining the fiction of a dishonest diagnosis becomes exceedingly difficult. Everybody on the health care team has to maintain the same story, and eventually, something goes wrong. Fletcher said that to benefit the patient, in the long run, the consequences are better if the truth is told. That is still staying within the Hippocratic principle, but the consequences are recalculated for a period of high-technology, complex hospital-based medicine.

A Possible Shift to an Ethic of Respect for Persons   The other possibility is that, at about this same period of time, people began saying that something was simply inherently wrong about not being honest with patients and that the morally right thing to do would be to tell the patient the truth. Particularly if one is already committed to informed consent, relevant information must be disclosed. How can one get informed consent for chemotherapy if the patient does not know he has cancer? He would be crazy to consent to radiation or chemotherapy if he thought that all that was wrong was that he had a cyst or a benign lump. He could not give an adequate consent, because he would not be adequately informed.

Case 4.6: Limits on the Physician's Duty to Promote Health

Jim Sullivan in his early thirties comes to Dr. Tom Wordsworth's office for a routine exam in conjunction with a new job. Dr. Wordsworth starts taking the history. It is obvious that Mr. Sullivan is grossly overweight. He tells the physician that he does not get any exercise, smokes two packs of cigarettes a day, and has since he was fourteen. He drinks a lot and generally does not take very good care of himself.

Dr. Wordsworth says to himself that this man is in for big trouble. He feels that he should encourage his patient to change his lifestyle. As he starts talking to Mr. Sullivan, he realizes it is not very likely he is going to change anything simply by telling the patient that he should not drink as much and should quit smoking. This is a man who is not likely to take up an exercise routine simply because this physician tells him to.

Dr. Wordsworth contemplates another approach. The plan is to do a chest x-ray, suspecting that some opacity will appear that will do the trick. When he examines the x-ray, there is nothing terribly alarming, but he notices some spots that will serve his purpose. He wants to shock his patient into changing his lifestyle. With an air of great alarm he brings the x-ray to his patient, saying that the spots are an indication of precancerous developments. He says that if Mr. Sullivan stops smoking now, there is a pretty good chance he can stop this development. But if he keeps smoking there is a high probability that he is headed for lung cancer. Intentionally overstating the risk, Dr. Wordsworth rationalizes that it is true that Sullivan's chances of developing lung cancer are higher if he continues to smoke and that it is an innocent, benevolent stretching of the truth to point to the meaningless spots and exaggerate the probability that the smoking would cause cancer. He believes that overstating the risk is the only way to benefit his patient. It is the only thing he can think of that will shock him into a new lifestyle.

Here is a physician lying to a patient about the risk for lung cancer and the meaning of his x-ray, but his purpose was to benefit the patient. If one is Hippocratic, he or she must at least sympathize with what this doctor was doing. But many people react saying that what Dr. Wordsworth did is still wrong. He told a lie to this patient. He deceived him. Those who include the principle of veracity in their list of ethical principles hold that it is simply wrong to tell a purposeful lie even for the benefit of the patient.

The philosopher Immanuel Kant (1909), classically associated with this respect for persons view, wrote an essay in the eighteenth century called "On the Supposed Right to Tell Lies from Benevolent Motives." He argued that "to be truthful or honest in all declarations is therefore a sacred and absolutely commanding decree of reason limited by no expediency." *Expediency* was the word of the day for calculation of benefits and harms. So no calculation of benefits and harms was relevant to deciding what a patient should be told, according to this respect for persons or Kantian view.

Not everyone who believes lying to be wrong takes as rigid a stand as Immanuel Kant. Most can imagine a situation so extreme that the only plausible course of action would be to lie. In military situations, prisoners captured by an enemy may feel obliged to lie when asked to disclose the position of their colleagues. In medicine, a physician also may feel that there are special cases, such as a mentally ill, temporarily suicidal patient who asks if a tumor is malignant. A physician may feel that the consequences of a truthful disclosure of the malignancy would be so severe in this case that a lie is justified, especially if it is only for a period necessary to overcome the suicidal tendencies.

The distinction between *prima facie* duties and *duty proper* may help clarify such situations. W. D. Ross (1939) was a philosopher who proposed the strategy of balancing two conflicting *prima facie* duties. What Ross said was that there is always a duty to tell the truth and there is also a duty to be beneficent. The two have to be balanced against each other. He used a balancing strategy for resolving conflict between principles. In this case there are two *prima facie* duties to consider. For Ross, one needs overwhelming benefit to justify overriding the principle of veracity. An equal balance between the two would not be sufficient; one needs to have a strong force in the direction of lying.

The AMA in 1981 published a new version of its principles of medical ethics, which says that "a physician shall deal honestly with patients and colleagues." There are no qualifications. That remains the current AMA position in their principles. What did the AMA have in mind? It could have been adopting a new Kantian view, that it is simply a duty to tell the truth. Or the AMA spokespersons could have been recalculating the consequences of lying and deception, thus holding to traditional consequentialist reasoning, but now believing that honesty tended to be beneficial to the patient.

The AMA's principles fit on one page at the beginning of a much larger document. The principles were adopted by the AMA's House of Delegates, but that group left interpretations to the AMA's Council on Ethical and Judicial Affairs. The interpretations, which constitute the rest of the large volume, suggest the reasoning of the council members. The principles on the first page seem to move all the way in the direction of insisting on honesty without exception, but the interpretations say that if disclosure poses such a serious psychological threat of detriment to the patient as to be "medically contraindicated," then the physician may withhold the truth (AMA, 1996, p. 120). The Council reopened a consequentialist justification for dishonesty that the House of Delegates had apparently closed. One explanation is that the House of Delegates, when it adopted the revised principles, was merely saying that it now believes that usually the way to benefit the patient is to deal honestly with him or her and the Council simply made clear that sometimes calculating consequences will lead to exceptions. The other possibility is that the House of Delegates was making a more fundamental shift to the view that there is simply a duty on the physician's part to deal honestly with patients, but the Council misunderstood that change, posing an interpretation that fails to take seriously the House's commitment to honesty.

Medically contraindicated is a term that arises frequently in medicine, especially in pharmacology. It sounds as if someone is stating a medical fact, but, on reflection, the term *medically contraindicated* is much more complex. Research may show that a drug or a disclosure may have a certain effect—that disclosure may be very depressing to the patient, for example. Still, it is a value judgment whether it is wrong to administer a drug or to disclose a diagnosis because it will cause depression. Likewise, research may show that a drug has an effect most people do not like. Nevertheless, calling that effect a "side" effect or saying that the effect makes the drug "contraindicated" requires a value judgment. It is merely a way of saying that the speaker believes on balance that the effect is undesirable.

In the case of disclosure of a diagnosis, the AMA's Judicial Council is saying that some information can apparently produce effects that the clinician should consider so bad that, in someone's judgment, the information should not be disclosed. That approach makes good sense from a Hippocratic perspective, but it would be rejected by one who holds to a strong principle of veracity (see Veatch 1991).

The three principles that give rise to duties and rights that have been discussed thus far—the principles of fidelity, autonomy, and veracity—are three important constituent parts of the notion of showing respect for persons, the main alternative to Hippocratic medical ethics. There is a final element that is sometimes included: the notion that respecting persons requires that they not be killed even if, hypothetically it would do no harm and might even do good to kill them. That principle, the principle of avoidance of killing, is the subject of the next chapter.

Key Concepts

Autonomy: A formalist or deontological moral principle that holds that actions or rules are morally right insofar as they involve respecting the autonomous choices of individuals. Autonomy is also a psychological state of an individual who is capable of being self-determining or self-legislating. The moral principle of autonomy holds that one has a duty to respect the self-determined choices of autonomous individuals.

Duty proper: One's duty, taking into account all relevant *prima facie* duties and the relevant rules for assigning priority to these *prima facie* duties.

Exceptionless duties: Duties that are binding in all circumstances. Logic tells us that two exceptionless duties that conflict with one another cannot both be binding simultaneously. Compare *Prima facie* duties and Duty proper.

Fidelity: A formalist or deontological moral principle that holds that actions or rules are morally right insofar as they involve keeping commitments, promises, or contracts.

Formalism: A type of normative ethical theory that holds that actions or rules are judged morally right insofar as they conform to a specified form rather than on the basis of the consequences they produce. See Deontological ethics (Key Concepts, chapter 3).

Lexical ordering: Ordering potentially conflicting ethical principles as in a dictionary, or lexicon; that is, all instances of one principle come before any instances of the next, just as in a dictionary all As come before any Bs.

Negative right (sometimes called a liberty right): A right to be left alone; to be free to act autonomously, free from the interference of others. Negative rights are often based on the principle of autonomy.

Positive right (sometimes called an entitlement right): A right not only to act autonomously but also to have access to the means necessary to carry out one's actions. Positive rights must be based, not on the principle of autonomy, but on the basis of some other principles such as beneficence or justice.

***Prima facie* duties:** Duties that are morally binding, other things being equal. Such duties may be overridden by other duties that are considered as having higher priority or as being weightier. Compare Exceptionless duties and Duty proper.

Professional standard: The standard for informed consent that requires that a physician disclose what colleagues similarly situated would have disclosed in similar circumstances.

Reasonable person standard: The standard for informed consent that requires that the physician must disclose what a reasonable patient would want to be told or would find significant, even if none of the physician's colleagues would agree.

Respect for persons: A term referring to a type of deontological or formalist normative ethics in which the principles of moral rightness specify certain duties owed to individuals (such as respect for autonomy, fidelity, veracity, or avoidance of killing).

Single-principle theories: Theories that determine the rightness or wrongness of actions or rules in all circumstances on the basis of a single principle. The Hippocratic principle (Key Concepts, chapter 1) and Social utility (Key Concepts, chapter 7) are two examples of single-principle theories.

Subjective standard: The standard for informed consent that requires that physicians disclose what the individual patient would want to know or would find significant.

Therapeutic privilege: The privilege that a Hippocratic physician will claim when withholding information that the physician believes would be harmful or upsetting to the patient.

Veracity: A formalist or deontological moral principle that holds that actions or rules are morally right insofar as they involve communicating truthfully and avoiding dishonesty.

Bibliography

American Medical Association. 1981. *Current Opinions of the Judicial Council of the American Medical Association.* Chicago: American Medical Association.

American Medical Association, Council on Ethical and Judicial Affairs. 1994. *Code of Medical Ethics: Current Opinions with Annotations.* Chicago: American Medical Association.

American Medical Association, Council on Ethical and Judicial Affairs. 1996. *Code of Medical Ethics: Current Opinions with Annotations, 1996–1997 Edition.* Chicago: American Medical Association.

American Medical Association, Judicial Council. 1984. *Current Opinions of the Judicial Council of the American Medical Association—1984: Including the Principles of Medical Ethics and Rules of the Judicial Council.* Chicago: American Medical Association.

Beauchamp, Tom L., and James F. Childress, eds. 1994. *Principles of Biomedical Ethics,* 4th ed. New York: Oxford University Press.

Benjamin, Martin. 1985. "Lay Obligations in Professional Relations." *Journal of Medicine and Philosophy* 10:85–103.

Berkey v. Anderson. 1 Cal. App. 3d 790. 82 Cal. Rptr. 67 (1969).

Bleich, J. David. 1979. "The Obligation to Heal in the Judaic Tradition: A Comparative Analysis." Pages 1–44 in *Jewish Bioethics,* edited by Fred Rosner and J. David Bleich. New York: Sanhedrin Press.

Brody, Baruch. 1988. *Life and Death Decision Making.* New York: Oxford University Press.

Canterbury v. Spence. 464 F.2d 772, 150 U.S. App. D.C. 263 (1972).

Cobbs v. Grant. 502 P.2d 1 (Cal. 1972).

DeGrazia, David. 1992. "Moving Forward in Bioethical Theory: Theories, Cases, and Specified Principlism." *Journal of Medicine and Philosophy* 17:511–539.

Faden, Ruth R., Catherine Becker, Carol Lewis, John Freeman, and Alan I. Faden. 1981. "Disclosure of Information to Patients in Medical Care." *Medical Care* 19, no. 7 (July 19):718–733.

Fletcher, Joseph. 1954. *Morals and Medicine.* Boston: Beacon Press.

Kant, Immanuel. 1909. "On the Supposed Right to Tell Lies from Benevolent Motives." Translated by Thomas Kingsmill Abbott and reprinted in Kant's *Critique of Pure Reason and Other Works on the Theory of Ethics.* London: Longmans, pp. 361–365. [Originally published in 1797.]

Kant, Immanuel. 1964. *Groundwork of the Metaphysic of Morals,* translated by H. J. Paton. New York: Harper and Row. [Originally published in 1785.]

Macklin, Ruth. "Moral Concerns and Appeals to Rights and Duties." 1976. *Hastings Center Report* 6, no. 5:31–38.

Meyer, Bernard C. 1968. "Truth and the Physician." Pages 159–177 in *Ethical Issues in Medicine,* edited by E. Fuller Torrey. Boston: Little Brown.

Natanson v. Kline. 186 Kan. 393, 350 P. 2d 1093 (1960).

Novack, Dennis H., Robin Plumer, Raymond L. Smith, Herbert Ochitill, Gary R. Morrow, and John M. Bennett. 1979. "Changes in Physicians' Attitudes toward Telling the Cancer Patient." *Journal of the American Medical Association* 241 (March 2):897–900.

Oken, Donald. 1961. "What to Tell Cancer Patients: A Study of Medical Attitudes." *Journal of the American Medical Association* 175 (April 1):1120–1128.

Rawls, John. 1971. *A Theory of Justice.* Cambridge, Mass.: Harvard University Press.

Richardson, Henry S. 1990. "Specifying Norms As a Way to Resolve Concrete Ethical Problems." *Philosophy and Public Affairs* 19:279–310.

Ross, W. D. 1939. *The Right and the Good.* Oxford: Oxford University Press.

Veatch, Robert M. (Ed.) 1977. "Case Studies in Bioethics: The Homosexual Husband and Physician Confidentiality." *Hastings Center Report* 7 (April): 17.

Veatch, Robert M. 1981. *A Theory of Medical Ethics.* New York: Basic Books.

Veatch, Robert M. 1991. "The Concept of 'Medical Indications.'" Pages 54–62 in *The Patient-Physician Relation: The Patient As Partner, Part 2.* Bloomington, Ind.: Indiana University Press.

Veatch, Robert M. 1995. "Resolving Conflict among Principles: Ranking, Balancing, and Specifying." *Kennedy Institute of Ethics Journal* 5 (September):199–218.

CHAPTER FIVE

The Principle of Avoidance
of Killing

A fourth element related to the notion of respect for persons has generated the most heated controversy in recent medical ethics. Many religious and philosophical commentators as well as health care professionals have held that human beings have a moral status that requires that life not be taken by human hands. The idea is sometimes expressed that life is sacred, that it is to be preserved (even preserved at all costs), or that one must refrain from killing. We shall discuss this notion as the principle of avoidance of killing and examine the differences among the various formulations.

As we did when examining the previous principles under the rubric of respect for persons—fidelity, autonomy, and veracity—we will see that the consequentialist ethics of beneficence and nonmaleficence (doing good and preventing evil) for the patient comes into conflict with an ethic of rights and duties.

The ethics of death and dying has in recent years included a significant controversy over exactly what it means to be dead. The definition-of-death debate, as it is sometimes called, has led to a shift in favor of a brain-oriented definition of death. These issues were taken up in chapter 2.

Here we take up the question of how we treat patients who are critically or terminally ill but are still alive according to the legal definition of death. Suppose a still-living but critically ill patient raises the question of whether it is necessary for that life to continue. These cases challenge us to clarify the meanings of terms such as *killing, allowing to die, forgoing treatment,* and *extraordinary means.* They also force us to clarify ethical questions, including whether it is acceptable to actively kill for mercy; to forgo treatment, allowing the patient to die; and just which treatments can be forgone, if that is deemed an acceptable choice. Here we confront the ethics of caring for the critically ill. In order to discuss this, we must make four distinctions that are going to be crucial: the distinctions between active killing and allowing to die,

I.   Active Killing vs. Letting Die (Action vs. Omission)
II. Withdrawing vs. Withholding (Stopping vs. Not Starting)
III. Direct vs. Indirect Killing
IV. Ordinary vs. Extraordinary Means

Figure 5.1: *Four Basic Distinctions in Death and Dying*

between withdrawing and withholding treatment; between direct and indirect killing, and between ordinary and extraordinary means (Figure 5.1).

Active Killing vs. Allowing to Die

The first distinction is the difference between actively killing the patient, on the one hand, and simply allowing the patient to die by forgoing treatment, on the other. This distinction is widely held throughout the world of medicine (Figure 5.2). It is generally believed that some moral difference exists between actively killing the patient and simply letting the patient die. The moral distinction has been accepted by the AMA (1996, p. 55), Roman Catholic moral theology (Sacred Congregation for the Doctrine of the Faith 1980), and the U.S.

Figure 5.2: *Active Killing vs. Forgoing Life Support (Action vs. Omission)*

Actions that kill are morally wrong, whereas forgoing life support may be acceptable depending on the circumstances.

Traditions tending to recognize this distinction

American Medical Association
Roman Catholicism
The President's Commission for the Study of Ethical Problems in Medicine and Biomedical and Behavioral Research

Traditions seeing no difference between killing and forgoing life support

Groups supporting active euthanasia
Judaism
Right-to-life groups

President's Commission for the Study of Ethical Problems in Medicine and Biomedical and Behavioral Research (1983).

It is not accepted by orthodox Judaism. In Judaism, letting a patient die is violating the sacredness of life just as much as actively killing (Bleich 1979). An orthodox Jewish patient who does not accept a recommendation to turn off a ventilator or to forgo some other treatment is expressing a long-standing Jewish position that all life is a gift from God and to be preserved, even if it is for a short period. Only when the patient is *goses* (moribund) will traditional Talmudic scholars accept the termination of life support. In fact, in that case it becomes a moral duty not to interfere with God's plan for the patient.

Distinguishing Active Killing from Allowing to Die

Invalid Arguments for Keeping the Distinction between Active Killing and Letting Die   Is there really a valid distinction between these two? Some arguments for the distinction really do not make much sense (Figure 5.3). For example, the argument that killing the patient just intuitively feels morally very different from letting the patient die cannot prove that there is truly a moral difference. It may be that they feel different only because people have been taught all their lives that it is worse to actively kill than it is to let die. If a feeling has been taught over the years by people who think there is a difference, that feeling cannot be used as evidence that a difference really exists. Citing that feeling as evidence is merely a circular argument.

Second, it is sometimes argued that active killing is illegal in almost all jurisdictions, whereas letting die is legal everywhere, at least under some conditions. It is true that active killing, even on the request of the patient, is illegal in almost all jurisdictions of the world. In the Netherlands, an arrangement exists between prosecutors and the medical profession that if physicians follow agreed-upon rules they will not get prosecuted for active killing. Active killing, however, even at the persistent and voluntary request of the competent patient remains illegal. The Northern Territory of Australia in 1995 was the first jurisdiction in the world to legalize active killing for mercy, but that action was overturned by the national legislature. By 1999, the only other place where any kind of active killing of the terminally ill was apparently legal was in the state of Oregon and that law continues to face legal challenges and makes legal only physician-assisted suicide not homicide on request (discussed later in the chapter).

Regardless of the state of the law, one cannot use what the law says to determine what is ethical. Imagine someone in a jurisdiction where the legislature is trying to figure out what the right law is to pass. He or she cannot argue that because it is illegal, it should stay illegal. Some people argue that it

Invalid Argument	Reason It Is Invalid
They intuitively feel different.	They may feel different because we have always been taught they are morally different.
Active killing is illegal, but forgoing treatment is legal.	The fact that one is legal and the other is illegal does not establish that there is moral difference or that there should be a legal one.
Active killing would change the role of the physician.	Physicians need not be the ones doing the killing.

Figure 5.3: *Invalid Arguments for the Distinction between Commission and Omission*

is time to change the law, but first one needs to decide the basis on which one might modify the law.

Third, sometimes it is argued that active killing is different from letting die because if physicians were allowed to actively kill, their role would be changed in a way that would be fundamentally different from simply letting critically ill patients die. But it would theoretically be possible to approve active killing ethically without making it legal. It would be possible to legalize active killing while still prohibiting physician participation. We could insist on a division of labor prohibiting physician participation and leaving the role of euthanizer to some other person or group. So whatever one thinks about the impact on the role of the physician, that problem could be isolated from the role of active killer for mercy. We could have a moral judgment that authorizes active killing but keeps certain special roles out of the active killing process. If one believes that the physician's role is healing and that healing is incompatible with killing, then we might say, "No one in this special role should kill, but other people could." Likewise, if active killing for mercy were legalized, we might also want to exclude people in certain other social roles from the practice. Elementary schools teachers, for instance, might have responsibilities that would make it difficult aesthetically and practically to permit them to moonlight as euthanizers.

Consequentialist Arguments For and Against Distinguishing Active Killing and Letting Die Are there arguments that really can be sustained for maintaining the distinction between commissions and omissions? Let's look first at the consequentialist argument. The consequentialist argument says that, on the one hand, the result is going to be the same whether the terminally ill patient is actively killed or is simply allowed to die. The patient is going to be dead soon either way, so it really does not make any difference. Other consequentialists come back and say that there is an argument based in consequences for a difference. The consequences to the society, they might argue, are actually worse if we permit active killing than if we continue to forbid it and permit only forgoing of treatment. That is an empirical question. What will the world be like if we legalize active killing? Will there be spillover effects, so that some people get killed who should not have been killed?

In the Netherlands, for the last several years, there has been an agreement between the medical profession and law enforcement officials that, even though it is illegal for the physician to actively kill a patient, if proper procedures are followed the physician will not be prosecuted.[1] The proper procedures include getting persistent and voluntary requests from an informed, freely choosing patient, consulting with another physician, and reporting the death as a euthanasia.

An important series of studies was conducted by the Remmelink Commission, a governmental commission established to examine the effects of the Dutch tolerance for active physician euthanasia (Netherlands Ministry of Welfare, Health and Cultural Affairs 1992; also see van der Maas et al. 1991). The commission made its best estimate of the number of physician interventions to end life in a twelve-month period. In the Netherlands, euthanasia is defined as a physician intervention to kill the patient after a persistent and voluntary request. The report estimated that there had been 2300 such interventions in the year of the study. That number did not include about 400 assisted suicides, which were already considered legal in the Netherlands. The critical finding was that the commission estimated that 1000 additional life-terminating acts occurred without an explicit and persistent request from the competent patient (Netherlands Ministry of Welfare, Health and Cultural Affairs 1992). Thus, almost one in three life-terminating interventions by physicians did not conform to the stipulated terms of the arrangement, which included that the request from the patient had to be voluntary and persistent. The commission also found that, of the total of 3724 actions by physicians to provide medical assistance in actively ending life, only 486 were reported on death certificates

---

[1]Various accounts of the guidelines to avoid prosecution appear in "Final Report of the Netherlands State Commission on Euthanasia: An English Summary," *Bioethics* 1, no. 2 (1987): 163–174; H. J. J. Leenen, "Dying with Dignity: Developments in the Field of Euthanasia in the Netherlands," *Medical Law* 8 (1989):517–526; and M. A. M. De Wachter, "Active Euthanasia in the Netherlands," *Journal of the American Medical Association* 262 (1989):3316–3319.

as such. The net result was that only 16 percent of the acts in which physicians actively assisted in causing the death of a patient were completely within the terms of the agreement. It is not possible to know whether the quasi-legalization of active euthanasia in the Netherlands increased the number of nonvoluntary and extralegal killings by physicians, but critics of the law claim that the number of nonvoluntary deaths increases when voluntary mercy killing is made acceptable.

The Argument from Implications for Incompetent Patients   In the previous section we examined the argument that the real, long-term consequences of accepting active killings for mercy might be a greater tolerance for active killing of incompetents and others who have not requested to be killed. Many proponents of the acceptance of active killing recognize this problem and make great effort in their policy proposals to ensure that only a very limited class of active mercy killings would be permitted. They insist that the patient make a voluntary request while competent and that the patient be certified to be terminally ill, usually by having a second physician confirm the diagnosis as well as the competence and voluntary choice of the patient. But those very safeguards may have unexpected implications for one who is arguing that active killings are morally the same as withdrawal of life support. Some of those implications come to light when one considers groups that cannot meet the criteria for the safeguards.

One such group includes patients who have never been competent to express wishes about terminal care. (We shall examine the issues related to such cases in the next chapter.) Their problem is very relevant to whether it is justifiable to maintain a distinction between commissions and omissions. If defenders of the thesis that there is no difference between active killing and letting die have their day, and if they gain support for their view by insisting that patients must be competent and voluntarily ask for either forgoing of support or active mercy killing, suffering incompetents will be left stranded. As we shall see in the next chapter, most commentators agree that it is morally justifiable to withdraw life support from incompetents on the basis of the same criteria that are used for competents. If, however, there were no difference between commissions and omissions, then there would be no reason to use different criteria for deciding when to accept commissions and omissions. If we were committed to the view that active, merciful killings are justified only when the patient is competent and terminal and voluntarily requests the behavior that leads to death, and if the same criteria applied to omissions, then it would always be unacceptable to withdraw life support from incompetent patients. In fact, it would even be unacceptable to withdraw life support from competent persons who were not terminal. The premise that there is no difference between commissions and omissions combined with the belief that commissions are acceptable only for terminal, competent patients leaves the incompetent and the nonterminal not only without active killing but also without relief that would come from forgoing life support. They are condemned by the logic of the premise that there is no difference between commissions and omissions. The only other option is for the defenders of active killing for mercy to revise their belief that active killings are acceptable only when patients are terminal and voluntarily ask to be killed after being certified as competent. In fact, many more honest defenders of active killing for mercy acknowledge that there is no logical way to limit such killings to the terminal and the competent. The same concern for compassion in the face of suffering would seem to support mercy for the nonterminal and incompetent as well. If there is no difference between active killing and letting die, then either both are acceptable for everyone or neither is acceptable for the nonterminal and the incompetent. This logic leads some people to conclude that even though the distinction is hard to maintain, there must be something to it. Two other arguments have been put forward to attempt to sustain the distinction between active killing and letting die.

The Argument from the Principle of Avoidance of Killing   A third argument in defense of the traditional distinction between active killing and letting die rests on the belief that there is a principle of avoidance of killing. According to this view, there is something inherently *prima facie* wrong about killing a human. (Whether this principle extends to nonhuman species was a question raised in chapter 2. There, we also considered exactly who counts as having this full moral standing such that it would be wrong to kill them.)

The principle of avoidance of killing is, according to many, a fourth part of "respect for persons." Just as there is something inherently *prima facie* wrong with violating autonomy or veracity or fidelity, so, according to this view, there is something morally wrong with killing a human being even if, hypothetically, it would be in the interest of the one being killed and even if the one being killed voluntarily requested to be killed. This is the position held by Jews and ancient Christians. It is also held by Muslims, Buddhists, and Hindus. It is also accepted by many secular thinkers including Marxists, and many physicians.

Some versions of this commitment to avoid killing extend to treating all human life as sacred; so it is wrong not only to actively kill but also to let any preventable death occur. Sometimes, in this form, this position is referred to as the principle of the sacredness of life. Holders believe that all life is sacred and must be preserved whenever possible.

Taking such a view literally, however, would require extremely rigorous demands: preserving as long as possible the lives of the terminally ill and comatose and actively intervening to prevent all deaths not only in war and violence but also in famine and natural disasters. Most people believe that it is not one's moral duty in the strict sense to prevent all preventable deaths no matter how remote and how difficult to prevent. They accept the naturalness of death but interpret the principle of avoidance of killing to disapprove morally, at least *prima facie*, any actions that will hasten death. If this principle of avoidance of killing applies only to active interventions to hasten death, then there is a basis for distinguishing between active killings (commissions) and omissions.

Surely, some omissions that lead to death are morally wrong as well. Someone who had an affirmative duty to save a life and failed to do so would have violated some moral principle. A parent who fails to feed his child or an emergency room physician who fails to deliver basic emergency care that could be life-saving would have violated specific duties to act affirmatively. Perhaps those failures can be viewed as violations of the principle of fidelity—that is, failing in a fiduciary relation. They might not, however, have violated the principle of avoidance of killing.

The Argument from Autonomy There is a fourth way in which some people argue that commissions and omissions that result in the death of a patient are morally different. This can be called the argument from *autonomy and informed consent*. Proponents of this view point out that letting die at the request of the patient or surrogate is always *prima facie* right because it is required to respect autonomy. By contrast, autonomy never requires that a physician kill a patient. Autonomy is an ethical principle requiring noninterference with the life plans of others. It does not require that one facilitate those plans. Autonomy is associated only with *negative*, or *liberty*, *rights*, or the right to be left alone, to be free to engage in actions of one's own choosing. Autonomy does not involve *positive*, or *entitlement*, *rights*, by which one would have a claim to goods or services or resources needed to carry out one's plans. At least in the law, many liberty rights do not entail entitlement rights. Hence, as we saw in chapter 4, women legally have a liberty right to abortion but not an entitlement to the resources necessary to obtain one. Thus omissions, according to this view, are morally different from commissions in that they are mandated by the principle of autonomy whereas commissions never are.

New Legal Initiatives for Physician-Assisted Suicide

Distinguishing Homicide on Request from Assistance in Suicide Recently, advocates of more-active interventions to hasten death have made some additional conceptual distinctions. They have separated cases in which one person would actively kill another at that person's request from cases in which one would merely assist in the person's suicide. The key, they argue, is whether the helper takes the last critical step that causes the death. On the basis of this distinction, injecting a lethal drug would be homicide. (If it were done at the patient's request, it would be called *homicide on request.*) On the other hand, prescribing an oral form of the drug that was then taken by the patient would be considered assistance in suicide because the last key step (taking the drug) would have been taken by the patient. In the 1990s there was a significant movement attempting to legalize assisted suicide when the assistance is provided by a physician and when the assistance is provided to a mentally competent, terminally ill patient who has requested the assistance. Part of the moral argument is that if the cases are limited to patients certified as terminally ill who have documented requests for assistance and if the patient must physically take the key step that results in death, the risk of abuse is lessened.

Initiative Petitions   The ethics of physician-assisted suicide will be a major issue in the twenty-first century. Dr. Jack Kevorkian's suicide machine was just a foretaste. The Michigan Supreme Court confirmed that the law prohibiting assisting in suicide is not unconstitutional (*People v. Kevorkian* 1994). Initiative 119 in the state of Washington in 1991 was the first recent attempt to legalize physician-assisted suicide. This was an initiative placed on the ballot by petition. It did not pass, but it got 46 percent of the vote and was a sign of things to come (McGough 1993). In 1991, another citizens' initiative was attempted in California, and it did about as well (Capron 1993).

In Oregon in 1994 a referendum legalizing physician assistance in suicide for competent, terminally ill patients passed by a close vote (Oregon Death with Dignity Act 1994). It has been sustained on court review. If that initiative continues to survive further legal challenges, it will be the first law in the United States legalizing physician participation in suicide. It still would not legalize actual killing by physicians, but only assistance by means of providing information, prescriptions, and the like.

Two Court Challenges to the Prohibition of Physician Assistance   While the people of Oregon were pursuing a referendum to legalize physician assistance in suicide, two courts each temporarily found a reason why state laws prohibiting physician assistance should be considered unconstitutional. First, on March 9, 1996, the U.S. Court of Appeals for the Ninth Circuit ruled that the Washington law banning physician assistance in suicide was unconstitutional. Although this ruling was later overturned by the U.S. Supreme Court, its arguments are worth examining. The Court of Appeals ruled that the prohibition on physician assistance in suicide violated a constitutionally protected liberty (*Compassion in Dying v. Washington):* the freedom to commit physician-assisted suicide.

Then on April 12, 1996, the Second Circuit Court of Appeals issued a ruling with a similar effect, providing that a prohibition on physician-assisted suicide violated the equal protection clause of the Constitution (*Quill et al.*

v. Vacco et al.). The reasoning in this case was that those persons who wanted to end their lives by terminating life support had the legal right to do so and that prohibiting physician-assisted suicide treated the group who preferred assisted suicide unequally.

The ethics of physician assistance in suicide is now four-square on the agenda for moral and public policy debate. One issue raised is whether there is any principled difference between physician assistance in suicide and physician killing for mercy. Many are claiming that, if physicians may morally and legally legitimately assist in suicides of patients, they may, for the same reasons, actually intervene to commit the lethal act—for instance, by injecting a barbiturate. Imagine, for example, a patient who is mentally lucid but so immobilized by disease as to be unable to take any action on his or her own. If the concern is that persons who want assistance in suicide deserve protection equal to those who want merely to refuse life support, then it would seem that the immobile patient—one with ALS, for example—could rightfully have the physician perform the lethal act. This patient would have a right to have assistance not merely by the physician's providing information but by having the physician actually do the injecting, since this patient could not take lethal medication on his own.

One practical argument remains for a distinction between committing the active euthanasia and merely assisting in suicide. If we are concerned about the potential for abuse and about some physicians who might irresponsibly attempt to pressure difficult patients into ending their lives, then possibly it makes sense to hold on to the requirement that the patient must himself or herself actively take the decisive step in ending his or her own life. Of course, some are concerned that even permitting physician assistance will run the risk that patients will be pressured into committing suicide. Some, pointing to Dr. Kevorkian, are concerned that the personality of many physicians prepares them to intervene aggressively, taking matters into their own hands. This is the personality that is ideal for an emergency room when a patient has a blocked airway and needs instant, aggressive intervention to save a life, but it could be just the wrong personality type for terminally ill patients who are candidates for having their lives ended.

Many of those who oppose such interventions do so on ethical grounds rooted in the principle of avoidance of killing or the doctrine of the sacredness of life. They are unlikely to be persuaded that pragmatic checks that will minimize abuse are relevant in deciding the matter. Some who continue to hold out for a difference between all active killings (both homicides on request and assisted suicides) and merely letting die may appeal to the difference between the negative rights autonomy provides and the positive rights that are beyond its grasp. It is likely that the matter of legalization of active life-ending interventions will remain controversial.

Stopping vs. Not Starting

Besides the basic distinction between commissions and omission, a second distinction creates difficulties in the ethics of the care of the dying. It is common to feel that it is morally worse to withdraw a treatment once it has been begun than to avoid starting it in the first place. It is understandable why physicians and nurses would have such an instinct. To those who physically have to withdraw a ventilator or other treatment, it feels psychologically as if they are actively killing just as certainly as if they had injected an air embolism. But it makes no sense as a practical matter or if the moral basis for drawing lines is between what is derived from autonomy as a negative right—a right to be left alone—and what is based on positive rights. It seems wiser to follow a policy of trying a treatment and then withdrawing it if it is not working.

The law treats stoppings as "forgoing treatment"; that is, it views them as the same as not starting in the first place. Withdrawing is viewed as withholding treatment not as active killing. The argument from autonomy explains why stopping treatment is morally the equivalent of not starting. Stopping is morally required by autonomy when consent to treatment is canceled. By contrast, killing is never obliged by the autonomous action of the patient or surrogate. If the principle of autonomy is significant in understanding why commissions are different from omissions in the first place, it should help us understand why withdrawing a treatment is morally like an omission rather than a commission. Now, most commentators, legal judgments, and hospital policies that recognize the legitimacy of the omission/commission distinction will classify withdrawing as comparable to withholding. That is the position of the President's Commission for the Study of Ethical Problems in Medicine and Biomedical and Behavioral Research (1983, pp. 73–77) and other groups (Figure 5.4).

Figure 5.4: *Withdrawing vs. Withholding*

**Some groups that see no moral difference
between withdrawing and withholding**

American courts
American Medical Association
The President's Commission for the Study of Ethical Problems
    in Medicine and Biomedical and Behavioral Research
Roman Catholicism
Talmudic Judaism

The Distinction between Direct and Indirect Effects

A third distinction is often confused with the active/passive or commission/omission distinctions: that is the distinction between direct and indirect effects. This notion is also sometimes referred to as the *doctrine of double effect*. The basic idea is that in some situations an action can lead to two effects: one intended and desirable, the other unintended and undesirable. The doctrine of double effect holds that the unintended, undesirable effect is morally tolerable if the action itself is not immoral, the undesirable consequence is not a means to the desirable one, and the desirable effect produces a great enough amount of good to outweigh or be proportional to the undesirable effect. A killing that is "direct" results from an action (or omission) in which the intention of the actor is the death of the individual. A nurse who refuses to answer a code because he wants the patient dead is directly killing by omission.

An indirect effect, such as a death, results from an action (or omission) in which the effect may be foreseen by the actor but is not intended and is not a means to a desired effect. An anesthesia accident in high-risk surgery would certainly not have been intended, although it might have been foreseen as a possible outcome. Deaths in such cases are morally tolerable according to those who subscribe to the doctrine of double effect.

Consider a physician who is morally opposed to abortion and who is caring for a pregnant woman with cancer of the uterus. Removing a cancerous uterus in a pregnant woman would certainly be known to cause the death of the fetus. That outcome is foreseen with absolute certainty. Nevertheless, even opponents of abortion, such as those who subscribe to the main tenets of Catholic moral theology, would find such a death morally tolerable although they would oppose all directly intended abortions. In this case, could they save the fetus, they would do so, but in the case of the previable fetus that would not be possible. The death of the fetus would not be the intended purpose of the action. Defenders of the removal of the uterus who nevertheless oppose directly intended abortion would say that, in this case, the physician was performing the act of removing the uterus. The physician could say that this act has a double effect: that is, two consequences—one desired and intended, the other undesirable and foreseen but not intended.

Giving high doses of narcotic for the purpose of relieving pain may also be known to run the risk of respiratory depression and even death. Once again, such a death would be morally tolerable if it had not been intended even though it might have been foreseen. If an analgesic could have been used that would have avoided the risk of death, then it would have been used. The Roman Catholic Church opposes all direct killing, as does the AMA. The courts generally accept the distinction as well.

The Distinction between Ordinary
and Extraordinary Means

The Meaning of the Terms

Having made the previous distinctions we can limit our attention to forgoing of treatments in situations in which the death is not directly intended, whether the treatment is withheld or withdrawn. We need to try to determine which among the treatments that are possible are morally required. The traditional terms for treatments that could acceptably be forgone was *extraordinary* means, and those that were morally required were called *ordinary*.

That language was unfortunate and very confusing. There are at least three ways to distinguish ordinary from extraordinary treatments. The first two are older, largely rejected meanings. Treatments could be distinguished statistically by separating common from uncommon ones and considering the common ones as ordinary. That would seem to be the normal meaning of the term *ordinary*. They could also be distinguished by the complexity of the technology, separating simple from complex, high-tech interventions.

Neither distinction makes much sense. Just because a treatment is common, it is not necessarily morally required for every patient. For some patients even common procedures may be inappropriate. They may serve no purpose, or the patient may be known to react poorly to them. Likewise, some very unusual procedures may be just right for some patients. By the same token, it makes no sense to decide which treatments are required by asking how complex the technology is. Some everyday, simple procedures may not be right for certain patients, while complex, high-tech ones may be exactly what some patients need. Medical ethicists have never used the term *ordinary* to mean either common or simple; they have not used *extraordinary* to mean either uncommon or complex. Rather, the terms have been used to refer to morally required (ordinary) and morally expendable (extraordinary) treatments.

Currently, the terms *ordinary* and *extraordinary* are being abandoned and replaced by language that makes more clear the inherently normative character of the distinction that needs to be made. We are increasingly simply referring to *appropriate* and *inappropriate* treatments. That language does not reveal the criteria for appropriateness, but it at least makes clear that the reference is not to how common or how complex the treatment is.

This new terminology does not constitute a real change in meaning. The terms *ordinary* and *extraordinary* have the same normative meanings among the philosophers and theologians who use them. These terms simply refer to treatments that are morally required or fitting and those that are not. The key question is what are the criteria that make the treatment appropriate.

The Criteria for Classifying Treatments as Morally Expendable

Uselessness Traditionally, a treatment has been considered morally expendable if it does not serve a useful purpose. That judgment just seems like common sense. But, as we shall see below, figuring out whether a treatment serves a useful purpose turns out to be more complicated than it may appear.

Grave Burden Even if a treatment serves a useful purpose, such as prolonging life, it may still be expendable if it involves a *grave burden*. Both these criteria are cited by the President's Commission for the Study of Ethical Problems in Medicine and Biomedical and Behavioral Research (1983, p. 84).

The language came from Catholic moral theology and was used by Pope Pius XII in a statement on prolonging life in which he said:

> But normally one is held to use only ordinary means—according to circumstances of persons, places, times and culture—that is to say, means that do not involve any grave burden for oneself or another (Pope Pius XII 1958, pp. 395–396).

In this statement Pope Pius XII referred only to grave burden. Other Catholic moral theology literature includes uselessness as a criterion as well. Note, however, that Pope Pius XII included burden to others as well as burden to the patient, a foreshadowing of the social medical ethics that we shall encounter in chapter 7. For the remainder of this chapter, we shall focus on the burden to the patient as a basis for forgoing life-sustaining medical treatment.

Proportionality In considering both uselessness and grave burden we are really dealing with the question of benefit/harm ratios. An absolutely useless treatment would be one with a zero benefit and therefore one that would have an unfavorable benefit/harm ratio.[2] A gravely burdensome treatment would often be one that would have some benefits, but those benefits would be ex-

---

[2] We can view an unfavorable benefit/harm ratio as one that is 1 or less. If the benefits equal the harms, then the ratio is 1. Most would assume that such a treatment is not worth pursuing and not morally required. A ratio less than 1—that is, a treatment with greater harms than benefits—is surely expendable. There is an older, more conservative interpretation of grave burden that implies that the harms must substantially exceed the benefit before a treatment is morally expendable. According to this view, if a life could be saved with burdens only modestly greater than benefits, apparently one would have a duty to preserve life. However, if one includes life preservation itself as one of the benefits, presumably a great benefit, it is hard to imagine why the burdens would have to greatly exceed the benefits in order for a treatment to be expendable.

ceeded by the burdens.[3] Recognizing that both these criteria reduce to a notion of an unfavorable benefit/harm ratio, the Vatican Declaration of 1980 (Sacred Congregation for the Doctrine of Faith 1980, p. 8) urged the adoption of a single criterion of *proportionality* as the basis for deciding which treatments may morally be omitted.

This notion was accepted by the U.S. President's Commission (1983, p. 88), but, in characteristic American fashion, it gave the criterion a patient-centered twist, emphasizing that the values that underlie the judgments of benefit and burden are subjective and must be the patient's values:

> Extraordinary treatment is that which, *in the patient's view,* entails significantly greater burdens than benefits and is therefore undesirable and not obligatory, while ordinary treatment is that which, *in the patient's view,* produces greater benefits than burdens and is therefore reasonably desirable and undertaken. [Italics added.]

The Subjectivity of All Benefit and Harm Assessments

The emphasis in the President's Commission report on the subjectivity of the value judgments in all benefit and harm assessments is becoming a critical dimension in all judgments about the appropriateness of medical treatments. As we saw in chapter 3, determining whether an effect is a benefit or a harm and, in either case, how much of a benefit or a harm, is invariably a subjective process. There is no reason why being an expert in medicine gives one special expertise in making these judgments. Of course, being an expert in medicine helps in knowing what the effects are likely to be, but once the effect has been specified, it is crucial to evaluate it by assigning it a positive or negative value. It is this task that is inherently subjective and beyond the expertise of the health professional. In fact, insofar as we are concerned about the benefit or harm to the patient, it is not going too far to say that the health professional cannot know without asking the patient, whether the treatment will be beneficial and, if it will, how beneficial. It is the patient who is likely to be the authority on making the assessment insofar as it is the effects on him or her that are concerned. If one includes the principle of autonomy in any assessment of the

---

[3]One can imagine a treatment that, although its benefits exceed its burdens, might still be expendable. One interpretation of the grave burdens criterion is that, there is only so much we can ask of a person. If the burdens are *great enough,* the treatment is expendable even if the benefits are larger. Most secular commentators would accept the idea that *whenever* the burdens exceed the benefits the treatment is expendable, even if the burdens are not great, and most commentators seem to agree that in any case in which the benefit exceeds the burdens, the treatment is morally appropriate.

morality of a treatment option, then, even in those cases in which it seems clear that the patient is not the best judge of how beneficial the treatment will be, it may still be the patient's right to decide whether it is provided. The patient's point of view is determinative.

In chapter 3, we found that there is a movement from more-subjective assessments of treatments, in which it is the individual physician's judgment that is central, to a more-objective standard, in which peer review and outcomes research provide the basis of the assessment. It is now clear that, although objective standards are needed to assess what the outcome will be of a particular treatment, it will be impossible to place a value on that outcome without making the assessment patient-centered. We are moving beyond the Hippocratic perspective to a more patient-centered basis for the subjective assessment of benefits and harms.

Determining when a burden is a grave burden is perhaps more obviously subjective than is determining when a treatment will have an effect. Two medically identical patients may have very different subjective responses to treatments. One may experience dialysis as unpleasant, but bearable, while another experiences it as intolerable. For the latter, the burden is surely greater than it is for the former. When the burden gets great enough, then, using the criterion of proportionality, the treatment becomes expendable.

It may be somewhat harder to understand that uselessness is also a subjective judgment. Uselessness sounds like a matter of objective fact. But uselessness must be defined as a function of what counts as worthwhile. Consider the possibility of using a ventilator to maintain a patient in a permanently vegetative state. If the purpose is to restore the patient to consciousness, then the ventilator is useless. If, however, someone views even vegetative life as precious and worth maintaining, then the ventilator could be very useful.

Withholding Food, Fluids, CPR, and Medications

If the morality of a treatment is a function of the benefit/harm ratio from the patient's point of view, are there any universally required treatments? What about antibiotics for infection, CPR, fluids, nutrition, and routine nursing protocols such as turning a patient?

Three views can be considered: (1) These are simple, therefore required; (2) these are expendable as objectively useless; (3) their usefulness is a function of patient (or surrogate) preferences. Controversy exists over whether there is some abstract sense in which there is an objective theory of value for determining whether these treatments are serving a worthwhile purpose. Even if there is, it seems obvious that mere mortal, finite human beings, whether they be physicians or philosophers, are incapable of rendering a definitely correct account of whether these are useful or useless in a given case.

Increasingly these are seen, like all other medical treatments, as requiring benefit/harm determinations. In many cases providing food, fluid, CPR, antibiotics, and routine nursing procedures will be very worthwhile on balance and, in those cases, they should be provided. In other cases, however, they may actually do no good for the patient—from the patient's perspective. They may even deliver burdens that are greater than the expected benefits. In those cases, according to the proportionality view that now prevails, they are morally expendable. They are "extraordinary" means no matter how routine and simple.

This means there can be no such thing as a routine DNR (do not resuscitate) order or an inherently necessary provision of fluids and nutrition. As a matter of law, the Baby Doe regulations may require that all infants must be provided with antibiotics, fluids, and nutrition—apparently even when they serve no purpose or offer a substantially grave burden. Many observers, however, including the authors of the President's Commission Report, the spokespersons for the Catholic Church, and other conservative commentators, are now acknowledging that there are times when these treatments serve no purpose and can be omitted (President's Commission 1983, p. 90, William E. May et al. 1987).

With the incorporation of all medical treatments into the framework of benefit and harm assessment under the criterion of proportionality, there is increasing agreement on how to analyze decisions involving competent patients and how patients should go about making those decisions. The real controversies for the future center on the problem of active intervention by health professionals to assist in suicide and to kill for mercy and on how these difficult life-or-death decisions can be made on behalf of incompetent patients.

Key Concepts

Assisted suicide: Providing help to another to facilitate that person's suicide—normally by education or by supplying the means for committing suicide.

Doctrine of double effect: The doctrine that, when an action can lead to two effects, one intended and desirable and the other unintended and undesirable, the unintended, undesirable effect is morally tolerable if the action itself is not immoral, the undesirable consequence is not a means to the desirable one, and the desirable effect produces a great enough amount of good to outweigh or be proportional to the undesirable effect.

Extraordinary means: Medical treatments that are not morally required.

Forgoing treatment: The term often used to refer to either withholding or withdrawing of treatment.

Homicide on request: Killing of another at that person's request—in medicine normally as an act of mercy—such as by injecting a lethal drug.

Ordinary means: Medical treatments that are morally required.

Proportionality: The criterion for determining whether a medical treatment is required or expendable by assessment of the benefit/harm ratio. Treatments are disproportional if the benefits do not exceed the harms (i.e., if the ratio is 1 or less).

Bibliography

American Medical Association, Council on Ethical and Judicial Affairs. 1996. *Code of Medical Ethics: Current Opinions with Annotations, 1996–1997 Edition.* Chicago: American Medical Association.

Bleich, J. David. 1979. "The Obligation to Heal in the Judaic Tradition: A Comparative Analysis." Pages 1–44 in *Jewish Bioethics,* edited by Fred Rosner and J. David Bleich. New York: Sanhedrin Press.

Capron, Alexander-Morgan. 1993. "Even in Defeat, Proposition 161 Sounds a Warning." *Hastings Center Report* 23, no. 1 (January–February):32–33.

Compassion in Dying v. Washington 1996. No. 94-35534 D.C. No. CV-94-119-BJR, U.S. Court of Appeals for the Ninth Circuit.

May, William E., et al. 1987. "Feeding and Hydrating the Permanently Unconscious and Other Vulnerable Persons." *Issues in Law and Medicine* 3, no. 3:203–217.

McGough, Peter M. 1993. "Washington State Initiative 119: The First Public Vote on Legalizing Physician-Assisted Death." *Cambridge Quarterly of Healthcare Ethics* 2, no. 1 (Winter):63–67.

Netherlands Ministry of Welfare, Health and Cultural Affairs. 1992. *Medical Practice with Regard to Euthanasia and Related Medical Decisions in the Netherlands: Results of an Inquiry and the Government View.* Rijswijk, Netherlands: Ministerie van WVC.

Oregon Death with Dignity Act [Ballot Measure 16]. 1994. Oregon. *Trends in Health Care, Law-and-Ethics* 9, no. 4:29–32.

People v. Kevorkian. 447 Mich. 436, 527 N.W.2d 714 (1994).

Pope Pius XII. "The Prolongation of Life: An Address of Pope Pius XII to an International Congress of Anesthesiologists." *The Pope Speaks* 4 (Spring 1958):393–398.

President's Commission for the Study of Ethical Problems in Medicine and Biomedical and Behavioral Research. 1983. *Deciding to Forego Life-Sustaining Treatment: Ethical, Medical, and Legal Issues in Treatment Decisions.* Washington, D.C.: U.S. Government Printing Office.

Quill et al. v. Vacco et al. 1996. Docket No. 95-7028, U.S. Court of Appeals for the Second Circuit.

Sacred Congregation for the Doctrine of the Faith. 1980. *Declaration on Euthanasia.* Rome: The Sacred Congregation for the Doctrine of the Faith, May 5, 1980.

Van der Maas, Paul J., Johannes J. M. Van Delden, Loes Pijnenborg, and Casper W. N. Looman. 1991. "Euthanasia and Other Medical Decisions Concerning the End of Life." *The Lancet* 338 (September 14):669–674.

CHAPTER SIX

Death and Dying

The Incompetent Patient

A fair amount of agreement exists today about the things said in chapter 5 about competent patients. People generally accept the framework presented with relatively little controversy. For incompetent patients, by contrast, the situation is one of moral chaos, where physicians and others simply do not know how to handle the stoppage of treatment on terminally and critically ill patients. One reason for the chaos is that there are three separate kinds of incompetent patients. Each of the three kinds must be handled separately. In this chapter, I am going to take them in order, first talking about formerly competent patients who have expressed their wishes, then never-competent patients without family or other pre-established surrogates, and finally never-competent patients who do have such surrogates. The ethical principles and legal standards used to guide decisions for each group are summarized in Figure 6.1.

Figure 6.1 *Types of Incompetent Patients and the Standards Used in Surrogate Decisions*

Type of Patient	Ethical Principle	Legal Standard
Formerly competent	Autonomy extended	Substituted judgment
Never-competent without family	Hippocratic utility	Best interest
Never-competent with family	Limited familial autonomy	Limited familial autonomy

Formerly Competent Patients

Some patients who are presently incompetent were once competent. Some of them may have expressed their wishes while competent. The first task in caring for formerly competent patients is to find out whether they ever expressed their wishes. This can be done orally, by talking to other people who know the patient or, increasingly today, it is done with what is called an *advance directive* (President's Commission 1983, Cantor 1993). An advance directive is a written expression of the patient's wishes. There are two forms. A *substantive directive* records the patient's substantive wishes about medical treatment if he or she should ever become incompetent to express wishes directly. Usually, but not always, it is designed to apply when the patient is terminally ill or in a permanently vegetative state (also commonly called persistent or permanent vegetative state). Patients can write out certain things they would not like. Ventilators, chemotherapy, medically supplied nutrition and hydration, and other means of aggressive life support are often mentioned. They can also record certain treatments that they would want to have provided. These may include palliative care but could also include medically supplied nutrition. If a patient has unusual desires to receive life-sustaining technologies, it is important that those wishes be recorded because, increasingly, the norm is not to provide them for terminally ill and permanently unconscious patients.

Alternatively, people may write what is called a *proxy directive,* in which they specify the person they want to serve as their surrogate decision maker in the event they are unable to speak for themselves. An advance directive naming a proxy is particularly crucial for those who do not want their legal next of kin to be their agent. Feuding spouses (legally the spouse is the next of kin) may want some other relative or friend to function as decision maker. Those whose spouse is incapacitated or for whom taking the active role as decision maker would be too much of a burden may name someone else. A brother or sister, an adult son or daughter, a friend next door, or someone else may be so named.

One can combine these two forms of directives into a single document that serves both to specify the general types of treatment one would want and names someone to interpret what the patient's wishes would be in ambiguous cases.

The Principle of Autonomy Extended

A decision that is made while competent is usually deemed valid and binding when one lapses into incompetency. It is extended into the period of incompetency. The moral principle underlying this form of advance decision making could be called the *principle of autonomy extended*. Whether it is legitimate to extend that autonomy has recently become a matter of increasing controversy. There is particular difficulty in cases in which the patient has become so incompetent that there is no remaining memory of the former self, the one that wrote the advance directive. The advanced Alzheimer's patient may be quite content with a new lifestyle even though the former self who wrote a treatment-refusing advance directive would have militantly refused to continue life in the patient's present form. We usually assume today that the advance directive is still binding, but some would argue that in some cases it should not be (Buchanan and Brock 1989, pp. 184–189; Dresser and Robertson 1989). The issue is one of whether the autonomous decisions of the individual made while competent should continue to control after the individual's life and values have changed radically and the individual has become incompetent. If one thinks of the present person as radically different from the one who wrote the directive, the tendency will be to question the authority of the directive. Some defenders of this view go so far as to say that the incompetent one may actually have become a "new person" to whom the advance directive written by the "other person" does not apply. It is in those cases, in particular, that questions have arisen about the status of advance directives. On the other hand, if one views the entire life of the writer of the directive as a biosocial whole so that there is continuity even if the person cannot presently remember the writing of the directive, then one will be more inclined to want the directive to control the decisions of the now-incompetent one. Proponents of this view suggest that the directive should remain valid because if the now-incompetent person were still competent, that is our best estimate of what the person would still say.

Substituted Judgment

In law, we talk about *substituted judgment*. A substituted judgment is a judgment made by a proxy on the basis of the patient's beliefs and values. It fills the gaps, the ambiguities, in an advance directive by drawing on what is understood to be the patient's value framework, so that in a case in which a proxy knows the patient would not want a ventilator even though the proxy would find the ventilator appropriate, the proxy must go by the patient's own values, not the proxy's. For example, a patient who has a very special fear of suffocation may generally be prepared to die and oppose all aggressive or experimental treatments but may insist that he receive any therapy, including a ventilator, that will help him avoid the feeling of suffocation. If he now lapses into incompetency, it is the responsibility of his proxy to draw on what the proxy knows of the patient's special value system to disapprove of aggressive therapies except for the ventilator or other interventions needed to avoid feelings of hypoxia.

An advance directive is supposed to express the patient's own unique beliefs and values. Some of them will make no sense to the physician at the bedside, who may not understand the patient's own history. The clinician needs to rely on the surrogate's substituted judgment, meaning drawing on the patient's own beliefs and values to try to do what the patient would have chosen had she been able to speak competently.

Going Beyond Advance Directives

What if a patient is in a jurisdiction that does not have a statute authorizing an advance directive? Some countries have no relevant statutes, although increasingly we are seeing them adopted, not only in the United States but in many other countries as well. All states in the United States now have statutes or case law that authorize advance directives (Choice in Dying, Inc.), but some cover only very special circumstances. For instance, in many states the law applies only when the patient is terminally ill.

That limitation may not appear to be a problem, but the law usually defines terminal illness very narrowly. To be terminally ill a person must be dying in a relatively short time period *regardless of life-supporting therapy.* A person who is stable in a permanently vegetative state is technically not terminally ill. A permanently unconscious patient, such as Nancy Cruzan or Karen Quinlan, is technically not terminally ill, and someone anticipating the possibility of ending up in a situation like theirs may still want the advance directive to apply. Is there a way advance directives can be used even though they are not covered by state statute?

If the relevant moral principle is respecting the autonomy of the patient, and if the patient once expressed himself while competent, extended autonomy still prevails. From the point of view of the ethics involved, it makes no difference whether the patient is terminally ill or not. If the correct moral principle is autonomy extended and the patient's wishes can be surmised, then the patient's wishes ought to be followed. Under common law in British and U.S. legal traditions, the wishes of the patient to refuse a treatment are still valid, even though they are not formally in writing. In the U.S. Supreme Court decision in *Cruzan* (*Cruzan v. Director, Missouri Dept. of Health,* 110 S.Ct. 2841 [1990]), the court said, "For the purposes of this case, we assume that the United States Constitution would grant a competent person a constitutionally protected right to refuse lifesaving hydration and nutrition." Although this is not a definitive conclusion from the court, it suggests where the court will come out, and it extends even to nutrition and hydration, so refusal of other, less controversial treatments would almost certainly be protected. Especially if the patient's wishes are not in writing, the clinician needs to make sure that the next of kin or the surrogate really is expressing what the patient wanted. In rare cases, if doubt exists about what the patient would want and there is no agreement among the relevant parties, they may actually have to go to court to clarify whether the surrogate is interpreting the patient's wishes correctly.

Case 6.1   Surrogate Refusal of Nutrition without an Advance Directive: The Limits of Substituted Judgment

Helen Corbett was a 75-year-old woman who suffered a stroke in March of 1982. She was left in a persistent vegetative state—that is, she was permanently unconscious—and her life was being maintained on a nasogastric feeding tube. She did not have a written advance directive, but evidence indicated that she had been preparing to sign one that would allow for her disconnection from life-support machines. Her husband, who was presumed to be her surrogate, finally concluded that no further life support would be appropriate. He even decided that he wanted to remove her feeding tube, which had been providing her nutrition.

The Florida state living will statute excluded refusal of nutrition and hydration, making his decision problematic. Could a patient's surrogate refuse a treatment that was specifically excluded from the state's advance directive statute and do so even if there was no signed advance directive?

There was general agreement that Mr. Corbett was acting in good faith and was presenting his wife's true wishes. On April 18, 1986, the Florida Court of Appeal ruled that a constitutional right to refuse treatment exists that takes precedence over the statute.[1]

From the point of view of the ethics involved, the principle of autonomy suggests that a person ought to be able to decline treatment even if she is not dying rapidly, even if she has not reduced her views to writing, and even if she is refusing something that is not covered under a state advance directive statute.

Mechanisms for Expressing Wishes

Advance Directives

The Euthanasia Educational Council's "Living Will"   The written advance directive had its origins in proposals for what was originally called a "Living Will." First proposed by Luis Kutner in the 1930s, the written instruction

---

[1]Based on Corbett v. D'Alessandro, 487 So.2d 368 (Fla. Ct. App. 1986).

directive was promoted starting in the 1970s by the Euthanasia Educational Council, the forerunner to the group Choice in Dying. The living will used the language of "artificial or heroic means," terms that we now know are too ambiguous for such documents. The model implied that one type of refusal was the answer for all persons and that refusing treatment was the only thing one who wrote a living will would ever want to do. (Now those wanting aggressive life support may consider writing a directive insisting on such treatment.) It and other advance directives are prospective rather than ad hoc; that is, they normally state wishes while one is still healthy, before one knows exactly how one will die. They are therefore often rather vague.

One physician, who had an unusual capacity to understand the nature of the choices involved, was able to be more specific. He refused life support in the event of a cerebral vascular accident but then excluded "cerebral vascular accidents of the subarachnoid space." Another physician, in his advance directive, rejected artificial respiration to prolong life "if I have lost the ability to breathe for more than two or three (not five or six) minutes." Most of us would not know the difference between three and five minutes of anoxia well enough to write such specific instructions. It is for problems such as this that a proxy who understands the patient's values is often needed.

An advance directive was in its original form permissive rather than mandatory. It authorized the physician to stop rather than instructing that he or she must stop. Now most advance directives are more firm in specifying what the patient wants, giving instructions rather than mere permission.

Catholic Health Association "Christian Affirmation of Life" The Catholic Health Association at one time produced a document in which the operative sentence was nearly identical to that of the Euthanasia Educational Council's living will. It stated that if "there is no reasonable expectation of my recovery from physical and mental disability, I request that no extraordinary means be used to prolong my life." That document has now been replaced by one pamphlet that helps people prepare their own advance directives and another that helps them formally appoint a surrogate, or "durable power of attorney" as they are sometimes called. Although the "affirmation" contained a theological preamble that added a uniquely Catholic Christian perspective, it functioned in a way that is quite similar to the Euthanasia Council's document. There is essentially no difference in the moral commitment of the two groups to facilitating individual control over decisions to forgo life support at the end of life.

The President's Commission for the Study of Ethical Problems in Medicine and Biomedical and Behavioral Research The 1983 report on *Deciding to Forego Life-Sustaining Treatment* of the U.S. President's Commission (p. 136) endorsed a combined substantive and proxy directive. Such proposals had existed since the mid-1970s (Bok 1976, Veatch 1976).

Problems with Advance Directives   A number of problems have been raised with advance directives. One of the first was whether the wishes of the author necessarily remain valid when the person has lapsed into incompetency. Another was the need to permit variation in wishes. People have infinitely varied opinions about how they want to be treated during a terminal illness, but the early model forms were drafted without room for variation and seemed to presume that everyone would want to refuse exactly the treatments and to refuse them in the same manner. This issue has been addressed by encouraging an individually tailored advance directive, by using forms permitting recording of explicit patient preferences in a range of medical scenarios (Emanuel and Emanuel 1989), or by using value assessments that attempt to produce a written record of the patient's values pertaining to terminal care (Doukas and McCullough 1991, Kielstein and Sass 1993).

Legislation   An alternative to individually prepared advance directives might solve the problems. Some people have advocated legislation clarifying the legal options for terminal care decisions.

Attempts to Legalize Active Mercy Killing and Assisted Suicide
Some of the boldest, if crudest, attempts at legislation have been designed to legalize active killing for mercy. This was tried first, without success, in Great Britain in 1937, then in 1947 in New York, then in Idaho in 1969, in Montana in 1973, and in Oregon in 1973. None had gotten anywhere until recently when, as described in chapter 5, the strategy shifted, attempting to legalize only physician assistance in suicide of terminally ill, competent patients. At that point the Washington Initiative (1991) and the one the following year in California, both of which were limited to assisted suicide, were narrowly defeated. In 1994 Oregon passed such an initiative. It allows terminally ill adults to make a voluntary informed choice to obtain a physician's prescription for drugs to end life ("The Oregon Death with Dignity Act," in Beauchamp and Veatch 1996, pp. 199–206).

Legalizing Active Killing for Mercy   Meanwhile, two important developments internationally have changed the legal scene regarding legalization of active killing for mercy. The Netherlands agreement between the prosecutors and the medical profession (see chapter 5), in effect, "Quasi-legalizes" euthanasia. The second development occurred in 1995, when the Northern Territory of Australia temporarily became the first jurisdiction to legalize voluntary active killing for mercy before the national government overrode their law.

Natural Death Act Legislation   Before this recent legal activity directed toward physician-assisted suicide and voluntary active euthanasia, most legal efforts had been designed to clarify the status of advance directives for terminally ill, formerly competent patients. All U.S. jurisdictions now have this type of legislation, either to provide a substantive directive or a proxy directive. They generally make clear that an advance directive written while the individual was competent is valid and must be obeyed provided certain conditions are met (including provision for confirmation of diagnosis and prognosis). Some of the issues to be addressed are listed in Figure 6.2.

Issues to Be Addressed in an Advance Directive

The most important lesson from the past two decades of discussion of advance directives is that they need to be specifically based on the values and desires of the individual person. However, several categories of information should be covered.

What Treatments Are Being Refused?   If the writer of an advance directive simply refuses "extraordinary" means, he or she is begging for trouble in interpretation. As we have seen, *extraordinary* can mean many different things to different people. Such language should be avoided. Even references to "machines" is ambiguous. Specific machines should be named, if they are to be

Figure 6.2   *Issues to Be Addressed in an Advance Directive*

Main Issues

What treatments are being refused?
What treatments are desired?
When should directive take effect?
Is a durable power of attorney to be appointed?

Additional Items to Consider

What hospital (or jurisdiction) should be used?
What physicians should be consulted?
What lawyer should be consulted?
What ethics consultants should be consulted?
Should there be consultation with a priest, neighbor, teacher, or other
    trusted confidant?
Is refusal under common law or statute or both?

excluded. Is an intravenous drip a "machine," or is the reference only to ventilators and dialysis machines? Does a refusal of machines imply a desire for other kinds of treatment such as antibiotics for infection, surgery that is meant to be an attempt to cure, or radiation? If one refuses CPR, is that refusal meant to apply to temporary and potentially reversible situations resulting from choking, an anesthesia accident, or an accidental drug overdose?

Another traditional term is *gravely burdensome.* It makes sense to say that one wants to refuse such treatments, but one must be aware that such terms are subject to tremendous variation in interpretation. At least one should designate whose judgment about grave burden should be governing. Does gravely burdensome mean the writer refuses only if the burden is very large, only if the burden is much larger than the benefits, or that any treatment with an excess of burden over benefit is refused?

Advance directives should make clear whether the writer is refusing or accepting food, fluids, antibiotics, and CPR and under which circumstances. Because it is very difficult to anticipate all possible circumstances, it is particularly important that someone be named to interpret what the patient really wants.

What Treatments Are Desired? It is at least as important to specify which treatments are desired and when. Does the patient want nutrition medically supplied? What about oral nutrition? Is fluid necessary for the purpose of keeping the patient alive or only for comfort, and who is to determine whether it is needed for comfort? If the person has refused surgery, is she also refusing pain-relieving surgery?

When Should the Directive Take Effect? The standard language is that the directive should take effect only when the patient is terminal and is dying imminently. That may be what some people have in mind, but it is for others the time when an advanced directive becomes irrelevant. If the patient is going to die soon regardless of treatment, then it is too late to make the decision to avoid prolonged dying. Does the advance directive include cases in which the person might be permanently vegetative but not terminally ill in the sense of dying imminently regardless of treatment? Does it ever come into effect when the person is neither dying nor vegetative, such as when the patient is in prolonged painful illness or is suffering from a decline of mental capacity? Should it come into play whenever the surrogate wants it to regardless of the patient diagnosis as long as the patient is not competent to speak for himself?

Is a Durable Power of Attorney to Be Appointed? Is a durable power of attorney (a proxy or surrogate) to be appointed, and, if so, is there a secondary proxy? If two or more are named, must their decision be unanimous or can anyone authorize nontreatment? What happens if they disagree?

Additional Items to Consider   Some people may have special concerns that will lead them to include other items in their advance directive. These have included:

What hospital (or jurisdiction) should be used?
What physicians should be consulted?
What lawyer should be consulted?
What ethics consultants should be consulted?
Should there be consultation with a priest, neighbor, teacher, or other trusted confidant?
Is refusal under common law or statute or both?

Never-Competent Patients without Family or Other Pre-existing Surrogates

Formerly competent patients have received a great deal of the attention in the debates over decisions for incompetent patients who are terminally or critically ill, but they are probably not the most difficult cases to resolve. A second group is those who have never been competent and are without family or any agents who could act as surrogates. These could be elderly people who have no living relatives or isolated adults estranged from family. (In referring to never-competent patients, we can include a special group who were once competent but have left no record of their wishes upon which a substituted judgment could be made.)

The Principles

Morally, the principle to be used with the familyless, never-competent patient cannot be autonomy. By definition, autonomy is impossible in this group. We must revert to the next principle, which is to maximize the net welfare of the patient. This is the principle of individual (Hippocratic) utility.

Using this principle, however, requires some assumptions. It requires assuming that incompetent persons have interests. In the case of the most severe cases of incompetency (anencephaly, for example), some would question whether it is meaningful to speak of the interests of the incompetent one at all. Even if an incompetent can be said to have interests, there must be agreement on what counts as welfare for the patient. We must believe that there is enough agreement on a theory of value to determine what is in this incompetent one's interest. Note that we probably are not interested just in his medical welfare. We saw in chapter 3 that reasonable people will normally want to trade off medical for other kinds of welfare, and the terminally ill patient in particular may be one for whom other kinds of welfare are decisive.

There is no legal or moral basis for a physician as a physician to decide to stop treatment on a patient who has never been competent and has no family to speak for him. On the other hand, clearly some treatments that a physician thinks of are not worth pursuing. Someone has to decide and some standard has to be used for that decision.

The Legal Standard

Legally, the standard that must be used is called the *best interest standard.* The goal is to do what is best for the patient—at least until we move to the level of social ethics and consider whether social utility or justice can ever dictate limits on pursuing the best interest of such patients. There is beginning to be doubt over whether we must do literally what is best for such patients. Not only social considerations suggest possible limits; pragmatic patient considerations do as well. It seems unlikely that we would be required to fly a patient to Bethesda for the latest research protocol or to call in the best surgeon in the world to treat an almost certainly fatal condition if doing so created enormous burden for others. Whatever decision maker is identified, it is possible that the agent will come up with less than the absolute best course. If the agent has missed by very far what to others seems to be the best treatment, some review will be needed, but small deviances will probably be overlooked.

Who Should Be the Surrogate?

The critical question is who the surrogate should be for the never-competent patient without family. Presently no clear answer exists. As we have seen, there is no basis for assuming that the attending physician (or anyone else) has the authority to speak for this group of patients. We have two options. First, we could pass a law naming the primary physician as the surrogate. Still, there is no reason why he should be authoritative in deciding the patient's best interest. In fact, physicians may have systematic biases that will lead them toward certain kinds of decisions that may not be in the patient's real interest. In the 1950s and 1960s, for instance, physicians tended to have a strong commitment to preserving life at all costs. More recently, there may be tendencies to avoid what clinicians deem to be "futile treatments." Even if there are no systematic biases in the physician population as a whole, individual biases will always be present. One physician may be aggressively pro-treatment while the one on duty on the next shift may be equally militant in her decision to transfer the patient to a hospice. There is no reason why this group of patients should be subject to these random variations.

There is a second argument against using the attending physician as a de facto surrogate. The primary physician is in the best position to be a check on the surrogate, whoever that may be. Although he should not have the authority to override a surrogate, he can certainly insist on an outside review of the surrogate's judgment. If the primary physician becomes the surrogate that check is lost.

The alternative would be to insist that a guardian be appointed legally for every patient who has never been competent and has no family and who someone thinks would be better off dead. They are the most vulnerable group in our society. They deserve special precautions, and many argue that this is the case in which it would be better to err on the side of caution.

Never-Competent Patients with Family or Other Pre-existing Surrogates

This leaves us with a third group of patients for whom a decision-making structure must be found: those who have never expressed themselves while competent or who have never been competent but have family members or other pre-existing surrogates (close friends or loved ones) available to function as surrogates. There is an emerging consensus that the next of kin should be the presumed surrogate in such cases (President's Commission 1983, Areen 1987). They should serve until they are demonstrated (normally to a judge) to be too foolish, too malicious, or simply unwilling to serve. It seems clear that the family should try to serve the best interest of the patient. What happens, however, when there is a difference of opinion about what is in the patient's best interest?

This seems to have been the situation in the case at the beginning of this volume of the youngster named Yusef Camp who ate a pickle and was found unconscious, presumably because someone had laced the pickle with drugs causing respiratory depression. When he was diagnosed as being permanently unconscious in a vegetative state, his parents were asked whether they would agree to terminating life support; they refused any such suggestion. They pointed to the possibility of miracles and, in any case, insisted on the value of Yusef's unconscious life. Is there any objective basis to which physicians can appeal in challenging this decision?

The clinicians would have to admit that ventilatory support would be effective in changing the dying trajectory of this patient. And the family can make a case for benefit, at least from their point of view. There seems no medical basis on which to refute the claims that unexpected results can occur. Nor is there any grounds for refuting the family's claim that all life, even permanently unconscious life, is precious. The clinicians can counter with the claim that further life support will almost certainly not permit the patient to emerge from a coma, but that is not the same as proving that the treatment will do no good. The latter claim is surely not a scientific medical fact; it is a value judgment—a widely accepted one, but one not universally held. They might try to argue that continuing treatment is not the best course for the patient, although showing why it is contrary to the boy's interest to continue treatment when he is unconscious and cannot suffer from the interventions is a difficult task. Some clinicians in such cases have attempted to claim that it is a "moral affront" to continue treatment in such cases, but against that claim one would have to consider whether it would also be a moral affront to rely on the medical establishment or the state to make a child dead against the parents' wishes.

What happens when the family makes what appears to be a choice that is not best for the patient in the eyes of clinicians? The family may be the legally designated surrogate decision maker, but surrogates do not have unlimited discretion in making medical choices for their incompetent wards. There seem to be two options. First, society could insist that the surrogate choose what most reasonably is the single best course—as determined by a court or some other authority. Determining what is the best course may be difficult, but it is a standard often advocated. At first, this seems like the appropriate policy. Otherwise family is held to a lower standard than is the court in cases involving never-competent patients without family.

However, if the family must choose the best possible course, they have no choice at all (because some other authority will determine what that single course is and force the family to pursue it). Moreover, every case would have to go to a court or some other authority to determine exactly what is best. This suggests a second course that may be preferable. In the case in which a family member or some other pre-existing surrogate is making the choice, we could give some limited range of discretion among plausible choices. In the case of Karen Quinlan, when Mr. Quinlan was appointed her guardian, he was never told he must turn off the respirator. He was given some discretion, as are other families. With this option, something less than the best choice will be tolerable.

What Is the Standard Underlying This Family Discretion?

What standard would support granting this discretion to the family or other surrogate? It cannot be literally the best interest standard. That would require overriding parents whenever they were even slightly wrong. The answer seems to be that the standard is some version of the *principle of limited familial autonomy*. That is what moral theorists are saying. Although the courts have never formally articulated such a principle (and, hence it is shown in brackets as the legal standard in figure 6.1), their decisions reflect this idea. The family is a fundamental institution in our society. It has limited authority to choose the values of its incompetent members. It has the right and duty to inculcate a value system into its incompetent members. It need not choose the best value system, but some plausible set of values should be transmitted. It has been suggested that the family has autonomy analogous to the individual, but it cannot be unlimited familial autonomy as it is in the case of the individual.

Consider the analogy with what we tell parents about the education of their children. We require that they provide an education for their children. We expect that it will be a good education. We as a society, however, do not monitor every choice, insisting that it be the best possible education. Parents are permitted to choose parochial schools, military schools, or aggressive achievement-oriented schools. As long as the family is within reason, the state will not second-guess it.

But at some point the society must be willing to say that the family deviates too radically. If the family chooses no formal education at all for its children, the state will intervene *parens patriae* and take custody. The autonomy of the family is vitally important, but it is limited.

What are the foundations of limited familial autonomy? Some find it in religious traditions, the divine ordination of the family as a fundamental unit; others, in pragmatic considerations such as the probability that the family is more committed to the welfare of the child than any other social group or the need to reward families for their service by allowing some limited discretion. Whatever the foundation, it is widely agreed that familial autonomy exists. The President's Commission, for example, says:

> This society has traditionally been very reluctant to intrude upon the functioning of families, both because doing so would be difficult and because it would also destroy some of the value of the family which seems to need a fair degree of privacy and discretion to maintain its significance (President's Commission 1983, p. 215).

The nuance of the notion of limited familial autonomy within the limits of reason is suggested by the following case.

Case 6.2:   Chad Green: The Case of Limited Familial Discretion about Chemotherapy

---

A two-and-a-half-year-old boy named Chad Green developed leukemia that, according to physicians, needed chemotherapy if the boy was to have a chance at survival. The family, however, believed in an alternative diet. They felt that the chemotherapy would be too toxic and harmful for their son and that it would fail. They preferred treating his leukemia with a special diet of macrobiotic rice and

Laetrile, an extract from apricot pits that was believed to be a therapy for cancer by many committed to alternative therapies.

When the family refused the recommended orthodox chemotherapy, the physician, Dr. John Truman of Harvard Medical School, felt obliged to seek judicial review. He eventually won a court order taking custody of the child for purposes of providing the recommended therapy. The claim was, in effect, that the parents had exceeded the limits of reason in pursuing what was in the child's best interest.

The boy's parents protested vigorously, at one point taking the boy to Mexico for the purposes of obtaining the Laetrile. Although they could have been prosecuted, wise heads determined that no purpose would be served.

Dr. Truman continued to pursue the case. He realized that he might be able to work out a compromise that would respect the parent's views, at least to some extent, and still accomplish the ends he was seeking. He offered to treat the child with the special diet and Laetrile, obtaining safe and clean samples of the agents, if the parents would agree to let him simultaneously administer the chemotherapy. This solution did not completely satisfy either party, and neither was convinced that this compromise was the best possible course for the boy, but they each realized that it accomplished much of what they were seeking. The court eventually accepted this compromise. The court, in effect, found that even if this was not the best possible course, it was within reason and should be allowed to proceed.[2]

The notion of limited familial discretion gives us some possible basis for further analysis of the case of Yusef presented in chapter 1. As he lay permanently unconscious on a ventilator, the physicians were convinced that the best course would be to stop the ventilator and let him die. They could not persuade the parents, however, that this was best. Several strategies were available, none of which seemed to offer a satisfactory solution.

First, they could have tried to argue that the boy was already deceased on the basis of brain criteria for death. Of course, no physician is ever required to treat a corpse. If the boy was already dead, then treatment could cease even against the parents' wishes. As we saw in chapter 2, there is increasing agreement that some form of a brain-based definition of death should replace the more traditional cardiac-based definition. In this case, however, there was still some limited brain activity, at least in the opinion of one of the neurologists who examined the patient. Moreover, in the District of Columbia at the time there was no law authorizing death pronouncement based on brain function. Thus the strategy of declaring the boy dead would not work.

---

[2]Based on Custody of a Minor. Mass., 379 N.E. 2d 1053 (1978) and other published reports of the case.

Second, the medical team could go to court to attempt to have the parents overruled in their judgment about what was best for the patient. We have seen that this approach can work in cases such as that of Chad Green. But in this case showing that the continuation of life support is seriously contrary to the boy's interest is a difficult standard to meet. We have just seen that the parents will be given limited discretion in deciding what is in their ward's interest. In this case, the boy is permanently unconscious according to the physicians, so it is hard for them to show that the boy is being harmed in any way by continuing. The medical team was likely to fail if it went to court on the basis of the claim that the parental judgment was contrary to the boy's interest.

There is still a third possible basis for seeking to override these parents. It could be claimed that the continuation jeopardizes not the boy's interests, but the interests of third parties: of the other patients on that ward, of the nurses who have to deliver care, or of the citizens of the District of Columbia, who were funding the treatment through their Medicaid program.

Is it possible that the time has come to begin to set limits on patient care not on the basis of patient well-being or even patient rights, but on the basis of the interests of third parties? Seeing how third-party interests might justifiably enter these and other medical decisions is the focus of the next chapter.

Key Concepts

Advance directive: A written expression of a person's wishes about medical care, especially care during a terminal or critical illness.

Best interest standard: The standard used by a proxy for medical decision making in cases in which it is impossible to know what the incompetent person's beliefs and values are. Such judgments are based on what are taken to be objective beliefs about what is good for the patient.

Principle of autonomy extended: The moral principle that is sometimes cited as supporting the duty to respect the autonomous choices of persons even after they have ceased to be competent.

Proxy directive: An advance directive that specifies the person to serve as the patient's surrogate decision maker in the event the writer is unable to speak for himself or herself.

Substantive directive: An advance directive that records the patient's substantive wishes about medical treatment, specifying treatments that are desired or refused and/or criteria for making judgments. Usually, but not always, it is designed to apply when the patient is terminally ill or in a permanently vegetative state. Ventilators, chemotherapy, medically supplied nutrition and hydration, and other means of aggressive life support are often mentioned.

Substituted judgment: The standard used by a proxy for medical decision making based on an incompetent person's beliefs and values as they were expressed while the person was capable of expressing them.

Bibliography

Areen, Judith. 1987. "The Legal Status of Consent Obtained from Families of Adult Patients to Withhold or Withdraw Treatment." *Journal of the American Medical Association* 258, no. 2 (July 10):229–235.

Beauchamp, Tom L., and Robert M. Veatch, eds. 1996. *Ethical Issues in Death and Dying*, 2d ed. Upper Saddle River, N.J.: Prentice Hall.

Bok, Sissela. 1976. "Personal Directions for Care at the End of Life." *New England Journal of Medicine* 295:367–369.

Buchanan, Allen E., and Dan W. Brock. 1989. *Deciding for Others: The Ethics of Surrogate Decision Making.* Cambridge: Cambridge University Press.

Cantor, Norman L. 1993. *Advance Directives and the Pursuit of Death with Dignity.* Bloomington, Ind.: Indiana University Press.

Choice in Dying, Inc. *Refusal of Treatment Legislation: A State by State Compilation of Enacted and Model Statutes.* New York: Choice in Dying, Inc., updated regularly.

Choice in Dying, Inc. *Right to Die Law Digest Statutes.* New York: Choice in Dying, Inc., updated regularly.

Doukas, David J., and Laurence B. McCullough. 1991. "The Values History: The Evaluation of the Patient's Values and Advance Directives." *Journal of Family Practice* 32, no. 2: 145–153.

Dresser, Rebecca S., and John A. Robertson. 1989. "Quality of Life and Non-Treatment Decisions for Incompetent Patients: A Critique of the Orthodox Approach." *Law, Medicine, & Health Care* 17:234–244.

Emanuel, Linda L., and Ezekiel J. Emanuel. 1989. "The Medical Directive: A New Comprehensive Advance Care Document." *Journal of the American Medical Association* 261 (June 9): 3288–3293.

Kielstein, Rita, and Hans-Martin Sass. 1993. "Using Stories to Assess Values and Establish Medical Directives." *Kennedy Institute of Ethics Journal* 3 (September):303–318.

President's Commission for the Study of Ethical Problems in Medicine and Biomedical and Behavioral Research. 1983. *Deciding to Forego Life-Sustaining Treatment: Ethical, Medical, and Legal Issues in Treatment Decisions.* Washington, D.C.: U.S. Government Printing Office.

Veatch, Robert M. 1976. *Death, Dying, and the Biological Revolution.* New Haven, Conn.: Yale University Press. [See also revised edition, 1989.]

CHAPTER SEVEN

The Social Ethics of Medicine

Allocation of Resources, Transplantation, and Human Subjects Research

Thus far the issues addressed in this volume have focused on the level of the individual patient-physician relationship. The Hippocratic ethic committed the physician to benefiting the patient. The principles clustered under the idea of respect for persons add duties to the agenda that do not necessarily end up benefiting the patient, but the focus is nevertheless still on the individual receiving medical services. There were at least two points at which hints of a more social concern emerged. In chapter 4, we noted that some modern discussions of the ethics of confidentiality permit disclosure of confidential information if necessary to provide significant benefit to third parties. In chapter 5, we noted that Pope Pius XII considered medical treatments extraordinary if they involved a grave burden to other people as well as to the patient. In both cases we delayed exploration of these third-party interests. This chapter opens medical ethical considerations to a more social dimension, asking when, if ever, our duties should include promoting the welfare of others or fulfilling nonconsequentialist obligations to others.

The Need for a Social Ethic for Medicine

The Limits of the Ethics of Individual Relations

The Hippocratic formula calls for benefiting the patient in the singular. Ancient Hippocratic medicine was not oriented toward the health or welfare of the community or of other individuals. That has also been the case in modern medicine and in modern interpretations of the Oath. For example, the Declaration of Geneva states that "The health of my patient will be my first consideration." *Patient* is in the singular. Even those codes and oaths that express commitment to patients in the plural still focus only on the single physician's patients. There is no concept of moral community in the Hippocratic tradition. It focuses on patient welfare rather than more inclusive welfare of other persons or of society as a whole.

When modern ethics began to shift from a Hippocratic ethic of benefit to a more deontological ethic of rights and duties, drawing on the notion of respect for persons and the underlying principles of fidelity, autonomy, veracity, and avoidance of killing, the new ethic was still addressing problems of the individual patient-physician relation—problems of confidentiality, informed consent, disclosure of diagnoses, and the care of the dying patient. It was as if in all the world there were only one physician and one patient. The moral problem was figuring out how the patient ought to be treated. The dispute between the consequentialist Hippocratic ethic and nonconsequentialist ethic of respect for persons was one within the tradition of individualism. If respect for persons seemed to be winning the day, defeating the more traditional Hippocratic paternalism, it was because the controversies of the day posed questions of how to treat the individual patient. In that world, autonomy and the related respect for persons principles seemed paramount.

But autonomy's triumph was only temporary (Veatch 1984). The moral problems in the medicine of the future moved from individual to a more social model. This shift required confronting the problems of ethical individualism. Both Hippocratic beneficence and respect for persons ignore the question of duties to third parties. In the modern world, ignoring society becomes increasingly impossible. Medicine must confront the issues of allocating scarce medical resources, including organs for transplant, and conducting research on human subjects where the goal is not improving the welfare of the individual patient but producing knowledge for the benefit of the society. Before examining these issues we need to examine what ethical principles can be brought to bear on these problems.

The Social Ethical Principles for Medical Ethics

Social Utility   It seems, at first, as if the principle for a social ethic ought to be what can be called *social utility*. In chapter 3, we saw that the principles of beneficence and nonmaleficence can be combined into an overall measure of consequences called *utility*. In that chapter, we were examining Hippocratic utility: that is, benefits and harms that accrue to the individual patient. In Figure 7.1 we provide a final version of the diagram that appeared in chapters 3 and 4. In Figure 7.1 social utility takes its place as a consequence-maximizing principle at the social level.

The Nature of the Principle of Social Utility   Now, still working in a consequence-maximizing mode, we must address a more social form of conse-

	Consequentialist Principles	**Duty-Based Principles**
Individual	Subjective 1. Beneficence 2. Nonmaleficence ....**Hippocratic Utility**........ Objective 1. Beneficence 2. Nonmaleficence	**The Ethic of Respect for Persons** 1. Fidelity 2. Autonomy 3. Veracity 4. Avoidance of killing
Social	**Social Utility** 1. Beneficence 2. Nonmaleficence	**Justice**

**Figure 7.1.   *Ethical Principles—Final Form,
Including Social Principles***

quence maximizing. Beneficence and nonmaleficence applied at the social level take into account all benefits and harms to all parties affected, not just the individual patient. Here the goal is the greatest aggregate good. This is the ethical principle of the classical social utilitarians, people like Jeremy Bentham (1967) and John Stuart Mill (1967). This is the ethical principle underlying standard cost-benefit analysis. In such analyses, planners attempt to determine the potential benefits and the potential costs (economic, social, and medical) of alternative uses of resources. Then they follow the course that will produce the most net benefit per unit of cost. Their principle is social utility—that is, beneficence and nonmaleficence applied socially—to all parties potentially affected by an action. This is just like Hippocratic utility maximizing, except that it is not limited to the individual patient.

Critics raise questions about the social utility principle. Two kinds of problems arise: problems of quantification and problems of inequity.

Quantification Problems   First, enormous problems exist in determining what maximizes the net good. This problem is particularly severe in health care, where the benefits include such nebulous and subjective goods as relief of pain, keeping a patient alive until some important family event occurs, or relieving mental anguish. Critics of the social utility principle claim that these are almost impossible to quantify and that efforts to do so expose the planners to the risk of incorporating biases in assigning weights to certain outcomes.

Although the quantification problems are severe, social scientists have become very sophisticated in providing such quantifications. For example, considerable work has been done in developing scales that permit comparison of different disease states. Robert Kaplan's (Kaplan and Bush 1982) Quality of Well-Being Scales were used by the Oregon Health Services Commission (1991) in the initial ranking of diagnosis-treatment pairs for its experiment in allocating Medicaid funds. This project attempts to decide which of several hundred possible medical interventions deserve priority. The commission asked people to rank various conditions on a scale from zero to one, with zero being comparable to death and one being normal health. From this information, together with scientific data on the possible effects of the intervention and their costs, the commission staff could calculate the cost per unit of expected benefit. These studies have been developed with great care and sophistication. Others have attempted to develop a single unit that integrates both the number of years of survival from an intervention and the quality of life that survival brings. The unit, called the quality-adjusted life-year (QALY), permits comparison on a single scale of interventions that primarily extend life with those that primarily improve the quality of life. These sophisticated health planning measurements can be used in calculations of benefit/harm ratios so that alternative interventions can be ranked in terms of the amount of well-being or the number of quality-adjusted life-years bought per unit of resource invested.

Problems of Inequity   The real controversy in the use of these numerical scales for comparing the benefits and costs of different treatment interventions is in the assumption that the morally correct course is the one that will maximize the aggregate net benefit per unit of resources. Striving to maximize aggregate net social benefits may hide the fact that the benefits are very unevenly distributed. It is the nature of medicine that some conditions and some patients are much harder and less efficient to treat than others. Patients with multiple chronic illnesses are less efficient to treat than those with acute, treatable conditions. People living in rural areas or inner cities may be harder to reach with medical services than suburbanites. A cost-benefit analysis comparing a health care investment for upper-middle-class suburbanites with one for rural area or inner city patients will show that the suburban health plan produced more benefit (lives saved or quality-adjusted life-years per unit of investment).

The moral issue is whether giving such priorities would be ethical. It may turn out that the health care system that is the most efficient is not the most fair or just or equitable. Assuming that the most efficient system is not the most fair, what is the proper relationship between these two ethical concerns?

Justice as an Alternative Social Ethical Principle   If we are not satisfied morally with allocation of medical resources solely on the basis of maximizing the aggregate good, we need a principle that provides an alternative. The principle of *justice* is often put forward to play this role. It is a way of showing respect for persons at the social level, hence, it appears in Figure 7.1 in the lower right quadrant as a duty-based principle at the social level. Most generally, justice is the principle that people in similar situations should be treated equally. The key is in exactly how the situations of people are determined to be morally similar. Different theories of justice identify different characteristics. In Greek culture, noble or aristocratic birth was considered relevant in deciding what constituted a fair allocation. In modern cultures, especially those influenced historically by Judeo-Christian thought, justice is interpreted in a more egalitarian manner. Justice is seen as requiring that people have opportunities for equality of well-being. In health care, this view is often interpreted as leading to distributing health services on the basis of need. Although need could be determined in terms of relative overall well-being, health care is often allocated on the basis of *medical* need.

We saw in chapter 3 that medical well-being is a complex concept, including considerations of preventing death, curing disease, relieving suffering, and promoting health. The question of determining who is worst off medically will require some consensus on the value judgments to be made. These are the same problems that would be faced, however, by those who would strive to allocate medical resources on the basis of maximizing overall social utility. In either case, we need a metric for comparing medical well-being. Whereas the social utilitarian would use units of quality-adjusted life-years to determine how to maximize their number in the aggregate, a proponent of the principle of justice would strive to make the distribution of quality-adjusted life-years as equal as possible. There are many ways of conceptualizing opportunities for equality of well-being.

If all that is called for is an *opportunity* for well-being, some would hold that, if people have had opportunities to be healthy, they do not have the same claim as others even though they may be in equal medical need. A person needing a liver transplant as a result of a history of alcoholism might, according to this view, not be given the same claim as one with another cause of liver failure. To the extent that a health-risky behavior is voluntary, some would claim that those needing medical care as a result of these behaviors have a lesser claim (Veatch 1980, Moss and Siegler 1991).

In determinations of who is in the greatest need, there is also controversy over whether we should consider people's well-being in a "moment in time" or over a lifetime. A moment-in-time perspective would compare people at a particular time, focusing medical resources on those who were worst off at that time. Triage based on treating the sickest among those who can benefit is a way of allocating according to egalitarian justice from this moment-in-time perspective (Baker and Strosberg 1992). Some medical services, such as relief of acute pain, treatment for acute curable illness, and provision of preventive medical service such as immunizations seem to many to be distributed fairly on the basis of who has the greatest need at the moment. Other health care services might be distributed on the basis of who is the worst off over their lifetime. The key to the principle of justice is that spreading resources according to need is a duty of ethics even if it does not maximize the total good done.

Those who accept a principle of justice see it as at least a *prima facie* consideration in a social ethic of health care—for deciding how health care resources should be allocated, how a transplant program should be operated, or how human subjects research should be conducted. Whether justice also leads to a duty proper—that is, a duty after all other moral considerations have been taken into account—depends on how one ends up ranking and balancing the claims of the competing moral principles. A pure egalitarian basis for distribution of health care resources seems implausible because that could lead to reducing all patients to the lot of the worst off. All people equally dead would be purely egalitarian. A defender of egalitarian justice would have to explain how other principles might come into play to avoid that outcome.

Ways of Reconciling Competing Claims

If both social utility and justice are at stake in a social ethics for health care, we need to know how they are related to each other. In some cases, doing what maximizes social utility will turn out also to produce a just distribution. Thus, if an antibiotic is in scarce supply, providing doses to those who have the most serious infections may also produce the most medical good. The difficult case is the one in which the two principles conflict. Sometimes giving a scarce drug to the sickest may mean giving it to someone who has relatively small chance to benefit whereas giving it to patients in somewhat better shape may predictably do much more good. As we saw in chapter 4, several different methods of resolving such conflicts are available.

Treating Social Utility and Justice as Equally Important   One widely accepted view is that neither social utility nor justice nor any other principle can always be considered to prevail. If each principle tells us what is *prima facie* morally required, then, according to this view, when principles conflict they must be balanced off against one another. We shall see that the current formula for allocating kidneys for transplant follows this approach.

The Rawlsian Maximin Reconciliation of Justice and Utility   Treating social utility and justice as equally weighty is not the only method of resolving the conflict between competing social ethical principles. One of the most important developments in twentieth-century ethics is the work of the philosopher John Rawls (1971). Rawls examines at great length the theory of how equality of distribution should be related to maximizing social utility. His view operates at a very abstract level, but some of his followers have attempted to determine the implications for a health care delivery system (Green 1976, Shelp 1981, Daniels 1985, DeGrazia 1991, Veatch 1991). One interpretation relies on one of Rawls's principles, sometimes called the *difference principle*. It specifies that when basic goods are distributed they should be distributed equally unless the inequalities result in an advantage to the worst off. Theorists debate whether the difference principle can be applied to health care, but if it were, it could support a practice of paying high salaries to physicians, but only if it were necessary as an incentive to get physicians to expend effort to help the worst off. It could also justify shifting some resources to healthier patients if that made it possible to provide at least minimal comfort to the worst off. Although the Rawlsian difference principle is sometimes treated as a principle of justice, it can better be understood as a justification for abandoning purely egalitarian justice when certain kinds of social utility are served—that is, when advantage is gained by the worst off.

The Partial Lexical Ordering of Duty-Based Principles over Consequence-Maximizing Principles   Another approach to resolving the competing claims of social utility and justice would rely to some extent on the *lexical ordering* of principles, discussed in chapter 4, which places all manifestations of one principle prior to any instances of another. One partial lexical ranking scheme considered in chapter 4 would place all nonconsequentialist principles above any that are consequence-maximizing. Then within the non-consequence-maximizing duties the competing claims would be balanced, as would the competing claims of beneficence and nonmaleficence on the consequence-maximizing side. Thus all the duties of justice and respect for person would have to be satisfied before any concerns about beneficence and nonmaleficence would come into play. The consequence-maximizing principles would be used only after fidelity to promises, autonomy, veracity, avoidance of killing, and justice had been fully satisfied. These latter claims could be balanced against one another.

This approach easily explains why many people hold that it is not acceptable to kill someone in a research project to learn information for the good of others, no matter how much good could result. The killing would violate the principle of avoidance of killing and, unless the victim consented, would also violate autonomy. This ranking also explains why the autonomous refusal of treatment of competent patients always takes precedence over beneficence—a conclusion that those who would balance beneficence and autonomy cannot explain. The ranking of non-consequence-maximizing duties over the consequence-maximizing ones explains a great deal in medical ethics.

Can it, however, explain why the worst-off patient with an incurable disease would not command all the world's resources? This is sometimes called the *bottomless pit* problem (or more politely the *infinite demand* problem) and is probably the most difficult question for defenders of the priority of justice over social utility. Defenders of lexical ranking point out that there may be many ways to escape the infinite demand problem. First, some advantages for the worst off may be so trivial that they would voluntarily surrender their claim. The claims of justice surely are alienable. That is, they can be waived by their claimants. Second, other nonconsequentialist principles may come into play, offsetting some claims of justice. For example, a health care system's promises to other patients would legitimately compete with the claims of justice of the worst off. Any diversion of resources necessary to avoid a killing would also compete. The principle of justice itself provides considerable leverage for avoiding the implications of the infinite demand problem. If all resources were diverted to those who appear to be worst off, others would soon be medically impaired. They might themselves actually become worse off than the original claimants to that position. If polio immunizations were sacrificed to fund care for terminally ill patients, for example, some now healthy would soon contract polio and perhaps be worse off than the presently dying. Defenders of the ranking of non-consequence-maximizing principles have several responses available to the infinite demand problem.

Allocation of Health Care Resources

The area of medical ethics that poses social ethical questions most dramatically is the allocation of health care resources. In the era of escalating health care costs, managed care, and global budgets for health care, the most controversial ethical issue is how scarce resources should be allocated (Bayer, Caplan, and Daniels 1983; President's Commission 1983; Veatch 1986b; Blank 1988; Strosberg, Fein, and Carroll 1989; Callahan 1990; Menzel 1990; Morreim 1991).

The Demand for Health Care Services

In the United States we spend about 3 billion dollars a day on health care.[1] Even so, the health of Americans is in a sorry state. It is far from the top in life expectancy at birth. Infant mortality is 60 percent greater than in Sweden.[2] What is not recognized is that the continual recitation of aggregate social indicators such as life expectancy and infant mortality implies that

---

[1]See Katharine R. Levit, Helen C. Lazenby, Bradley R. Braden, Cathy A. Cowan, Patricia A. McDonnell, Lekha Sivarajan, Jean M. Stiller, Darleen K. Won, Carolyn S. Donham, Anna M. Long, and Madie W. Stewart, "Data View: National Health Expenditures, 1995," *Health Care Financing Review* 18 (Fall 1996): 175; also see the Health Care Financing Administration Web site: http://www.hcfa.gov/stats/nhe-oact/tables/t09.htm.

maximizing aggregate health is the morally legitimate goal. Today about 15 percent of the U.S. population has no health insurance at all.[3] Another 10 percent is woefully underinsured. Dreadful differences in health are correlated with income, education, and race. Enormous international differences exist as well.

The Inevitability of Rationing

There is an argument that we do not need to ration health care. If we just divert resources from foolishness and waste elsewhere in the system, there will be enough for health care. At this point, one can plug in his or her favorite budget target: the defense department, junkets for Congressmen, tobacco subsidies, and the like. This may be a good argument when we talk to people outside of health care, but still it is not realistic. The cost of doing everything we would like to do in medicine for everyone who would like to receive it exceeds the gross domestic product. And that is without considering obligations to others in less wealthy parts of the world. Rationing is inevitable. There will always be more demands for health care services (some of which are quite marginal) than there are resources. In such a world, rationing is morally necessary. Even if we recognize that there are enough funds to provide a decent minimum for everyone (and then some), every health plan must exclude some services—not only luxuries but also marginal tests and procedures for some patients who have high-priority needs.[4] Let's try to get at the moral logic of this rationing, what is often expressed as a movement for cost containment.

[2] *The World Health Report 1996: Fighting Disease, Fostering Development* (Geneva: World Health Organization, 1996), pp. 119–120.

[3] Katherine Swartz, "Dynamics of People Without Health Insurance," *Journal of the American Medical Association* 271, no. 1 (1994):64–66.

[4] The classic illustration is the test for occult blood in the stool used as an indicator of possible cancer. Everyone agrees that this test is worthwhile. A famous paper by Duncan Neuhauser and Ann M. Lewicki ("What Do We Gain from the Sixth Stool Guaiac?" *New England Journal of Medicine* 293, no. 5 [July 31, 1975]:226–228) showed that it costs (in 1975 dollars) $1175 to find a positive result, a wise investment. But when the test is performed, some 9 percent of the positives will be missed. The test can be repeated, finding most of those that were missed the first time, but still missing a few. The second time around, it costs $5492 to find a case, still what many would consider a good investment. If the test is repeated a third time, it will cost $49,150 to find a positive; the fourth time, $469,534, and still not quite all the positives will be located. The test can be repeated indefinitely, each time being more expensive because there are fewer and fewer positives to be located. The sixth test would cost $47,107,214 to find a case. By the time we get to the sixth test, the cost seems unreasonable, yet from the point of view of the patient whose case was found, it would be valuable. The problem is that there is no clear principle upon which to say we have gone far enough. The test is simple, virtually risk-free, and could be repeated over and over. At some point every insurance plan will say that the cost is too great for the expected benefit given the other uses to which the funds could be put.

Case 7.1: DRG Limits and Myocardial Infarction

DRG 122 is the Medicare diagnosis-related group designation for "acute MI without cardiovascular complications, patient discharged alive." All Medicare patients with this diagnosis in a given hospital generate a flat Medicare reimbursement to the hospital. Other hospitals would get the same reimbursement adjusted for regional and other variables. If the physicians at the hospital treat a patient for less than the cost of the reimbursement, the hospital keeps the difference; hospitals sometime share the surplus with the physicians as an incentive to treat economically. If the cost exceeds the reimbursement, the hospital must cover the difference.

If the hospital has other services with surpluses, it can "cost-shift" to cover any such losses. That practice raises ethical issues, however. Either the services generating surpluses are getting reimbursed at too high a rate or the patients in the services generating surpluses are being undertreated. Too high a rate should lead to "ratcheting down" the reimbursement to a more appropriate amount, but ideally there should be no surpluses in any services to make up shortfalls in any other services.

In a study of three hospitals conducted some years ago, it was found that the average cost was slightly over $10,000 per patient in DRG 122 (Veatch 1986a). Of course, this was not the actual cost for each patient. Some who were difficult to treat cost much more; other, easier, cases cost less. But this was the cost on average. The scheduled reimbursement was $7100 per patient. Thus, if those hospitals treated 100 patients in a given time period, the cost would be over $1,000,000, but their global budget[5] would be only 100 times $7100, or $710,000, to pay the costs of the care for the group. It does not take a degree in accounting to realize that the cardiology service cannot survive on this basis without some subsidy. Assuming no other services are generating surpluses—and they should not be in a well-adjusted system—ethically how should cardiologists respond?

The medical records of this group of hospitals showed that the average length of stay in the hospital for a myocardial infarction was thirteen days.[6] This was

---

[5]A global budget is an overall financial funding resource supplied to a hospital department, a managed care organization, a health system, or a national health care plan from which those responsible must provide all the care for all the patients in their system. Global budgets are often set by governments or by the collective funding received from insurers or subscribers in such a way that the total funding is not sufficient for health care providers to deliver all the services they would like to provide for each patient. The ethical task is to determine, first, whether the overall size of the budget is morally justified and, second, how the inevitably deficient resources should be allocated among the patients (Veatch 1994).

[6]Since these data were gathered, the average length of stay has been reduced considerably. The ethical problem, having an ideal length of stay that would generate more costs than the reimbursements would cover, remains the same.

the average time that clinicians in these institutions believed that their patients needed to stay to obtain ideal medical benefit.[7] Further analysis of the individual medical records revealed that one of the cardiologists consistently had lengths of stay well beyond the average. His patients averaged eighteen days of stay, with an average cost of $14,000. It was at first suspected that he might be a particularly skilled cardiologist who, therefore, assumed responsibility for particular difficult patients. This, however, proved not to be the case. There was no evidence that his patients had any different degree of severity than the other patients at these institutions. What is the proper response of the cardiologists to the economic pressure from the Medicare DRG system?

Ethical Responses to the Pressures for Cost Containment

The different ethical principles discussed in this volume will offer very different ethical responses to the dilemma of pressures for cost containment. Taking various principles from Figure 7.1 we can see their implications. Examining those implications will provide a summary of the alternative ethics available in health care.

Ethical Principles at the Level of the Individual

The Subjective Form of Hippocratic (Patient-Benefiting) Utility The Hippocratic Oath would have each physician treat for myocardial infarction by striving to benefit the patient according to the physician's judgment. That, of course, is exactly what these physicians, including the atypical physician who insisted on unusually long lengths of stay for his patients, were trying to do. The longer-than-average hospital stays were what was called for by subjective Hippocratic beneficence. That physician believed that the long hospital stays were best even though colleagues would disagree.

The graph in Figure 7.2 is a schematic representation of the cardiology resource problem. It can function as a general model of clinician investment of resources in patient care. The length of stay, which is represented on the horizontal axis, is an approximation of resources invested.[8] On the vertical axis, the aggregate net medical good done is represented. The curve shows that early units of investment are more efficient than later ones. They do more good

---

[7]Technically, the average length of stay may represent something less than the ideal length, since physicians may already have acted on their cost-consciousness to send patients home when they had received almost all the benefit that could be expected, rather than keeping them to the point when medical benefit was fully maximized.

[8]It is only an approximation because clearly the early days of hospitalization for a myocardial infarction consume resources more intensely than do the later days. Still, the graph represents the economist's notion of decreasing marginal utility of units of resources. The more invested, the lesser the incremental addition to the good that is done.

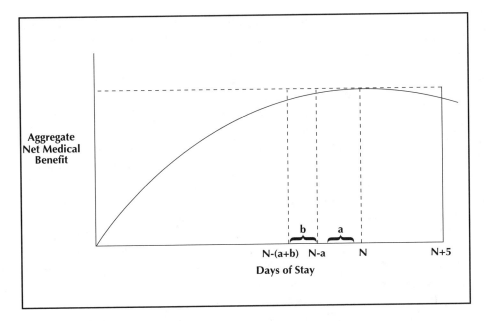

Figure 7.2 *Schematic Representation of Aggregate Benefit per Day of Stay in the Hospital*

than later units of investment. If one keeps investing in more and more days, eventually no more good will be done; the curve will become flat. A patient who is kept in the hospital even longer, statistically, may actually experience a net harm. Iatrogenic infection and other hospital-caused harms lead the curve to turn down, indicating that the aggregate good done for the patient may actually decrease.

The Objective Form of Hippocratic (Patient-Benefiting) Utility   What is striking is that shifting from the goal of patient welfare assessed subjectively by the individual clinician to a more objective measure of effects through peer review and outcomes research, may, by eliminating useless medical treatment, actually increase the net good done for the patient while as a side effect conserving resources. Imposing peer review constraints on the outlier intensive utilizer of days of stay will drive days of stay back to the consensus of colleagues.

This length of stay, symbolized by point *N* in Figure 7.2, approximates objective net medical benefit. Driving care back to this level by peer review is primarily motivated out of the modified Hippocratic concern of objectively promoting the patient's welfare, but resources are saved as a side effect. (Of course, peer review may also identify some underutilizers of treatment resources. Aggressive, patient-welfare–oriented peer review will increase expense in those cases. The net savings will be the reductions in overtreatment less adjustments for undertreatment.) The concern is still patient-centered; it focuses on patient welfare. With Hippocratic beneficence, cost containment is a fringe benefit.

The Principle of Autonomy The patient's estimate of his welfare may not be the same as the consensus of the peer review. The patient may rationally differ on what counts as a medical benefit. The patient may consider things other than medical benefits. The elderly patient may contemplate going home, longing for home cooking or to see grandchildren. The patient may decline what peer reviewers would determine to be real medical benefit.

No rational person wants resources spent on treatment he is trying to refuse. Patients are saying no to last-ditch cancer surgery when the face is half eaten away by cancer, to artificial hearts that leave one half comatose, and to respirators pumping oxygen into unconscious, decaying bodies. When patients say no, it is foolish to spend valuable resources forcing care on them even when the consensus of medical expertise favors intervention.

If we add the principle of autonomy to the calculus, we reach the conclusion that it is morally wrong to benefit a patient who does not want to be benefited.

The result of the shift to an objective form of Hippocratic utility and adding the principle of autonomy is a modified Hippocratic principle: Benefit the patient according to some objective standard of medical benefit rather than subjective judgments of benefit unless the patient (or surrogate) rejects the care being offered.

This modified Hippocratic formula is still patient-centered; but it now focuses on the rights as well as the welfare of the patient. It is based on autonomy as well as modified Hippocratic beneficence. We get another fringe benefit. If some of the hundred myocardial infarction patients decline some marginal hospitalization, the average days of stay drops further. An amount of additional care would be refused that can be symbolized by the interval a in Figure 7.2. Average length of stay would be driven back to the point labeled $(N - a)$. Costs would drop further.

The resource allocation question could be addressed by simply letting the principle of autonomy have free reign. Some propose a free-market solution to the problem of health care resource allocation. Instead of worrying about the shortfall in the Medicare funding, we could go entirely to a privately funded system in which people self-pay for their health care either by paying out of pocket with whatever resources they have or by buying private insurance in advance that defines the extent of the coverage available. Of course, some would get very inadequate health care by this free-market approach. Pure libertarians would, however, be willing to take these consequences. They claim that the fact that some would have to go without would be *unfortunate*, but not, they say, unfair (Engelhardt 1996). Individuals might be moved by charity to provide assistance, but there would be no right, no entitlement to any health care services. This would be a purely autonomy-driven health care system.

The moral reality, however, is that almost no one completely accepts this approach to resource allocation based solely on the principle of autonomy. Every nation in the world recognizes some entitlement to some health care services. Even the United States recognizes entitlements through Medicare, Medicaid, CHAMPUS (the military insurance system), and the right of access to hospitals for emergency care. The question is on the basis of what ethical principle will these entitlements rest. On the basis of what was said earlier in this chapter, two alternative social ethical principles are candidates.

Ethical Principles at the Social Level   We have now cut the fat out of the system. What if lowering the outlier in the name of patient welfare and granting autonomy still leave costs above reimbursement levels? Neither Hippocratic utility nor autonomy can help any more. Clinicians who stay focused on the level of individual responsibility would say that the cuts have gone as far as they should.

The principles considered thus far focus on the individual patient: his or her medical welfare, assessed either by the individual clinician or by more objective standards, and his or her autonomy. Physicians are quite comfortable with this situation. They operate on the top half of Figure 7.1, the principles that deal with the individual. Most clinicians now accept both the shift to objective standards for assessing outcomes and respect for patient autonomy. Still, resources may not be adequate to pay for all beneficial and desired care. In fact, in a world of scarce resources, some medical services will almost certainly be considered too trivial, too marginal, or too expensive to be covered in basic insurance plans.

In the case of the DRG for myocardial infarction, if treatments for which there is no objective evidence of real benefit and those that are not desired by the patient are eliminated, some savings will accrue. In the group of hospitals that provided the data, it was estimated that about $1000 in costs per patient would be eliminated by these reductions. That would reduce costs to an average of $9000. But that still leaves a gap of almost $2000 per patient between reimbursement and what clinicians and patients would agree is useful and desirable.

The ethical question raised is what should be done with regard to marginally beneficial but expensive care. In the graph in Figure 7.2, consider care in the range marked by small *b*. By definition, these services are beneficial. They do not offer great benefit, but peer review and objective outcomes measures lead both patient and professional peer reviewers to consider them on balance to be slightly beneficial after both the risks of side effects and the hoped-for benefits have been considered. They are, however, expensive in comparison to benefit. From the physician's point of view, they are beneficial; from the patient's point of view, they are desirable. Yet, from society's point of view, these services constitute marginal, inefficient care. The resources could be used much more effectively somewhere else. Perhaps they could also be used more fairly elsewhere. To address decisions of this sort, we need to move to the lower level of Figure 7.1, to the ethical principles labeled *social.*

Consider the choices that need to be made from the point of view of people planning their own insurance system. Would they want insurance to cover marginally beneficial care? For example, consider bone marrow transplant for metastatic breast cancer. Presently, it is an experimental therapy that may improve the possibility of survival for patients who have tried other therapies unsuccessfully. On the other hand, there is not yet any firm evidence of a benefit, and the cost is approximately $100,000. Would rational agents planning their own insurance, before knowing whether they or their loved ones would get breast cancer (but knowing the general probabilities of getting the disease), want to fund an insurance plan to cover this treatment? Note that if bone marrow transplant for breast cancer is not covered, resources will be available for some other good cause—either for other medical treatments or for a lower insurance premium so that funds can be used for other, nonmedical goods.

We do not insist on ideal care in any other sphere of life. We do not fund ideal levels of housing, food, or education. Almost certainly we should not fund as part of any basic insurance coverage (public or private) all possible beneficial and desired health care no matter how marginal the benefit. In basic health care plans we almost certainly will not fund cosmetic surgery, private psychoanalysis, or exotic infertility treatments, even though we should acknowledge that for some people they offer some benefits that are desired. Likewise, we probably should not fund every imaginable diagnostic test or therapy including those that produce very low probability of beneficial information or results. Funding all health care that is beneficial and desired would have to come at the expense of moving even further away from the ideal in other spheres of life. Insurance premiums and reimbursement should take all this into account. If we want resources left for other goods in life, we do not want to reimburse for all possible beneficial care. We do not even want to reimburse for all beneficial and desired care. Some care should not be provided even if it is beneficial and even if it is desired by the patient. The only question left is what social ethical principle we ought we to use for setting the limits.

In the case of Medicare reimbursement for myocardial infarction, funding will require "backing down the curve," moving somewhat to the left of the point $(N - a)$ to eliminate care in the range designated as b. It is apparent, however, that there is no obvious point that would identify the right amount of this marginally beneficial, desired care that should be eliminated. Social utility and justice provide different answers. It is not clear whether rational people planning their own insurance coverage would want to include bone marrow transplant for breast cancer. Perhaps subscribers to some plans would include it while others would not provide the coverage (providing either a lower premium or some extra funds for something else they valued more highly).

Social Utility   In the case of the limited reimbursement for myocardial infarction patients, social utilitarians would back down the curve in Figure 7.2, moving to the left from the maximal amount of good that could be done for the myocardial infarct patients. As long as the marginal resource would do more good spent somewhere else, they would keep eliminating services. They would stop at the point at which the marginal resource spent on the MI patients would do as much good as if it were spent on any other patients or in any other way. Mathematically, if the highest point on the vertical axis (point N) is designated as B_{MAX}, they would move to the left to the point where the slope of the curve for the MI patients would be as steep or steeper than the slope would be on any other curve representing expenditures for any other purpose. This is the approach any social utilitarian would use. It is the driving idea behind cost-benefit analyses. Social utilitarians strive to identify alternative benefits that could have been obtained for each dollar spent on marginal health resources. The Oregon Health Services Commission was doing precisely this process when it did an initial ranking of possible uses of its Medicaid dollars. It attempted to identify the most efficient uses and ranked them highest. Inefficient uses tended to be of two kinds: services for patients who would very likely do well even without them (For example, the later days of stay for myocardial infarction patients) and services for patients who were so ill that the services had almost no chance of helping (such as end-stage AIDS patients). When the commissioners and others looked at the list, however, they found that the results were morally unacceptable. Some patients who were, according to the Commission's data, inefficient to treat, nevertheless seemed to have moral claims, claims that are best characterized as claims of justice.

Justice   In the case of the allocation of limited funds for myocardial infarction patients, the justice theorists—at least those who interpret justice to require allocating on the basis of need—would back down the curve in Figure 7.2 to the point at which the myocardial infarct patients would be as poorly off or worse off than any other patients. As long as there were other patients in the system worse off, these justice theorists would divert the funds to the worse off patients. Of course, if the DRG system were properly designed and its goal were to target resources for the worst off, the reimbursement would be arranged precisely to accomplish that goal. A perfect reimbursement would exist, according to one who would give justice the first priority, if the $7100 was exactly the amount needed to keep the MI patients from being worse off than any one else.

If the cardiology department operates on a global budget (i.e., if it assumes it is to allocate its total income among its total group of patients) this approach would still leave the problem of how to allocate among its patients. If the system incorporates a principle of justice into its ethical mandate, then it would be wrong to allocate the department's global budget on the basis of utility maximizing. Some reconciling of social utility and justice is called for.

Reconciling Conflicts among Social Ethical Principles for Allocating Resources   The various methods of reconciling conflicts among moral principles are: giving absolute authority to one principle, balancing competing claims, lexically ranking competing claims, and some combination of balancing and ranking. The implications of using a single principle or lexically ranking competing principles are relatively straightforward. Several different approaches to balancing or combining ranking with balancing are possible, however. One might try to hold the ratio of ideal costs to actual expenditures constant, hold the ratio of maximum possible benefit to actual benefit constant, or give worse-off patients a proportionally greater percentage of their possible benefits. Those methods can be put into mathematical terms.

Holding Percentage of Ideal Costs Constant for Each Patient   One approach would be to, first, determine for any given health care service (a hospital, clinical department, or DRG) the costs of ideal care (point N on Figure 7.2). Then take the ratio of available budget to ideal funding and deliver to each patient that fraction of his or her ideal resources. This would generally give greater resources to those with greater needs, but would avoid an absolute priority of justice thereby giving better off patients some services as well. This would be one way of balancing social utility and justice. In mathematical terms everyone's actual costs (C_{ACTUAL}) should be a constant percentage of the ideal costs (C_{MAX}), where the percentage is the percentage of the ideal budget that is actually available. For each person:

$$\frac{C_{ACTUAL}}{C_{MAX}} = K \text{ (constant)}$$

That would treat each person equally in the sense of giving each person the same fraction of the services he or she needs while at the same time recognizing that concentrating all resources on the sickest would be very inefficient. Thus, if 80 percent of ideal funding were available, everyone would receive 80 percent of the services he or she could use. Of course, since there is declining marginal utility with health care resources, supplying 80 percent of the ideal resources should normally provide much more than 80 percent of the possible benefit one could receive with ideal levels of services.

Holding Percentage of Maximum Benefits Constant for Each Patient
There are refinements of this approach that may be even more satisfying. It is known, for instance, that if everyone is treated with the same percentage of their ideal resources, not everyone will achieve the same degree of success. Therefore instead of giving everyone the same percentage of their maximum usable resources, we could strive to give everyone the same percentage of his or her maximum benefit. Mathematically:

$$\frac{B_{ACTUAL}}{B_{MAX}} = K \text{ (constant)}$$

where the constant is the percentage dictated by available resources. As before, when we realize that the benefits from health resources tend to decrease as more resources are expended, a system that had only a tolerable fraction of its maximally useful resources ($7100/$9000, or about 79 percent in the case of the myocardial infarction example) would be able to provide a very high percentage of its maximal possible benefit, perhaps as high as 98 or 99 percent. The moral logic here is that justice is achieved by treating all patients equally in the sense that they all get the same percentage of their maximal possible benefit while utility is served by permitting some resources to be used for medically well-off people who can nevertheless be helped efficiently by modest treatments.

Giving Worse-Off Patients a Proportionally Greater Percentage of Their Possible Benefits   Defenders of egalitarian justice might see holding constant the percentage of maximum benefits as still giving too much of the resources to the already well-off. A possible alternative that would tip the balance more in favor of justice would be to give worse-off patients a proportionally greater percentage of their possible benefits. Someone who is already quite healthy and who is getting the same percentage of his available medical benefit as someone who was medically very poorly off might be seen as commanding too many resources. This situation could lead to a further adjustment. For example, an administrator might strive to balance utility and justice by making for each patient the ratio of the actual benefit to maximum possible benefit inversely proportional to how poorly off the patient is before treatment:

$$\frac{B_{\text{ACTUAL}}}{B_{\text{MAX}}} = \frac{K}{WB_{\text{BEFORE}}}$$

where WB_{BEFORE} equals the individual patient's well being before treatment.[9]

The Role of the Clinician in Allocation Decisions

There is one final question that must be addressed in the discussion of allocating scarce resources. Should saving resources be a goal of the clinician at the bedside? There is a real split among clinicians as well as among laypeople on this issue. Two options are available; neither is terribly attractive. One is to make the clinician the one who decides where to cut costs. The other option is to exempt clinicians from any involvement in cost considerations.

Make the Clinician the One Who Decides Where to Cut Costs   Making the clinician society's cost-containment agent has advantages. Clinicians may know where there is some fat in the system, where cuts can be made. This option also has the advantage of keeping bureaucrats out of decisions. Some clinicians are now advocating that they abandon their traditional commitment to being exclusively agents for their patients so that they will be free to decide to eliminate marginally beneficial services. They are, in effect, lobbying for moving from individual ethical principles to social ethical principles.

There are also very serious objections to asking clinicians to take on the role of cost-containment agent. First, there are pragmatic objections (physicians might systematically cut costs in the wrong places), and, second, there is a principled objection (the physician would have to take on a new moral role).

Problems Involving Physician Bias   We saw in chapter 3 that deciding what counts as a benefit and a harm is a complex, subjective task. Acting as a rationing agent inevitably involves trade-offs of competing goods. Clinicians may make trade-offs in systematically atypical ways. For example, some trade-offs will require comparing the value of the medical care being contemplated with the value of other medical goods. An extra day in the hospital for the myocardial infarction patient must be balanced against an extra day in the nursing home for the Alzheimer's patient, funding a well-baby clinic, or providing pain relief for cancer patients. It could be argued that cardiologists *should* make these trade-offs atypically. They probably will and perhaps ought to give too much priority to cardiology, just as other specialists would see special value in the services they provide. Recall we are speaking of eliminating real, if marginal,

---

[9]See Veatch 1994, for a further exploration of this strategy.

benefits. The specialist who has devoted his or her life to one particular medical service is in a poor position to decide how much value that service offers in comparison with the value offered by other medical services. Clinicians should be biased in these tasks. They are not malicious; this kind of bias is simply inherent in the nature of specialization. People grow to place unusual value on the services they provide. Surgeons are likely to advise cutting; radiologists prefer radiation; and medical oncologists prefer chemotherapy. None of these should be placed in a position of deciding when to sacrifice their services for others.

Likewise, clinicians will have to compare the costs and values of medical goods with those of nonmedical goods if they are to act as societal gate keepers. They must decide whether funds are better spent on medicine or on education, housing, or food stamps. Once again, they cannot be expected to be in a position to make these trade-offs. All experts ought to be biased. At least that is the claim of the critics of using the clinician as cost-containment agent.

Finally, the gate keeper role will require making choices between competing ethical principles and theories. There is increasing evidence that various professional groups have predictable preferences for various ethical principles. Physicians, having historically been consequentialists, tend to prefer the consequentialist principles. When they are forced to make resource allocation decisions they give special priority to social utility over justice. Other professions may have other orientations. There is some evidence, for instance, that clergy and lawyers tend to emphasize duty-based ethical principles. They are likely to give more weight to justice. The choice of ethical principles, clearly, is not based on medical expertise.

Clinicians simply have no basis for making choices among competing medical goods, between medical goods and competing goods from outside medicine, or among competing ethical principles. Even the clinician with the most noble intentions can be expected to make trade-offs in an atypical fashion.

Problems in Abandoning the Patient-Centered Ethic There is a second objection to using the clinician as a cost-containment agent. Traditionally the role of the clinician as an advocate for the patient was Hippocratic and paternalistic. As that ethic was replaced with a more duty-based respect for persons ethic, the clinician's role still remained patient-centered. It would now serve the rights as well as the interests of patients, but the patient was still the focus. Should clinicians also take responsibility for social ethical issues such as resource allocation?

Do we really want to ask clinicians to abandon their role as patient advocates? Especially if it can be shown that they might make trade-offs incorrectly in the first place, would it not be better to keep the clinician in the patient advocate role? Asking a clinician to take on resource allocation tasks is in effect asking him or her to remove the Hippocratic Oath (or any other oath to benefit patients) from the waiting room wall and replace it with a sign that reads:

> Warning all ye who enter here. I will generally serve your interests, but in the case of marginally beneficial expensive care I will abandon you in order to serve society as their cost-containment agent.

Make the Clinician Exempt from Social Ethics   The alternative is to give the clinician an exemption from social ethics for the normal case. This choice would still not mean a retreat to the subjective Hippocratic ethic. It could still require objective assessment of medical effects. It could still require respect for autonomy and rights of patients. But it would exempt the physician from any task of abandoning the patient at the margin, freeing him or her to remain loyal as an advocate for the patient. It would raise the clinician to the same high moral calling of the defense attorney, who is obliged ethically to remain loyal to the client even if the attorney believes the client is guilty. In law, the system relies on other actors—prosecutors, judges, and jurors—to see that the system as a whole is fair.

The corollary to this approach is that if physicians do not perform social ethical tasks someone else must. If it is correct that not all desired and beneficial health services can be funded through basic health insurance programs—that some will be so minimally beneficial and so expensive that other services will have moral priority—then society as a whole through the planning of the limits on its insurance coverage and through its delegated representatives will have to decide which services are morally of such low priority that they cannot be funded. Someone must take on the onerous moral responsibility of incorporating social ethical principles into a health care program. If the clinician can be expected to do the job in the wrong way and perhaps should have a special moral duty of serving the patient that is incompatible with taking on the duties of social ethical resource allocation, then the members of the society will have to find others to take on this responsibility.

Organ Transplantation

A second area in which medical ethics is necessarily social is organ transplantation. The ethics of transplantation generally involves three issues: the fundamental morality of moving body parts, the ethics of organ procurement, and the ethics of allocation. All of these involve social moral controversies.

Is Performing Transplants "Playing God"?

The fundamental moral issue is whether moving human body parts from one being to another is tampering with the human's basic nature in ways that go beyond what is acceptable human conduct. The controversy is exacerbated when the organs come from nonhuman animals. Some people consider organ transplantation to be not only psychologically repulsive but morally and religiously questionable as well. Nevertheless, the major Western religious traditions all are supportive of organ transplantation, even transplants involving the heart—that traditional, romantic "seat of the soul." The fundamental problem of whether modern medical interventions go beyond what is morally acceptable for humans is the subject of chapter 8.

Procurement of Organs

The procurement of organs for transplantation has been a more mundane, but no less controversial, issue. Procurement raises even more directly the question of the relation of the individual to society. Some commentators have held that human organs of the deceased cannot possibly be of any use to the dead person and should automatically become the property of the state to be used for good social purposes, including not only transplantation but also research, education, and other medical therapies. Some countries have now legislated that organs can be taken without consent provided the individual or family have not registered an explicit objection. This practice has been called "routine salvaging" (Dukeminier and Sanders 1968). It is the law in some Latin, Scandinavian, and Asian countries. The United States, Britain, and other Anglophone and Germanic countries, however, have remained committed to the model of donation of organs. They rely on the belief that the individual has rights against the state and these rights extend to control of the corpse. Organs may, therefore, be procured only with the consent of the person from which they are taken (or that person's surrogate). This view reflects the individualism of liberal Western political philosophy. The principles of informed consent, and the related respect for persons principles of fidelity to commitments and truth telling, control the procurement of organs in these countries.

Organ Allocation

Some of the most dramatic and contested social ethical issues today arise over the ethics of allocating scarce organs for transplant. There are presently over 64,000 people waiting for organs in the United States. The supply is inevitably scarce and will be for the foreseeable future—at least until artificial organs or animal organ sources become more routine.

When there is a short supply of a life-saving resource, the social ethics of resource allocation becomes crucial. What has been said earlier in this chapter made clear that, if a purely libertarian, free-market allocation is unacceptable, there are only two potentially governing principles: social utility and justice.

Case 7.2: Allocating Organs by Tissue Type

The United Network for Organ Sharing (UNOS) is legally responsible in the United States for allocating organs for transplantation. One basis for allocation would be to give the organs to the patients who will predictably get the most benefit.

In the case of kidneys, it is known that the success of a kidney graft is dependent on the degree of HLA histocompatability of tissue antigens. There are six possible antigens that can be matched. The better the match, the higher the probability that a graft will survive. Thus, if we want to maximize the chance of graft survival, we will give the kidney to the patient on the waiting list who has the closest HLA match with the donor.

We now know, however, that not all racial groups have the same likelihood of matching the donors in the donor pool. In particular, in the United States Caucasians are statistically more likely to be the best matches of any group. The reasons for this are complex. Middle class people (of whom more are Caucasian) are more willing to donate organs. Some minority groups have greater need for transplant. (Higher incidence of high blood pressure among blacks, for example, means they have a greater need for kidneys.) Moreover, even if the willingness to donate and the need were the same, Caucasians, being a larger proportion of the population, would have a better chance of having a closer match. The result is that if we strive to maximize the probability of graft survival, the allocation will tend to favor whites at the expense of blacks and other minority groups. The question is, Do we still really want to maximize the probability of graft survival knowing that unequal distribution among racial groups is one of the likely outcomes? Moreover, other social statistics can be used to statistically improve the number of years of graft survival. Males do slightly better than females; younger people better than the elderly; and middle-class patients better than lower-class patients. Thus the policy that would statistically maximize the number of years of graft survival would be one of giving organs preferentially to young, white, middle-class, males.

While such a policy can be shown to maximize the net benefit measured in years of graft survival, it obviously could be seen as an unfair, inequitable policy. If the goal is to give all patients equally ill an equal chance of getting an organ, we will want to adjust the allocation formula to ensure greater equity in access. This can be done by giving consideration to time on the waiting list and other factors to ensure that those who are less likely to be favored by standard matching criteria will get a more equitable opportunity at getting an organ (even though doing so will lower somewhat the total number of years of graft survival obtained from the available kidneys).

Social Utility　An ethic of allocation driven solely by the principle of maximizing social utility would clearly favor allocating on the basis of degree of HLA match, at least until we learn enough about control of tissue rejection to overcome the disadvantage of poor match. If poor matches were guaranteed to fail and good matches to be successful, the ethical problem would not be severe. In the era of immunosuppressive drugs, however, the difference between a poor and a good match is only marginal—a few percentage points difference in one-year graft survival. Nevertheless, if benefit is measured in terms of years of expected graft survival, a social utilitarian would favor allocating on the basis of HLA match. The surgeons involved in transplant overwhelmingly support HLA matching and other predictors of graft survival as a basis for allocation, consistent with their traditional consequentialism in ethics.

Justice　Those committed to the importance of the principle of justice in allocating scarce resources—including many of the nonphysicians involved in organ allocation—are not automatically swayed by the data showing that HLA matching increases marginally predicted graft survival. They claim that, especially with a public program such as organ transplantation, all persons should have an equal right to the benefits of the program regardless of their genetic makeup, whether those genes control race, gender, or HLA pattern. They tend to favor adjustments in the organ allocation formula to provide more-equal access by adding weight to factors such as time on the waiting list, blood type, and a marker for previous exposure to foreign tissue that decreases the chance of finding a suitable organ.

The United Network for Organ Sharing's (UNOS) Ethics Committee faced this problem directly. Some members, mainly physicians, were more inclined to give priority for kidney allocation to social utility as the basis for allocating while others were more inclined toward giving priority to justice. Kidneys are allocated by giving each candidate points for various factors relevant to allocation. Some points can be assigned for reasons having to do with predicted medical utility, such as a good tissue match. Other points can be assigned to try to promote justice in allocation, such as time on the waiting list, degree of medical urgency, or high levels of antibodies for foreign tissues.

Balancing Social Utility and Justice   The UNOS Ethics Committee, not being able to resolve the question of which principle deserves priority, reached a compromise. They endorsed a policy of giving half the weight in the allocation to considerations of medical utility and half the weight to considerations of justice (Burdick, Turcotte, and Veatch, 1992). The allocation formula has now been adjusted several times to try to balance the competing claims of medical utility and justice. Likewise, a public debate over the allocation of livers can be understood, in part, as a dispute between those who would give priority on the basis of needs-based justice and those who favor more-utilitarian concerns. Surgeon-dominated UNOS has traditionally favored an allocation first to local transplant centers. UNOS authorities believed that giving first priority to local centers would encourage organ procurement and would decrease the time from procurement to transplant (reasons related to maximizing the expected benefit of the transplant program), even though they knew that local allocation would prevent some sicker or more-desperate patients at more-distant centers from getting a transplant. Nonphysicians, favoring a more-equitable access for those who are sickest (i.e., a justice-based concern), have pressed for changing the allocation so that the sickest get organs first even though they are farther away and somewhat lower aggregate benefit can be expected. The federal government has recently ordered UNOS to change its allocation, redirecting the formula from one driven by social utility to one more committed to the principle of justice. Quite predictably, surgeons have protested, claiming that such an allocation will produce less benefit. It is clear that choosing an ethical principle determines some very practical matters, including who lives and who dies.

Research Involving Human Subjects

A third area in which medical ethics inevitably becomes social is research involving human subjects (Katz 1972, Veatch 1987, Levine 1988). It is striking that a physician whole-heartedly committed to the Hippocratic ethic of doing whatever will benefit the patient is logically committed to the view that all research involving human subjects is unethical.

Distinguishing Research and Innovative Therapy

Here it is important to distinguish between true *research* and what is sometimes called *innovative therapy*. Throughout history when a patient has had a condition that did not respond to standard treatments, physicians have felt compelled to try something that can be called innovative therapy. Through most of history innovative therapies, new things, were attempted without any systematic scientific plan or intention. The goal was to try to help the patient.

Risks were considered acceptable given the bleak alternatives. Medical research is a much more recent phenomenon, dating from only the nineteenth century. Its goal is not to benefit the patient. In fact, if one treatment, whether innovative or standard, is plausibly in the patient's interest it would be unethical to include the patient in a clinical trial in which he might receive something else. Medical research is undertaken for the purpose of producing generalizable knowledge for the benefit of society, not to benefit the subject. Research that involves placing groups of subjects chosen at random into two different treatments is ideal for isolating the critical variable being studied. It is morally justified only when researchers honestly do not know which of the two treatments is preferable—when they are at what is called the "indifference point" or "equipoise." In those situations, placing a patient in a randomized design cannot be to the patient's advantage compared to simply receiving the standard treatment since there is no basis at the inception of the study for believing anything else is superior.

Medical research involving human subjects must meet all the ethical criteria discussed in earlier chapters of this book. A potential subject must give an adequately informed consent meeting the standards discussed in chapter 4. The subject's autonomy must be respected. If private information is collected about the subject, the rules of confidentiality grounded in the principle of fidelity must be followed. The principle of veracity requires that investigators deal honestly with subjects. Hence, psychological studies built on the intentional deception of the subject have long been controversial. On the basis of traditional individual-focused principles of beneficence and nonmaleficence, risks to the subject must be minimized. But here is where medical research departs from traditional clinical medicine. The obvious way to protect subjects from harm in procedures that cannot be known in advance to be beneficial to them is to to avoid doing the research. If the standard treatment were thought to be comparable (if researchers have no reason in advance to believe the experimental treatment is better or worse than the standard treatment), the subject would always be protected by simply not doing the study. This point is true even more obviously in the case of research on normal subjects. If medical research is justified at all, it must be by appeal to some ethical principle other than those operating at the level of the individual.

Social Ethics for Research Involving Human Subjects

Social Utility An examination of the standard guidelines for research involving human subjects will always reveal that the first, minimal condition for justifying studies on humans is that they are believed to offer hope of producing knowledge valuable to the society that cannot be obtained in any other manner. The first criterion is that the study must be supported by the principle of social utility. It is clear that Hippocratic utility—patient-centered concern about benefits and harms—will not do to justify research. It is generalizable, scientific knowledge that is being pursued, not patient welfare.

Respect for Persons The Nuremberg code makes clear that social utility is not the only criterion for justifying medical research involving human subjects. As we saw in chapter 4, it gives a strong commitment to self-determination or what is now in ethical theory normally called autonomy. The most important document after Nuremberg summarizing the ethics of research on human subjects is the Belmont Report of the U.S. National Commission for the Protection of Human Subjects of Biomedical and Behavioral Research (1978). It is built on three ethical principles: beneficence (which it treats as if it were social utility—including duties to avoid harm as well as benefit), respect for persons, and justice. From respect for persons it builds a consent doctrine and could as well have developed its commitment to confidentiality.

Justice From the principle of justice the Belmont Report recognizes a duty to ensure fairness in recruiting subjects. No study can recruit subjects solely from wards that serve low-income patients or from prisons, mental hospitals, or other institutions that would provide for inequity in subject selection (unless the nature of the study required that only these subjects participate). More recently, the principle of justice has required that subjects be recruited so as to make it possible to apply the findings across racial and gender differences.

Other advocates of the principle of justice have claimed that the requirements of justice must go further. Consider the following case.

Case 7.3: *Justice in Design of Research*

Some years ago, researchers at a major medical center wanted to test several chemotherapeutic agents for toxicity and make an initial estimate of the effectiveness of the combination of drugs. One of the agents, methotrexate, can have serious side effects, but the protocol called for giving it in a high dose followed the next day with leucovorin, which is known to neutralize the methotrexate. The methotrexate would be administered every twenty-one days at the hospital. The controversy was over whether the leucovorin could be prescribed for the subjects to take at home, which would pose the risk of patients' accidentally or intentionally forgetting to take a dose—a mistake that could prove fatal.

Defenders of administering leucovorin in the hospital argued that it would be safer for the patients if they were hospitalized for three days out of every twenty-one, including the days on which they were to take their medication. They pointed out it would also provide for more carefully controlled science. Researchers would maintain better control over the amount of medication and the timing of its administration. They also were concerned that researchers not inadvertently be a party to a suicide by means of refusing to take the leucovorin.

On the other hand, defenders of permitting the leucovorin to be taken at home emphasized the burden of making sick patients come to the hospital for three days out of every twenty-one of their remaining time. Some suggested that because they were particularly sick, they had a special claim to have the research design as convenient and pleasant for them as possible. As long as they knew the risks of taking the medication at home they should be permitted to do so or should be given a choice whether to come to the hospital. It seemed that the safest course was also the best science, but that advantage would come at what some subjects would take as an additional burden on an already very difficult life.[10]

If the only ethical principle guiding this study were social utility, it seems obvious which research design should be chosen. Hospitalizing the patients for three days out of every twenty-one ensures better control and close monitoring of the subjects. Moreover, it seems to provide better protection for patients against the risk that they will not take the rescue agent. If home administration requires sending a professional staffperson to the patient's home to administer the leucovorin, hospital administration might even be cheaper. From a utilitarian perspective hospitalization seems the clear choice.

But these are very sick patients. Asking for them to spend three out of every twenty-one of the few days they have remaining seems a considerable burden for them. Many patients might legitimately prefer to stay at home and take their leucovorin without having to be in the hospital or under the watch of the researchers. If the subjects are among the worst off—as they well might be—then those who subscribe to a needs-based theory of justice would conclude that they have a special claim to have their interests served even if doing so does not maximize social utility. Especially if the proponents of the needs-based theory also minimized concern about the risk of the patients' committing suicide and held a strong commitment to self-determination, they may well

[10]The case is based on Robert M. Veatch, "Case Study: Risk-Taking in Cancer Chemotherapy," *IRB* (August/September 1979):4–6.

conclude that the morally correct protocol was at-home administration. Although at-home administration would sacrifice social utility, it would promote the well-being of these particularly needy persons.

Resolving Conflicts among Principles in Research on Human Subjects

If social utility and the other ethical principles at stake in research on human subjects sometimes come into conflict, how is the conflict to be resolved? The problem is by now a familiar one. Those who believe that principles in conflict must be balanced against each other will give priority to none of the principles. By extension, they are logically committed to the position that social utility may, at least in an extreme case, override the claims of autonomy and justice—that subjects may be conscripted into research without their consent or even against their vocal objections. The fact that very few people support compulsory participation in medical research is one of the pieces of evidence cited by persons who believe that it is ethically suspect to balance social utility and autonomy.

The alternative is to give some principles an absolute priority over others. If absolute priority were given to autonomy, subjects, in principle, could never be conscripted against their will no matter how beneficial doing so would be to the society. Although theorists often point out that such a position is hard to justify, that is actually very close to the operating rule in the case of compulsory participation in medical research. It is hard to imagine a real-life situation in which compulsory participation would be supported.

In the case of the methotrexate study, justice also seems to provide an appeal that conflicts with maximizing utility. Many would at least give justice some place against the strategy of simply designing the research so as to maximize the potential social benefit. Some might insist that the interests of the worst off should be given an absolute priority similar to that given autonomy. Then only when two or more of the duty-based principles came into conflict would they be traded off against one another. So, for example, if research had to involve compulsory participation in ways that minimally violated individual autonomy in order to serve the interests of the worst off, there would be a conflict between autonomy and justice and they might end up being balanced against each other.

It is striking that there is no clear discussion in research on human subjects guidelines or law regarding what should happen if some of the principles can be satisfied but others cannot. For example, seven criteria for acceptable research are listed in the federal guidelines for institutional review boards. One might assume that all seven must be met, including those requiring voluntary consent, protection of confidentiality, and justice as well as those pertaining to benefits to the society and protection of both subject and society from harm.

But some people interpret them to require only that they be satisfied "on balance." If all must be satisfied, then the principles of autonomy and justice apply as well as Hippocratic and social utility principles. As in the allocation of resources and transplantation, different policies and practices will be called for depending on how these questions are answered.

Key Concepts

Indifference point: In research involving randomized clinical trials, the state in which researchers honestly do not have reason to believe that one treatment is preferable to the others. Randomized clinical trials are normally believed to be ethical only if investigators are at the indifference point (sometimes also called clinical equipoise).

Innovative therapy: Therapy sometimes used by clinicians and laypeople in cases in which standard therapy is believed to be ineffective. The purpose is to try whatever is plausible for the benefit of the patient, not the production of generalizable, scientific knowledge. Compare Research.

Justice: The principle that an action is morally right insofar as it treats people in similar situations equally. Different theories of justice provide different bases for allocating resources justly. For example, egalitarian justice would distribute health care on the basis of need. Compare Social utility.

Research: The systematic pursuit of scientific knowledge for the purpose of advancing science. In medicine, research interventions using human subjects may turn out to benefit the subject, but that is not the purpose; in ethically acceptable research using human subjects the benefit from the research interventions cannot be known in advance.

Social utility: The principle that an action or rule is morally right insofar as it produces as much or more net good consequences as any alternative, taking into account the benefits and harms for all parties affected.

Bibliography

Social Ethical Theory

Bentham, Jeremy. 1967. "An Introduction to the Principles of Morals and Legislation." Pages 367–390 in *Ethical Theories: A Book of Readings,* edited by A. I. Melden. Englewood Cliffs, N.J.: Prentice-Hall.

Engelhardt, H. Tristram. 1996. *The Foundations of Bioethics,* 2d ed. New York: Oxford University Press.

Mill, John Stuart. 1967. "Utilitarianism." Pages 391–434 in *Ethical Theories: A Book of Readings,* edited by A. I. Melden. Englewood Cliffs, N. J.: Prentice-Hall.

Rawls, John. *A Theory of Justice.* 1971. Cambridge, Mass.: Harvard University Press.

Shelp, Earl E., ed. 1981. *Justice and Health Care.* Dordrecht, Holland: D. Reidel Publishing.

Veatch, Robert M. 1986. *The Foundations of Justice: Why the Retarded and the Rest of Us Have Claims to Equality.* New York: Oxford University Press.

Allocation of Scarce Medical Resources

Baker, Robert, and Martin Strosberg. 1992. "Triage and Equality: An Historical Reassessment of Utilitarian Analyses of Triage." *Kennedy Institute of Ethics Journal* 2 (June) 103–123.

Bayer, Ronald, Arthur L. Caplan, and Norman Daniels, eds. 1983. *In Search of Equity: Health Needs and the Health Care System.* New York: Plenum Press.

Blank, Robert H. 1988. *Rationing Medicine.* New York: Columbia University Press.

Callahan, Daniel. 1990. *What Kind of Life: The Limits of Medical Progress.* New York: Simon and Schuster.

Daniels, Norman. 1985. *Just Health Care.* Cambridge, England: Cambridge University Press.

DeGrazia, David. 1991. "Grounding a Right to Health Care in Self-Respect and Self-Esteem." *Public Affairs Quarterly* 5 (October):301–318.

Green, Ronald M. 1976. "Health Care and Justice in Contract Theory Perspective." Pages 111–126 in *Ethics and Health Policy,* edited by Robert M. Veatch and Roy Branson. Cambridge, Mass. Ballinger Publishing.

Kaplan, R. M., and J. W. Bush. 1982. "Health-Related Quality of Life Measurement for Evaluation Research and Policy Analysis." *Health Psychology* 11:61–80.

Menzel, Paul. 1990. *Strong Medicine: The Ethical Rationing of Health Care.* New York: Oxford University Press.

Morreim, E. Haavi. 1991. *Balancing Act: The New Medical Ethics of Medicine's New Economics.* Dordrecht, The Netherlands: Kluwer Academic Publishers.

Oregon Health Services Commission. 1991. *Prioritization of Health Services: A Report to the Governor and Legislature.* n.p.: Oregon Health Services Commission.

President's Commission for the Study of Ethical Problems in Medicine and Biomedical and Behavioral Research. 1983. *Securing Access to Health Care,* vol. 1. Washington, D.C.: U.S. Government Printing Office.

Strosberg, Martin A., I. Alan Fein, and James D. Carroll. 1989. *Rationing of Medical Care for the Critically Ill.* Washington, D.C.: The Brookings Institution.

Strosberg, Martin A., Joshua M. Weiner, and Robert Baker, with I. Alan Fein. 1992. *Rationing America's Medical Care: The Oregon Plan and Beyond.* Washington, D.C.: The Brookings Institution.

Veatch, Robert M. 1980. "Voluntary Risks to Health: The Ethical Issues." *Journal of the American Medical Association* 243 (January 4):50–55.

Veatch, Robert M. 1984. "Autonomy's Temporary Triumph." *The Hastings Center Report* 14, no. 5 (October): 38–40.

Veatch, Robert M. 1986a. "DRGs and the Ethical Reallocation of Resources," *Hastings Center Report* 16, no. 3 (June):32–40.

Veatch, Robert M. 1991. "Justice and the Right to Health Care: An Egalitarian Account." Pages 83–102 in *Rights to Health Care,* edited by Thomas J. Bole III and William B. Bondeson. Dordrecht, The Netherlands: Kluwer Academic Publishers.

Veatch, Robert M. 1994. "Healthcare Rationing through Global Budgeting: The Ethical Choices." *Journal of Clinical Ethics* 5, no. 4 (Winter):291–296.

Organ Transplantation

Burdick, James F., Jeremiah G. Turcotte, and Robert M. Veatch. 1992. "General Principles for Allocating Human Organs and Tissues." *Transplantation Proceedings* 24, no. 5 (October):2226–2235.

Dukeminier, Jesse, and David Sanders. 1968. "Organ Transplantation: A Proposal for Routine Salvaging of Cadaver Organs." *New England Journal of Medicine* 279:413–419.

Fox, Renée C., and Judith P. Swazey. 1992. *Spare Parts: Organ Replacement in American Society.* New York: Oxford University Press.

Moss, Alvin H., and Mark Siegler. 1991. "Should Alcoholics Compete Equally for Liver Transplantation?" *Journal of the American Medical Association* 265:1295–1298.

Task Force on Organ Transplantation. 1986. *Organ Transplantation: Issues and Recommendations.* Washington, D.C.: U.S. Department of Health and Human Services.

Research Involving Human Subjects

Katz, Jay. 1972. *Experimentation with Human Beings.* New York: Russell Sage Foundation.

Levine, Robert J. 1988. *Ethics and Regulation of Clinical Research,* 2d ed. New Haven, Conn.: Yale University Press.

U.S. National Commission for the Protection of Human Subjects of Biomedical and Behavioral Research. 1978. *The Belmont Report: Ethical Principles and Guidelines for the Protection of Human Subjects of Research.* Washington, D.C.: U.S. Government Printing Office.

Veatch, Robert M. 1987. *The Patient as Partner—A Theory of Human-Experimentation Ethics.* Bloomington, Ind.: Indiana University Press.

CHAPTER EIGHT

Human Control of Life

Genetics, Birth Technologies, and Modifying Human Nature

Many of the themes already discussed in this book are also relevant to new developments in genetics and reproductive technologies. Issues of autonomy and consent, veracity, fidelity in the patient-physician relation, and the allocation of scarce resources apply here as well. We now have the power not only to diagnose genetic disease and to advise potential parents about the characteristics of offspring but also to insert new genetic material into human beings to correct for defective genes and even to improve on the nature of the species. When any of these technologies is used on humans, the consent of the patient or surrogate for the patient is needed just as in any other medical treatment. Moreover, we have the ability to create new human life in a test tube and to implant the newly created embryo not only in the uterus of the woman who supplied the egg cell but also in another woman. Implantation can be done with the recipient's promising to return the newborn infant to the woman who supplied the egg—a process called surrogate motherhood—or with the understanding that the woman who gestates the pregnancy is to keep the newborn and raise the child whose genetic makeup is unrelated to her own. The process of offering an egg in this way is sometimes called egg donation. To the extent that promises of confidentiality or promises about relinquishing the newborn are made, the ethics of promise keeping arises just as in any other medical relation. The development of preimplantation and in utero diagnosis will raise the same issue about abortion that arises in other debates about abortion: When, if ever, is it ethical to terminate embryonic and fetal life? It will force us to deal again with the meaning of the principle of avoidance of killing. All of these new technologies of birth can be extremely expensive. In vitro fertilization, for example, costs on average $72,000 to produce a live birth.[1] Thus, using these technologies raises the same issues of justice in resource allocation that arise in any other health care–rationing controversy.

Yet, there is an additional dimension of medical ethics that arises with particular vigor in these contexts of genetics and birth technologies: Should human beings manipulate the very nature of the species? Is it the appropriate role of humans to be a passive part of nature or a more active controller of it? Is it the proper role of the human to tamper with creation in ways depicted in the Frankenstein myth or to take charge of nature and shape it for the human's own ends? This chapter will focus on these more basic philosophical issues while exploring the ethics of the new genetic and birth technologies. These broader issues cut across the more traditional normative disputes in medical ethics about ethical principles discussed in earlier chapters.

The Human as Created and as Creator

Medical Manipulation as Playing God

When Mary Wollstonecraft Shelley created the story of Frankenstein in 1817, she provided an alternative title, *The Modern Prometheus*.[2] Thus she harkened back to the legend of the Greek god who not only molded the clay figures that became humans but also stole fire from heaven to make it available to human beings, giving them powers they had never before possessed. The metaphor of "playing God" has become common in the era of the biological revolution.[3] It is used by persons who fear that humans are going beyond appropriate limits in remolding or "recreating" the human's nature. These critics suggest that genetic engineering and the "manufacture" or "fabrication" of new human beings take us beyond the normal mission of medicine—to save life, cure disease, and relieve suffering.[4] They believe that we are on the verge of changing the species so radically that we can be said to be changing its fundamental nature.

---

[1]Peter J. Neumann, Soheyla D. Gharib, and Milton C. Weinstein, "The Cost of a Successful Delivery with In Vitro Fertilization," *New England Journal of Medicine* 331 (1994):239–243.

[2]The brief story is well worth reading. Mary Wollstonecraft Shelley, *Frankenstein; or, The Modern Prometheus* (New York: Collier Books, 1961).

[3]A number of books exploring these themes have appropriated the metaphor: R. C., Sproul, ed, *Playing God: Dissecting Biomedical Ethics and Manipulating the Body* (Grand Rapids, Mich.: Baker Books, 1997); Gerald A. Larue, *Playing God: Fifty Religions' Views on Your Right to Die* (Wakefield, R.I.: Moyer Bell, 1996); Ted Peters, *Playing God?: Genetic Determinism and Human Freedom* (New York: Routledge, 1997); June Goodfield, *Playing God: Genetic Engineering and the Manipulation of Life* (London: Sphere Books, 1977); Thomas J. Scully, and Celia Scully, *Playing God: The New World of Medical Choices* (New York: Simon and Schuster, 1987).

[4]For a forceful early statement of this perspective see Ramsey 1970.

The critical underlying question is whether it is moral to make these radical changes. Some commentators, influenced by conservative religious traditions, hold that the human is a finite creature prone to make mistakes. Thus, they tend to be pessimists, fearing that changes initiated by humans will ultimately be for the worse. They point to the dangers of atomic energy, environmental disasters, and medical experiments that have gone horribly wrong. Their premise is that basic changes in the human species will lead to sinister biological effects that, on balance, are bound to be terribly harmful. For others, the objection goes beyond the seriousness of the consequences to a more fundamental issue: There are moral limits on how far humans should go in using their knowledge of science to change their nature. They point to the religious symbolism of a Biblical creation story in which the human sins by eating of the forbidden fruit of knowledge.

Having Dominion over the Earth

Other people have quite a different set of moral intuitions. They claim that, on balance, humans' use of science has dramatically improved the human situation and, drawing on another religious metaphor, speak of humans as "co-creators" having a moral duty to use knowledge of science not only to combat disease but also to improve on nature. They opt to make human reproduction and human existence more progressive, rational, and planned.[5] These more optimistic and interventionistic advocates have appropriated a different religious symbol, pointing to the other Biblical creation story in which the human is to have dominion over the earth and to "subdue it." In this chapter, our primary concern is whether interventions in genetics and birth technologies push the limits of human authority to manipulate or rationalize (depending on one's perspective) the basics of human nature.

Genetics and the Control of Human Reproduction

Genetics

For centuries, humans have had a vague idea that parents somehow influence the characteristics of their offspring. The science of genetics, which nineteenth-century Austrian botanist and priest Johann Gregor Mendel is credited with founding, provided a basis for beginning to understand the biological influence of parents on their children.

Early in the twentieth century, vague notions of inheritance of disease and mental incapacities led to a eugenics movement leading not only to

---

[5]For a dramatic example of this pro-interventionist commitment see Fletcher 1974.

extermination campaigns in Nazi Germany but also to compulsory sterilization laws in thirty U.S. states. In the famous 1927 U.S. Supreme Court decision *Buck v. Bell* (274 U.S. 200), Justice Holmes, heavily influenced by the
eugenics movement, misleadingly declared that "three generations of imbeciles is enough."[6]

Genetic Counseling   These naive, often confused understandings of the
science of genetics combined with a moral subordination of the rights of
the individual to purported societal interests produced a sorry chapter in early
medical ethics. However, by the end of the 1960s, the complexities of genetics
were beginning to become clearer. Moreover, the focus on societal interests
was gradually being replaced with a more traditional medical perspective in
which the motivation for intervention was the prevention of human suffering.
This shift gave parents, for the first time, a scientific basis for making reproductive choices in the light of their interests and those of their offspring. Legal
abortion in the United States in the 1960s was limited to so-called hard cases,
those that threatened the life and health of the pregnant woman and those
that involved rape, incest, and "fetal deformity." Thus we had not only more
complete scientific information and a more rights-oriented ethic but also a
law that would permit at least modest choices about whether to carry preg-
nancies through to delivery.

Since then, genetic counseling has gradually emerged as a field that makes
information available to individuals and couples potentially at risk for genetic
disease or whose offspring might be affected. In the case of such autosomal
recessive genetic diseases as Tay-Sachs syndrome, sickle-cell anemia, or cystic
fibrosis, each parent must contribute a copy of the defective gene for the disease to manifest itself. This means that, even before marriage, people who have
these diseases in their family can be tested to learn whether they have a copy
of the disease-causing gene. If both prospective parents have the gene, they
can be counseled about remaining childless (through contraception, sterilization, or other strategies) or, if the genetic status of the fetus can be tested in
utero, whether to terminate the pregnancy.

Genetic counseling can also be used for other conditions. Autosomal
dominant conditions such as Huntington's disease, retinoblastoma, and neuro-
fibromatosis express themselves if only a single copy of the gene is present.
Thus, a single affected parent can transmit them. In the case of retinoblastoma, a tumor of the eye that will be fatal if untreated, surgical removal of at
least one eye may prevent death but will leave the patient with compromised

---

[6]For an analysis of how the court erroneously interpreted the facts of this case, see Paul A. Lombardo, "Three
Generations, No Imbeciles: New Light on *Buck v. Bell*," *New York University Law Review* 60 (1985):30–62.

vision or no sight at all. Huntington's disease does not manifest itself until the affected person is in his or her thirties or later, but then it leaves the person with progressive muscular paralysis that eventually leads to early death. It was the disease of folk singer Woody Guthrie. Each child of an affected person has a 50 percent chance of having the defective gene. Because symptoms do not occur until adulthood, affected persons in the past often reproduced and passed the gene along to their offspring before they knew whether they were affected. Now it is possible to test persons at risk of Huntington's disease so they can make choices about reproduction. However, in the process they will learn, perhaps years in advance, whether they themselves have the disease. Some claim that healthy people should not know in advance how they will die; others insist that persons at risk should have this information, perhaps even when they are still children, so that they can plan marriage, career, and other life choices in light of it.

We can also test for such chromosome conditions as trisomy-21, or Down syndrome, which leads to varying degrees of mental retardation and perhaps accompanying physical problems with the heart and digestive track, and trisomy-18, a rapidly debilitating and fatal disease. These often result from abnormalities in the process by which chromosomes combine during fertilization so they are not passed from parents. In other cases, parents may also have the condition (as in some cases of Down syndrome). When the parent has the chromosomal abnormality, he or she can be tested and the condition identified. Even if the parent does not have the abnormality, fetal chromosomes can be screened, making possible choices about abortion of affected fetuses. Some chromosomal abnormalities are sex-linked, meaning that normally only males will be affected. Some of these conditions, such as Duchenne muscular dystrophy, are quite serious; others, such as color-blindness, can be quite minimal. Often the only prenatal screening possible is determination of the sex of the fetus. Since normally only males are affected, aborting all male fetuses of those with a family history of the condition will prevent births of affected infants. However, this will also mean aborting normal males half of the time.

Making choices in the context of genetic counseling poses not only traditional ethical problems of deciding about abortion, fertility regulation, informed consent, confidentiality, forgoing life support, and allocation of resources but also whether humans should be choosing the genetic makeup of their children. Some people—for example, those who reject advance knowledge of their Huntington's disease status—believe that it is more "natural" and appropriate to let the disease evolve without knowing whether they are at risk, even though they will have to make reproductive decisions without knowing whether their children have a 50-50 chance of inheriting the gene. Others insist that it is irresponsible to make reproductive choices in ignorance of one's genetic status. Similar controversy exists about whether individuals should learn the sex and genetic status of the fetus or should adopt the traditional approach and wait until delivery to gain this information.

Genetic counselors and others who advise prospective parents professionally, such as clergy and physicians, also face moral choices in the context of genetic counseling. A basic question for them is how they should interact with their clients. Many now take the position that they should be "nondirective"; that is, they should not attempt to transmit their own moral views to their clients. Instead, they maintain, they should provide their clients with scientific, social, and psychological information and leave the evaluative choices up to them. These counselors are aware of the issues raised in chapter 3 about how difficult and subjective it is to determine what counts as a good outcome. Thus, they give priority to client autonomy, letting the client control the value judgments and the ethical choices.

However, this value-neutral position is increasingly being called into question. Contemporary philosophy of science now suggests that value neutrality may be impossible, that counselor values will inevitably seep into the information the counselors transmit and that deciding which information is *important enough* to provide will necessarily require some value judgments on the counselor's part. Moreover, some evaluations seem to pose such clear-cut choices that many would consider it unethical to fail to voice an opinion about them. For example, parents can now decide to abort a fetus simply because it is not the preferred gender or because it has a minor medical condition such as color-blindness. They can also choose to bear children despite horrendous, painful, and fatal conditions such as trisomy-18. Many genetic counselors consider either of those sorts of choices so obviously wrong that it would call for more-directive counseling. Deciding whether to be directive in these situations will depend not only on one's views about abortion and autonomy but also on how one feels about intervening into life's most mysterious and important processes.

This discussion suggests a serious problem for the future of genetic counseling. If counselors cannot be completely neutral and feel that some choices are so obviously immoral that they cannot in good conscience refrain from conveying their disapproval, how can prospective parents and others being counseled protect themselves from undue and distorting influences from their counselors? It is not clear why the moral beliefs of genetic counselors should be determinative for decisions made by counselees who are regarded as autonomous and self-determining moral agents (even though they cannot make their decisions without the assistance of such counseling). One approach would be to strive to have counselors try to be as fair and unbiased as possible while still realizing that their communications will inevitably contain value perspectives.

If those being counseled understood that all counseling conveys value judgments, and if counselors openly expressed their points of view, clients could pick their counselors and the institutions in which the counselors work on the basis of compatibility of values as well as availability of factual information. For important decisions they might seek out other counselors for second opinions, intentionally pursuing counselors whose values are quite different. A traditional Catholic might first get counseling from someone from within that tradition and then seek out a counselor whose values are quite different, in order to see how different the messages are. Even if these counselors try to present "just the facts," and present them as fairly as possible, in at least some cases, the messages are bound to be quite different.

Genetic Screening   Genetic screening carries the process of genetic counseling to a new and more systemic level. For many genetic conditions, one can test for the presence of a gene that predisposes the individual or that person's offspring to genetic disease by using a blood test or some other procedure that is simple and inexpensive. Thus, it is feasible to screen whole groups of people. The earliest population screening was carried out on African Americans for the gene for sickle-cell disease and on Ashkenazi Jews for Tay-Sachs genes. With screening, prospective parents would know before marriage or before conceiving children whether each carried a gene for the disease. If they did, in the simplest recessive conditions, then one in four of their children would have the disease and two in four would carry a single copy of the gene, meaning that they would not have the disease but could pass a gene on to their children.

Because such screening is targeted at whole communities, it is difficult for counselors who propose testing to be value-neutral. One would not advocate the expense and effort of a communitywide program unless one were committed to the position that the disease in question was quite serious and worth preventing. Moreover, many of the earlier conditions for which screening was done involved ethnic minority communities and often led to the recommendation that couples limit child-bearing or abort affected fetuses. These proposals smacked of a campaign designed to eliminate significant numbers of the future generation of the group involved. More-radical commentators termed this a form of genocide. More recently, screening has become available for such diseases as cystic fibrosis and phenylketonuria (PKU), which affect nonminority Caucasians. However, suspicions about screening continue, and a concern about eugenics still lingers.

Within the past few years, evidence has become available that specific genetic tests can identify people who are at risk for serious diseases such as breast cancer and certain forms of colon cancer. It is believed that specific genes, such as the BRCA1 gene for breast cancer, predispose individuals for disease that in some cases can be treated only by radical procedures such as bilateral preventive mastectomy. Genes for other conditions, such as familial polyposis colon cancer, can be detected in children before the disease manifests itself in adulthood. Regular monitoring can be undertaken for those with the predisposing gene to identify early appearance of the disease.

Both genetic testing and screening pose serious social problems for persons who are identified as having the predisposing genes or even the carrier state. There is increasing concern that insurance companies may discriminate against those with such genes or that employers may resist hiring them for fear that their health insurance costs will increase. Even more subtle is the question of whether knowing that one carries such a gene will be stigmatizing or lead to lower self-image. Some maintain that it is better not to know one's genetic makeup and thus avoid the risk of discrimination and social-psychological sequellae. Others believe that it would be distressing to persons at risk for a disease to know that the tests are available and yet not to know whether they were affected. The risks of genetic discrimination would not deter them from being tested.

The Human Genome Project   The potential for genetic testing and intervention escalated in 1990 when the United States Congress formally committed to the Human Genome Project. Part of an international genetic research initiative, it is expected to cost $3 billion and take at least fifteen years. Its goal is to identify the position of every one of the 50,000–100,000 genes in the human body and eventually be able to intervene to diagnose and modify, if appropriate, any of those genes. The project is utopia for those who believe in the "dominion and subdue" view, but it is the worst nightmare of the anti-tampering school.

Because we are likely to be able to diagnose problematic genes before we can remove and replace them or provide other therapy to respond to their impact, the Human Genome Project is viewed with great suspicion by those who believe that abortion is ethically unacceptable. On the other hand, those who are technological optimists see the possibility of heading off medical problems at their genetic source one by one, thereby leading to a healthier population and great reductions in suffering and medical costs. The more realistic understand that many diseases are not genetic in their origin and, of those that are, many are *polygenic,* that is, they involve many genes. This means that medical scientists will still have to determine how genes interact in order to address such major chronic diseases as many cancers, heart disease, stroke, and diseases of senescence. It is likely that we will find that the same genes that increase risk for some undesirable conditions also are essential for preventing or mitigating the effects of other equally unattractive outcomes.

The crucial question from the point of view of ethics is whether the goal—full knowledge of the human genome—is an ideal worthy of pursuit or a malicious, Promethean quest that takes humans beyond the knowledge that is appropriate for them and opens up possibilities for intervention that are best left untouched.

Genetic Engineering What many of the "dominion and subdue" school take as their ultimate goal is subsumed under what is sometimes called *genetic engineering*. Whereas genetic counseling and screening are devoted primarily to identifying problematic genes and avoiding their transmission, genetic engineering is direct and aggressive. It strives to overcome the effects of the bad genes by inserting the proper genetic information and eventually removing the genes that cause problems. The first genetic engineering efforts merely added a gene that was missing, such as the gene for producing a crucial enzyme.

Therapy vs. Enhancement The ultimate goal is to identify and remove harmful genes as well as to add missing ones. A distinction can be made, that some consider morally significant, between therapy and enhancement. Some people have conditions that can be clearly identified as diseases, bodily conditions that people evaluate negatively and that are deviations from some imagined normal state. The first formally documented attempt at gene therapy in humans, described below, is an example of a therapeutic intervention.

Case 8.1: *Adenosine Deaminase Deficiency (ADA Disease)*

Physicians were stumped by the cause of sickness in a young girl by the name of Ashanthi DeSilva. Her luck changed on the day she and her parents went to see pediatrician Dr. Ricardo Sorensen. Sorensen immediately recognized Ashanthi's condition as a rare genetic disorder known as severe combined immunodeficiency (SCID). Although only a handful of people are afflicted with SCID, he recognized the disease in Ashanthi because another of his patients, Cynthia Cutshall, was afflicted as well. In fact, on the day Ashanthi came to visit Dr. Sorensen, Cynthia was just leaving the doctor's office. This meeting marked the beginning of a long friendship between the two girls, bonded through a disease that threatened their lives, and a cure that made medical history.

Both Ashanthi and Cynthia had inherited a genetic mutation that prevented their cells from producing the enzyme adenosine deaminase, or ADA. This enzyme is crucial to immunological response in humans. Without it, even minor infections such as the common cold can be lethal. Throughout their short lives, Ashanthi and Cynthia had been constantly faced with the perils of infection and a depressed immune system. Their situations changed when French Anderson, a National Institutes of Health (NIH) scientist, decided to employ a radically new technique known as gene therapy as a potential cure. Using viral particles as carriers, Anderson sought to insert functional ADA genes into Ashanthi and Cynthia. He hoped that the functional genes inserted into their white blood cells would produce the necessary ADA and thus restore their immunological function.

Although this technique had never before been used on human subjects, Anderson was optimistic. After a series of deliberations with various review boards, he was granted permission to go forward with the treatment. The results were astonishing. Tests showed that both Ashanthi's and Cynthia's immune systems were significantly improved. Both girls would return to NIH to receive their life-giving gene on a regular basis. The next step, however, is to insert the functional genes into the stem cells in their bone marrow. Stem cells are the mother cells of the immune system, and, if they retain the functional genes, then Ashanthi and Cynthia's bodies will be capable of producing the ADA on an ongoing basis—no more trips to NIH and no more ADA deficiency. If the technique works, Ashanthi and Cynthia's disease will be forever gone. Their contribution to medical science, however, will be far from over. Their treatment has opened the floodgates for potential cures to many other genetically derived diseases.[7]

By contrast, enhancement involves improving on a normal healthy body. Some people would like to be able to add to the normal lifespan or to improve on what are considered normal human characteristics. Perhaps they would like to have a more pleasant personality or less of a desire to eat. These are likely to turn out to be polygenic characteristics that do not lend themselves to gene modification. It is possible, however, that some conditions could be controlled by a single gene responsible for a simple enzyme. We have recently seen that drugs changing the metabolism of a single body chemical such as serotonin can have major effects on personality and weight.

This distinction between therapy and enhancement rests on some hypothetical point that some call "normal health." Bringing people up to that point could be considered therapy, while taking them beyond that point might be considered enhancement. Providing "therapy" generates considerable support, but enhancement is considered much more controversial. Moreover, the dividing point between them may be very hard to define. For example, would

---

[7]Based on Larry Thompson, "The First Kids with New Genes," *Time,* June 7, 1993, pp. 50–53.

someone who comes from a long line of very short people and who is himself short be considered normal (compared with his ancestors) or abnormally short (compared with the rest of the population)? Would a female who is short be considered as "abnormal" as a male of similar height? Would parents who wanted their daughter to grow to be as tall as her brother (who happens to be tall enough to have a lucrative basketball career) be thought of as pursuing therapy or enhancement?

The simple cases of therapy for serious genetic diseases generate the most sympathy. Even persons reluctant to tamper with genes cannot help feeling sympathy for Ashanthi and Cynthia with their ADA deficiency. On the other hand, enhancement generates nervousness even among the "dominion and subdue" people. They may worry, for example, that if some people in a population engaged in enhancement others would be forced to copy them just to stay competitive.

Somatic vs. Reproductive Cell Changes   A second moral distinction in the genetic engineering debate is also considered important. To date, attempts to add genes to people with genetic diseases have involved inserting new genetic material into somatic cells. This means that the effort, if successful, will affect only the individual treated, not that person's offspring. The reproductive cells of that person will still contain the genetic defect. That person's offspring will be similarly affected. In the case of some autosomal recessive conditions, in which a second gene is needed from the mate before the disease can occur, leaving the reproductive cells unchanged may not pose an immediate problem. However, for dominant conditions it could. The more aggressively interventionistic camp advocates eliminating the problematic gene permanently so that it is not passed from one generation to the next. This is sometimes called *germ-line* or *reproductive cell gene therapy* because an attempt is made to fix the egg or sperm cells, not just the somatic cells.

Such reproductive cell gene therapy is potentially riskier than somatic cell therapy. If inserting a new gene or replacing a defective one is done somatically and the effect is unexpectedly deleterious, the problem has been created for only one generation. In the case of reproductive cell therapy, in contrast, the problem would be perpetuated in future generations unless some additional gene therapy were invented to reverse the changes. Reproductive cell genetic changes have already been carried out in animal studies. A strain of "shiverer" mice has been bred so that their nervous system lacks myelin, a basic protein; shiverer mice are missing a gene responsible for production of this protein. Researchers have microinjected the necessary gene into zygotes of shiverer mice. In at least one case, the gene was successfully incorporated into offspring that went on to transmit the gene to successive generations (Walters and Gage Palmer 1997, pp. 60–61). Researchers, ethicists, and social commentators are now beginning to take seriously the possibility of attempting similar germ-line genetic changes in humans.

New Reproductive Technologies

Closely related to the controversy over genetics is the newly emerging tension over new reproductive technologies. Here the conflict between those who fear tampering with nature and those who favor human rational control reaches new heights.

Artificial Insemination Contemporary issues of human control of the means of reproduction have their roots in some older techniques. For centuries it has been known that male infertility and concern about male-transmitted genetic disease could be addressed by relying on some source of sperm cells other than the husband. The sperm are introduced into the mother by some artificial means: AID (artificial insemination by donor) or, in cases in which the husband's sperm are viable but other problems arise, AIH (artificial insemination by the husband). Undoubtedly, using a source of sperm other than the husband has also been done by NID (natural insemination by donor), either with or without the husband's knowledge.

All of these methods have been rejected by some traditional ethics as being "unnatural." Their concern is partly directed to the fact that a third party is involved, meaning that the conception is, in some sense, out of wedlock. However, some among them object even to AIH. This is the view of the Catholic church, which maintains that all sexual relations must be "natural": that is, consistent with the *natural moral law*. Sexual relations must be reserved for fulfilling the natural or proper ends of marriage, which involve both procreation and a unitive function. (The latter is sometimes referred to as the "bonding of man and woman"; Ashley and O'Rourke, 1989, p. 250). According to this view, every sexual act must be open to both of these functions (and hence artificial birth control is forbidden as "unnatural"). More recent interpretations recognize the acceptability of sexual acts in which procreation is not possible. Holders of this view accept as moral the rhythm method of controlling fertility, and some also accept the use of oral contraceptives, holding that these pose no artificial or morally unacceptable barriers to sexual relations. Nevertheless, persons within this tradition still insist that any method used must be within the context of a marriage relation in which at least some sexual relations take place when the reproductive function can be fulfilled. Moreover, intentional manipulations that place artificial barriers or involve artificial separation of the procreative and unitive functions are still unacceptable (Sacred

Congregation for the Doctrine of the Faith 1987). This means that not only artificial birth control but any reproductive acts that do not involve natural coitus are unacceptable.

Of course, many outside this tradition do not share the view that the morality of reproduction is determined by assessing whether these so-called natural ends or purposes have been met. In varying degrees, they have grown to accept various techniques that have been labeled "artificial": barrier methods of contraception, sterilization, artificial insemination using a husband's sperm, and artificial insemination using donor sperm. The moral choices involved in deciding about artificial insemination escalated in subsequent decades as undreamed-of manipulations of reproductive processes began to emerge.

In Vitro Fertilization The change can be dated. On July 25, 1978, Louise Brown, the world's first so-called test tube baby, was born. Doctors Patrick Steptoe and Robert Edwards developed the technique of removing eggs from a woman's ovary and fertilizing them with semen in a Petri dish.[8] At first, in vitro fertilization, as the procedure is called, was used exclusively for treating infertility in married couples.

In the early days of in vitro fertilization, one of the moral issues involved what amounts to controversy over doing research on human subjects without consent. It seemed that these babies who had been brought into existence in such a novel way were at risk of trauma. We could not be sure that they would not have terrible malformations. Critics argued that the procedure could not be said to be for the benefit of the babies that would not otherwise have been alive.

Now that hundreds of infants have been born because of these techniques, that concern has lessened, but a more fundamental concern remains. Is there something about in vitro fertilization that pushes human manipulation of the beginnings of life too far? The generation of human life has traditionally been thought to be a mystery, something largely out of human hands. Some people believe that that is the way it ought to be. They consider it hubris to put control of fertilization into human hands, literally bringing it out into the open and placing the process under glass.

In vitro fertilization not only divorces reproduction from sexual relations; it also permits a substantial opportunity for human control. Now it is standard practice to fertilize several eggs, permitting physicians to select the most desirable ones for implantation. Preimplantation genetic testing is on the horizon. Excess embryos will be discarded, frozen for later use, consigned

---

[8]Patrick C. Steptoe and Robert G. Edwards, "Birth after the Reimplantation of a Human Embryo," *Lancet* 2, no. 8085 (1978):366.

to research, or donated to other infertile couples. The metaphors of manufacture, (re)production, and fabrication are used by critics to suggest manipulation and tampering in a process that has an almost sacred quality to it. In the meantime, the group that supports such endeavors points to the values symbolized by the image of having dominion and subduing. They see human control of the generation of life itself to be the ultimate triumph in the rationalization of planning, selecting, and improving the chances of eliminating disease as well as infertility.

Surrogate Motherhood   Once the technology of in vitro fertilization had been developed, there was no technical reason for limiting its use to married couples. The same techniques could be used for unmarried partners and, with the help of sperm donors, lesbian couples. Even more controversial was the fact that there would be no technical reason for the fertilized egg to be implanted in the woman from whom it was taken. Surrogates could be used to gestate the embryo; they would agree to return the newborn to the woman who contributed the egg and her partner. Surrogate motherhood could be used either for medical reasons—for women whose uterus would not support pregnancy or for those who would be endangered by pregnancy—or for reasons of convenience—for women who preferred not to be pregnant. A woman who lacked ovaries but wanted to become pregnant could receive a "donated" egg that would be fertilized by her partner and implanted in her. Thus, she could become pregnant and gestate a fetus that, although not genetically hers, was hers to gestate and raise. All those procedures, and more, have now become commonplace. In fact, it is now possible for there to be at least five "parents" involved in the creation and birth of a child: the man who is the source of the sperm, the woman who is the source of the egg, the one who gestates the fertilized egg, and the two who take responsibility for nurturing the postnatal child.

Case 8.2:   *The Mary Beth Whitehead Case*

William and Betsy Stern wanted to have a child, but Mrs. Stern had chosen not to bear her own child because of a medical condition that she believed would have been dangerously aggravated by carrying and delivering her own child. In February 1985, Mr. Stern signed a surrogacy agreement with Mary Beth Whitehead in which Ms. Whitehead agreed for a $10,000 fee to be artificially inseminated with Mr. Stern's sperm and to carry the offspring to term. She agreed that after delivering the baby she would turn the child over to the Sterns and that they would become the legal parents.

A baby girl was born on March 27, 1986. Ms. Whitehead called her Sara; the Sterns called her Melissa; and eventually the courts called her Baby M. After the birth, Ms. Whitehead refused to relinquish parental rights. In her book A Mother's Story, *Mary Beth Whitehead recalls one of many confrontations she had with the Sterns after the birth.*

> I looked at Betsy Stern and thought to myself, "Betsy, I'm not selling this child. I started this when I actually believed it wasn't my child. Everyone convinced me that it was your child, but going through the pregnancy and the pain of labor, and then seeing the baby has made me realize that this is my baby, not yours."[9]

In the following months, a series of confrontations occurred between Mary Beth Whitehead, her husband at the time, Rick, and the Sterns. The infant was in the Sterns' possession for only a short while after her birth before Ms. Whitehead took her and fled from her home in New Jersey to Florida, where she led a life on the run for several weeks. Eventually, the police seized the child, and she was returned to the Sterns.

But the battle was far from over. Although "Sara," or "Melissa," remained in the Sterns' care, a lengthy legal battle was waged to determine who should have custody of the child. On March 31, 1987, the New Jersey Superior Court ruled that Baby M would remain in the sole custody of her father William Stern. Mary Beth Whitehead's parental rights were terminated.

Mr. Stern had filed suit claiming that his rights had been violated. He claimed that he was being denied equal protection under the fourteenth amendment of the Constitution. He argued that, since men who provide sperm for artificial insemination legally surrender their parental rights, women should be treated similarly. The debate centered on whether women are bound by contractual commitments signed before conceiving as surrogate mothers to surrender parental rights.

The Supreme Court of the State of New Jersey, which eventually reviewed the lower court opinion, ultimately awarded custody of Baby M to the Sterns but denied the equal protection argument, thus apparently undermining binding surrogacy contracts. Mary Beth Whitehead's parental rights were restored, and she was later allowed (in a separate court decision) unsupervised, uninterrupted "liberal" visitation privileges. In future cases, the possibility remains that a surrogate mother who changes her mind about a commitment to surrender parental rights could gain custody.[10]

---

[9]Mary Beth Whitehead, with Loretta Schwartz-Nobel, *A Mother's Story: The Truth about the Baby M Case* (New York: St. Martin's Press, 1989), p. 22.

[10]This summary is based on In re Baby M, 109 NJ 396, 537 A.2d 1277 (1988); Lauritzen 1993; and Whitehead, *A Mother's Story.*

As the complexity of these relations increases, the moral issues also increase. When only two people contribute to the process, their motivation is clear. As soon as a third party becomes involved, even in AID, the question of compensation to motivate that person's assistance arises. Sperm donors have always been paid, raising the issue of why women who provide an egg cell or a womb for gestation should not also be compensated. It is argued that there are significant differences in the time, burden, and risk involved, but it is not clear whether that fact implies that payment would be more or less justified. Presently, markets to pay surrogates who provide a womb (or a womb plus an egg, as Mary Beth Whitehead did) are considered highly suspect and actually are prohibited in some jurisdictions. Excluding compensation is believed to make the decision to participate, particularly by poor women, less coercive, but it also raises questions about fairness for women who accept considerable burden for the benefit of others.

The central issue in the controversy over surrogacy contracts is whether women who agree to serve as surrogates are bound morally or legally to follow through on their commitment to hand over the child to the people who originally were to become the postnatal parents. The Whitehead case poses the issue dramatically. Those committed to the right of competent persons to form binding contracts consider policies permitting surrogates to cancel their commitment unfair. They ask, in terms of chapter 4, is there a duty of fidelity to promises? These defenders of surrogacy contracts hold that people should be screened to ensure that they are mentally competent and stable before they make such a commitment but that, once the commitment has been made, they have a moral duty to keep it. To do otherwise would be unfair to both the man and the woman who were promised that the child would be theirs to nurture and who made emotional, social, and psychological commitments based on that promise.

Critics are not satisfied with that defense. They point out that women who agree to become surrogates are often of lower socioeconomic and educational status. Payment for surrogacy is sometimes considered de facto coercive for such persons. Moreover, pregnancy is not a mere business transaction, for bearing a child is an enormous and an emotional undertaking. Bonds are created between the pregnant woman and the fetus she is carrying that may not be predictable. They claim that women need a period of time after the pregnancy to reassess and determine whether they can continue to commit to relinquishing the child they have borne. One problem with this argument is that it seems to suggest that women, in at least this one respect, are unique in that, even if they are adults deemed mentally competent, they cannot make autonomous, rational commitments that are free from nonrational, emotional factors beyond their control. Defenders of autonomy and the right and duty to contract insist that women as a group cannot be held hostage to those who cannot predict the emotional impact of their pregnancy. That argument, in turn, has reinforced opposition from those who doubt the legitimacy of extra-corporeal manipulations of life's beginnings.

Cloning   Just when one begins to believe that the technological manipulation of life's processes can get no more Promethean, news breaks that a Scottish scientist has cloned a sheep. Cloning is the asexual reproduction of an organism by taking the nucleus, along with its chromosomal material, from a cell of an existing creature and implanting it into an enucleated egg cell or other cell of another creature. This modified cell, once charged by an electric shock, has the potential to grow and develop into a new being. The resulting creature, barring mutations, will be a genetically identical copy of the original one, a being who preexisted it by a significant amount of time. It is like an identical twin, but with the critical difference that the clone can observe its biological future insofar as it is genetically determined.

Of course, there is more to a creature, especially a human, than his or her genes. A being is shaped by environment, time and place, and nurturing. Therefore, even a genetic clone will not be truly identical to its genetic parent. But this asexual reproduction is controversial in part because of the concerns we are tracing in this chapter: the concerns about tampering with human nature and its rational control. Even seeing the genetic future is a radical change from the mysterious unknown of more traditional organic development.

Cloning also raises the specter of producing multiple copies of people who are particularly suited for certain roles—warrior, intellectual, sex object. In reality, the chance of such a Brave New World enterprise seems remote. Far more likely are the agricultural applications of cloning and, among humans, some unusual, if sympathetic needs. One imagined scenario is of a couple who, perhaps after a long period of attempting to bear a child, finally conceives and has a baby. Then, after one or the other parent becomes incapable of reproducing, the baby is critically injured in an accident. As the child is dying, the couple realizes that their only opportunity to bear another child that is genetically their own would be to clone the dying baby. The technology involved is relatively simple, at least compared with research in space or nuclear physics. They might persuade some reproductive medicine specialist, perhaps motivated out of scientific curiosity and ego as well as sympathy for the couple, to attempt to clone another child.

The real controversy clearly is not scientific or legal. It is ethical. The issue of cloning involves decisions about what constitutes benefit and harm, whether parents should have the autonomy to choose to pursue creating a clone, whether the risks to the clone can be justified when there is no being, no patient, to benefit before the act of cloning, and whether resources are justly and fairly devoted to such reproductive technologies. But the cloning controversy is ethical not only or even primarily in the sense of raising the questions of ethical principles that have dominated most of this book and most of the late-twentieth-century medical ethical debate. Cloning, as well as the other technologies in this chapter, have captured the public imagination because they force us to decide whether some medical technologies go beyond what is morally tolerable human manipulation of the very processes of life. That is a question that takes us beyond the controversy between the Hippocratic ethic (in either its original subjective or more recent objective form) and the ethic of respect for persons of liberal political philosophy. It takes us beyond the tension between individualistic ethics and social ethics—whether the benefit-maximizing ethic of social utilitarianism or the distribution-oriented ethic of social justice. Ultimately, the ethics of medicine will force patients and well as physicians, laypeople as well as professionals, not only to deal with choosing among the different ethical principles but also to decide what the role of the human should be in re-creating the species.

Key Concepts

Gene enhancement: Genetic engineering designed to improve on the normal genetic constitution of an individual.

Gene therapy: Genetic engineering designed to correct a genetically caused medical problem.

Genetic engineering: Genetic intervention that strives to overcome the effects of bad genes or to improve the genetic constitution of an individual by removing unacceptable genes or inserting more acceptable ones.

Genetic screening: The testing of groups at risk for genetic disease for the purposes of identifying those who possess certain genes that make individuals susceptible to genetic disease or carrier status.

Germ-line gene therapy or enhancement: Gene therapy or enhancement targeted on the germ cells, that is, those cells that are involved in reproduction. The intention is that the effects will be transmitted to future generations.

The Human Genome Project: An international genetic research initiative that has as its goal the identification of the position of all of the 50,000–100,000 genes in the human body. The United States Congress formally committed to the support of this project in 1990 when it was expected to take fifteen years to complete.

In vitro fertilization: The medical procedure whereby an egg is fertilized by sperm outside the woman's body, normally followed by implantation into the uterus. "In vitro" is the Latin for "in glass." Hence, the popular expression "test tube baby." In fact, other pieces of laboratory equipment are usually used.

Somatic cell gene therapy or enhancement: Gene therapy or enhancement targeted on the somatic cells, that is, those that are not involved in reproduction. The intention is that the effects will not be transmitted to future generations.

Surrogate motherhood: An arrangement whereby a woman bears a child for another woman with the intention that the other woman become the nurturing parent. This can involve implantation of the embryo following in vitro fertilization of the other woman's egg cell or artificial insemination of the surrogate mother.

Bibliography

Alpern, Kenneth D., ed. 1992. *The Ethics of Reproductive Technology.* New York: Oxford University Press.

Ashley, Benedict M., and Kevin D. O'Rourke. 1989. *Healthcare Ethics: A Theological Analysis,* 3d ed. St. Louis: The Catholic Health Association of the United States.

Bayles, Michael D. 1984. *Reproductive Ethics.* Englewood Cliffs, N.J.: Prentice-Hall.

Cohen, Cynthia B., ed. 1996. *New Ways of Making Babies: The Case of Egg Donation.* Bloomington, Ind.: Indiana University Press.

Fletcher, Joseph. 1974. *The Ethics of Genetic Control: Ending Reproductive Roulette.* Garden City, N.Y.: Anchor Books.

Gostin, Larry, ed. 1990. *Surrogate Motherhood: Politics and Privacy.* Bloomington, Ind.: Indiana University Press.

Heyd, David. 1992. *Genethics: Moral Issues in the Creation of People.* Berkeley: University of California Press.

Holtzman, Neil A. 1989. *Proceed with Caution: Predicting Genetic Risks in the Recombinant DNA Era.* Baltimore: The Johns Hopkins University Press.

Hull, Richard T. 1990. *Ethical Issues in the New Reproductive Technologies.* Belmont, Calif.: Wadsworth Publishing.

Kitcher, Philip. 1996. *The Lives to Come: The Genetic Revolution and Human Possibilities.* New York: Simon and Schuster.

Lauritzen, Paul. 1993. *Pursuing Parenthood: Ethical Issues in Assisted Reproduction.* Bloomington, Ind.: Indiana University Press.

Murray, Thomas H., Mark A. Rothstein, and Robert F. Murray Jr. 1996. *The Human Genome Project and the Future of Health Care.* Bloomington, Ind.: Indiana University Press.

New Jersey Commission on Legal and Ethical Problems in the Delivery of Health Care. 1992. *After Baby M: The Legal, Ethical and Social Dimensions of Surrogacy.* Trenton, N.J.: New Jersey Commission on Legal and Ethical Problems in the Delivery of Health Care.

Ramsey, Paul. 1970. *Fabricated Man.* New Haven, Conn.: Yale University Press.

Robertson, John A. 1994. *Children of Choice: Freedom and the New Reproductive Technologies.* Princeton, N.J.: Princeton University Press.

Sacred Congregation for the Doctrine of the Faith. 1987. "Instruction on Respect for Human Life in Its Origin and on the Dignity of Procreation." *Origins* 16, no. 40 (March 19):698–711.

UNESCO, International Bioethics Committee. 1995. *Proceedings 1995.* Paris: UNESCO.

Walters, LeRoy, and Julie Gage Palmer. 1997. *The Ethics of Human Gene Therapy.* New York: Oxford University Press.

Whitehead, Mary Beth, with Loretta Schwartz-Nobel. 1989. *A Mother's Story: The Truth About the Baby M Case.* New York: St. Martin's Press.

Appendix

Hippocratic Oath

I swear by Apollo Physician and Asclepius and Hygieia and Panaceia and all the gods and goddesses, making them my witnesses, that I fulfill according to my ability and judgment this oath and this covenant:

To hold him who has taught me this art as equal to my parents and to live my life in partnership with him, and if he is in need of money to give him a share of mine, and to regard his offspring as equal to my brothers in male lineage and to teach them this art if they desire to learn it without fee and covenant; to give a share of precepts and oral instruction and all the other learning to my sons and to the sons of him who has instructed me and to pupils who have signed the covenant and have taken an oath according to the medical law, but to no one else.

I will apply dietetic measures for the benefit of the sick according to my ability and judgment; I will keep them from harm and injustice.

I will never give a deadly drug to anybody if asked for it, nor will I make a suggestion to this effect. Similarly I will not give to a woman an abortive remedy. In purity and holiness I will guard my life and my art.

I will not use the knife, not even on sufferers from stone, but will withdraw in favor of such men as are engaged in this work.

Whatever houses I may visit, I will come for the benefit of the sick, remaining free of all intentional injustice, of all mischief and in particular of sexual relations with both female and male persons, be they free or slaves.

What I may see or hear in the course of the treatment or even outside of the treatment in regard to the life of men, which on no account one must spread abroad, I will keep to myself holding such things shameful to be spoken about.

If I fulfill this oath and do not violate it, may it be granted to me to enjoy life and art, being honored with fame among all men for all time to come; if I transgress it and swear falsely, may the opposite of all this be my lot.

Reprinted by permission from Ludwig Edelstein. Ancient Medicine: Selected Papers of Ludwig Edelstein, p. 6. © 1967 by Johns Hopkins University Press.

Principles of Medical Ethics (1980)
of the American Medical Association

Preamble

The medical profession has long subscribed to a body of ethical statements developed primarily for the benefit of the patient. As a member of this profession, a physician must recognize responsibility not only to patients, but also to society, to other health professionals, and to self. The following Principles adopted by the American Medical Association are not laws, but standards of conduct which define the essentials of honorable behavior for the physician.

I. A physician shall be dedicated to providing competent medical service with compassion and respect for human dignity.

II. A physician shall deal honestly with patients and colleagues, and strive to expose those physicians deficient in character or competence, or who engage in fraud or deception.

III. A physician shall respect the law and also recognize a responsibility to seek changes in those requirements which are contrary to the best interests of the patient.

IV. A physician shall respect the rights of patients, of colleagues, and of older health professionals, and shall safeguard patient confidences within the constraints of the law.

V. A physician shall continue to study, apply and advance scientific knowledge, make relevant information available to patients, colleagues, and the public, obtain consultation, and use the talents of other health professionals when indicated.

VI. A physician shall, in the provision of appropriate patient care, except in emergencies, be free to choose whom to serve, with whom to associate, and the environment in which to provide medical services.

VII. A physician shall recognize a responsibility to participate in activities contributing to an improved community.

Reprinted by permission from American Medical Association, Council on Ethical and Judicial Affairs. Code of Medical Ethics: Current Opinions with Annotations, 1998–1999 Edition. Chicago: American Medical Association, 1998, p. xiv.

Index